Publisher

Published by

THE BIBLE FOR TODAY PRESS
900 Park Avenue
Collingswood, New Jersey 08108
U.S.A.

**Church Phone: 856-854-4747 BFT
Phone: 856-854-4452 Orders:
1-800-John 10:9**
e-mail: BFT@BibleForToday.org
website: www.BibleForToday.org
fax: 856-854-2464

Publishing assisted by:
The Old Paths Publications, Inc
www.theoldpathspublications.com

ISBN #978-1-56848-038-1

**We Use and Defend
the King James Bible**

November, 2003 BFT2988BK

Copyright, 2019
All Rights Reserved

Acknowledgments

I wish to thank and to acknowledge the assistance of the following people:

- **The Congregation** of the Bible For Today Baptist Church, for whom these messages were prepared, to whom they were delivered, and by whom they were published. They listened attentively and encouraged their Pastor as he preached;
- **Yvonne Sanborn Waite**, my wife, who encouraged the publication of these sermons, read the manuscript several times, suggested the various boxes, and gave other helpful suggestions and comments;
- **Dianne W. Cosby**, for typing these messages from the original cassette tapes and put them in computer format;
- **Dr. Edward R. Smith**, for editing the messages in the computer format, inserting the texts of various verses used, and paragraphing the exposition;
- **Daniel S. Waite**, the Assistant to the Bible For Today Director, who guided the book through the printing process, and made important suggestions;
- **Barbara Egan**, our Bible For Today secretary who also read the manuscript and offered helpful suggestions and comments.
- **Joann Nawrocki**, one of our Bible For Today Baptist Church friends who also read the manuscript and gave us some helpful suggestions and comments.

Foreword

- **The Beginning.** This book is the **fifth** in a planned series of books based on expository preaching from various books of the Bible. It is an attempt to bring to the minds of the readers two things: (1) the **meaning** of the words in the verses and (2) the practical **application** of those words to the lives of both saved and lost people. Since the book of Philemon was also written from prison and is only one chapter in length, I have included it in this book with Colossians.
- **Preached Sermons.** These are messages that have been preached to our **Bible For Today Baptist Church** in Collingswood, New Jersey, broadcast over radio, and placed on our website as follows:

(http://www.BibleForToday.org/audio_sermons.htm)

This site is for people all over the world to listen to, should they wish. As the messages were originally preached, I took half a chapter during our Sunday morning services, spending about forty-five minutes on each message.
- **Other Verses.** In connection with both the meaning and application of the verses in these two books, there are many verses from other places in the Bible that have been quoted for further elaboration of Paul's discussion. One of the unique features of this study is that all of the various verses of Scripture that are used to illustrate further truth are written out in full for easy reference.
- **A Transcription.** It should be noted that this book is made up largely from the transcription of the tape recordings of the messages as they were preached. These recordings are available in both audio and video formats (**BFT#2988/1-4**; or BFT #2977VC1-2 and **BFT#2996TP**; or **BFT #2996-VCR**). Though there has been some editing, the words are basically the same as the ones I used as I preached the sermons. Though different in emphasis, this was also the method Dr. H. A. Ironside used in his Bible exposition books.
- **The Audience.** The audience intended is the same as the audience that listened to the messages in the first place. These studies are not meant to be overly scholarly, though there is some reference to various Greek words used by Paul. My aim is to help lay people to understand the Words of God. It is my hope that I can get as many as possible of my expositions in print so that my children, grandchildren, and all children in the faith may be able to rejoice with me in the things the Lord has brought to my attention as I have preached from the verses in Colossians and Philemon.

Yours For God's Words,

D. A. Waite

Pastor D. A. Waite, Th.D., Ph.D.
Bible For Today Baptist Church

Table of Contents

Publisher's Data i

Acknowledgments ii

Foreword iii

Table of Contents iv

Colossians Chapter One 1

Colossians Chapter Two 49

Colossians Chapter Three 89

Colossians Chapter Four 125

Philemon 161

Index of Words and Phrases 193

About the Author 223

Order Blank Pages 225

Notes 232

Colossians Chapter One

Introductory Remarks

Colossians is one of four prison epistles, the others being the books of Ephesians, Philippians, and Philemon. Colosse is a city in Asia Minor which is now Turkey. Colosse is about 50 miles east and a little south of the city of Ephesus. Paul is writing from Rome, Italy, clear across the Mediterranean Sea.

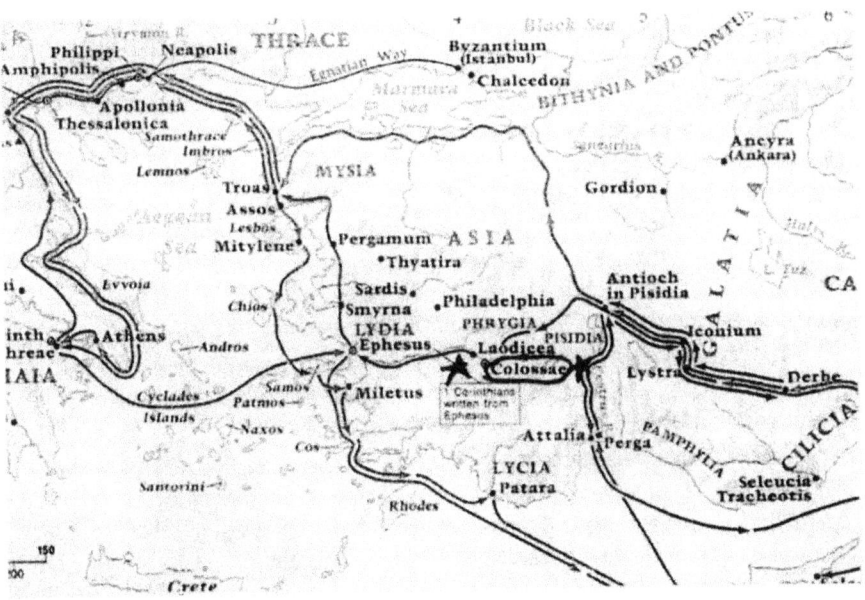

Colossians 1:1

"Paul, an apostle of Jesus Christ by the will of God, and Timotheus *our* brother"

"Paul, an apostle of Jesus Christ" The author of this book is named in this first verse. It was *"Paul."* He identifies himself as an *"apostle of Jesus Christ."* The Greek word for *"apostle"* comes from the verb, APOSTELLO. This means *"to send out or to send forth."* Paul was commissioned and sent forth by the Lord Jesus Christ. I don't believe it was Matthias (see Acts 1:15-26) who was the one that God intended to replace the traitor, Judas Iscariot. I believe it was Paul. Peter led the 120 assembled disciples in an election. The Lord Jesus Christ had told them:

- **Luke 24:49**
  And, behold, I send the promise of my Father upon you: but **tarry ye in the city of Jerusalem, until ye be endued with power from on high.**

He said to *"tarry"* until they were *"endued with power from on high."* This would be the descent of the Holy Spirit on the day of Pentecost. Then, and only then, they were to be missionaries to the entire world.

- **Acts 1:8**
  But **ye shall receive power, after that the Holy Ghost is come upon you: and ye shall be witnesses unto me both in Jerusalem, and in all Judea, and in Samaria, and unto the uttermost part of the earth.**

I believe that Paul was that special *"apostle"* who was *"sent forth with orders."* That is what that word, *"apostle,"* means. The Lord Jesus Christ is the One Who gave Paul these orders. The Lord Jesus saw Paul, found him, and saved him while he was on the road to Damascus, getting ready to kill Christians. Acts Chapters 9, 22, and 26 tell the story of Paul's conversion in his own words. The Lord Jesus Christ blinded Paul with a light brighter than the sun.

"by the will of God" Paul was an *"apostle,"* not by his own will, but *"by the will of God."* It is important that every one of us who are saved become servants of the Lord by God's will, not by our own will.

"and Timotheus *our* brother" *"Timotheus"* (or Timothy) was Paul's friend, who apparently was visiting Paul when he wrote this letter from his first Roman imprisonment. His name means *"honoring God."* According to Acts 16:1, Timothy was a resident of Lystra. His father was a Greek. His mother was a Jewess. He was one of Paul's traveling companions on his missionary journeys. Paul wrote two letters to Timothy, 1 Timothy and 2 Timothy. Timothy was the pastor of the church at Ephesus.

Colossians 1:2

"To the saints and faithful brethren in Christ which are at Colosse: Grace *be* unto you, and peace, from God our Father and the Lord Jesus Christ."

"To the saints" Notice that Paul is writing *"to the saints."* By the word, *"saints,"* Paul does not refer to those whom the Roman Catholic Church has canonized. This word refers to every person who is born-again and saved by personal faith in the Lord Jesus Christ. In our King James Bible, believers are called *"saints"* many times. We ought to recognize that and understand it.

- **Romans 15:25-26**
  But now I go unto Jerusalem **to minister unto the saints**. For it hath pleased them of Macedonia and Achaia to make a certain **contribution for the poor saints** which are at Jerusalem.

"Saints" here were living. They were not dead and canonized by the Roman Catholic Church only after they have died. They are believers. Paul wanted to take a certain contribution to the *"poor saints"* who were at Jerusalem. You can even be *"poor"* and be a *"saint."* You don't have to be rich. Anyone who is saved is a *"saint."*

- **Romans 15:31**
  That I may be delivered from them that do not believe in Judea; and that my service which I have for Jerusalem may **be accepted of the saints**;

- **Romans 16:2**
  That ye **receive her in the Lord, as becometh saints**, and that ye assist her in whatsoever business she hath need of you: for she hath been a succourer of many, and of myself also.

The Greek word for *"saints"* is HAGIOUS. It means *"set apart ones or sanctified ones"* for the Lord's use.

- **Romans 16:15**
  Salute Philologus, and Julia, Nereus, and his sister, and Olympas, **and all the saints which are with them**.

The *"saints"* should live saintly and in a sanctified manner. Saint Nicholas is a figment of the misguided imagination. Saint Christopher on the dashboard of some cars to protect the riders is a Roman Catholic saint. All believers are *"saints."* If you are reading this book and you are saved then you are a *"saint"* according to God's Word.

"and faithful brethren in Christ which are at Colosse"
Paul is writing *"to the saints and faithful brethren in Christ which are at*

Colosse." The believers are not only called "*saints,*" but they should also be "*faithful*" in all things as "*brethren.*" To be "*faithful*" is important. Are we "*faithful*" or faithless? The Greek word for "*faithful*" is used of "*persons who show themselves faithful in the transaction of business, the execution of commands, or the discharge of official duties.*"

"Grace *be* unto you, and peace" "*Grace*" is from the Greek word, CHARIS. A form of this word is still used in the modern Greek language as a greeting. It means both "*hello*" as well as "*thank you,*" and everything else that goes along with it. "Peace" is the Jewish greeting. It is SHALOM.

God's Peace

If you are a Christian, "peace" has been defined as "*the tranquil state of the soul assured of its salvation through Christ, and so fearing nothing from God, is content with its earthly lot of whatsoever state that is.*" That is "*peace.*"

There is a "*peace with God*" that people can have.
- **Romans 5:1**
  Therefore being justified by faith, **we have peace with God** through our Lord Jesus Christ:

There is also the "*peace of God*" which is possible to have for those who first have received "*peace with God.*"
- **Philippians 4:6**
  Be careful for nothing; but in every thing by prayer and supplication with thanksgiving **let your requests be made known unto God.**

"from God our Father and the Lord Jesus Christ" The only source of "*grace*" and "*peace*" is from the Father and the Son. They are the only Ones who can give us true "*grace*" and true "*peace.*" Notice the equality of the two Persons of the Godhead here. The Lord Jesus Christ is every bit as much Deity as God the Father is or God the Holy Spirit. There is a unity in the Godhead, and they are coexistent and coeternal and copowerful in all their attributes.

Colossians 1:3

"We give thanks to God and the Father of our Lord Jesus Christ, praying always for you"

"We give thanks to God and the Father of our Lord Jesus Christ" Paul was in continuous thanksgiving for these Christians who were at Colosse. We ought to be thankful for everyone we know who is saved. Be thankful for them that God has touched their hearts and redeemed them from the wicked world and made them His sons or daughters because they are *"in Christ."*

"praying always for you" Though Paul was in prison he was still *"praying always"* for others. He hoped that others were *"praying"* for him I am sure.

Colossians 1:4

"Since we heard of your faith in Christ Jesus, and of the love *which ye have* to all the saints"

"Since we heard of your faith in Christ Jesus" There was a time when Paul did not even know the Colossians. In time, however, he was not the one who led them to Christ. As soon as he heard of their *"faith in Christ Jesus,"* especially, he remembered them daily in prayer. He thanked God for them. That *"since"* is a time factor. There must be a time when you trusted in the Lord Jesus Christ as your Saviour, otherwise you are lost. There must also be a place where this event in your life took place. If you have trusted Christ by faith then you have been redeemed by trusting in Him and believing on His Name. If there has never been a time when you trusted the Lord Jesus as Saviour, you have not been born-again. You have not received Him by faith. You are not saved. You don't have faith in the Lord Jesus Christ. I urge you to trust the Lord Jesus Christ if that is your need at this moment.

"and of the love *which ye have* to all the saints" In the Colossian church, there was no separate *"love"* for just some of the *"saints."* Those who are saved should have a *"love"* for *"all the saints,"* as well. In some churches there does not seem to be *"love."* There seems to be much that could be termed war, fighting, bickering, division, hatred, and all kinds of things. I am glad that our *Bible For Today Baptist Church* here in Collingswood is a peaceful and a loving church. We want to keep it that way always. Some of you saints may be rich, poor, fat, skinny, or whatever your status is, but if you are a believer in the Lord Jesus Christ, we have a love for you. We want you to *"grow in grace and in the knowledge of our Lord and Saviour Jesus Christ"* (2 Peter 3:18). We want you to be comfortable in Him and to do His will. Praise God for the *"love"* that we can have one for another in the things of Christ. This is not the case in so many different churches today.

You might ask, *"How can a church exist without love one for another?"* Well, I don't know how these kinds of churches exist. They take offerings. They pay their preachers. But in their churches, you have some of the saints seated in one section, and some in another section, and they don't talk to each other. It is a terrible travesty in our churches today. I don't mean only in modernistic and liberal churches, but I mean in fundamental churches that claim to know and love the Lord Jesus Christ. We must keep that true Christian "love" burning one for another. The *"love"* for *"all the saints"* should be seen and felt among us.

Colossians 1:5

"For the hope which is laid up for you in heaven, whereof ye heard before in the word of the truth of the gospel"

"For the hope which is laid up for you in heaven" Paul was not only praying for the saints, but also *"for the hope"* which was *"laid up"* for them *"in Heaven."* He is thanking God for this *"hope."*
- **1 Corinthians 15:19**
  If in this life only we have **hope in Christ**, we are of all men most miserable.

Hope Beyond the Grave
There is a *"hope"* beyond the grave for those who are saved.

When born-again Christians die, they go to Heaven. That is what Paul is speaking about. That laid up hope is set aside, reserved, in Heaven. Peter talked about this inheritance in Heaven.
- **1 Peter 1:4**
  To an inheritance incorruptible, and undefiled, and that fadeth not away, **reserved in heaven for you.**

Heaven is a special place. Paul said that these Colossians who have faith in Christ and love for the saints have a *"hope"* laid up in Heaven.
- **Acts 23:6**
  But when Paul perceived that the one part were Sadducees, and the other Pharisees, he cried out in the council, Men and brethren, I am a Pharisee, the son of a Pharisee: **of the hope and resurrection of the dead I am called in question.**

Here, Paul talked about the *"hope of the resurrection."* He was speaking of that future life with Christ with our resurrected bodies. He used that *"hope"* to divide the group. Some were Sadducees who did not believe in the resurrection, and some were Pharisees who did believe in the resurrection. When Paul said that he believed in the resurrection, there was mumbling, there was groping for words, there was fighting and bickering in that *"council"* meeting. He was freed from this council because he believed in the *"hope and the resurrection of the dead."*

- **Acts 24:15**
And have hope toward God, which they themselves also allow, that there shall be a resurrection of the dead, both of the just and unjust.

That was the Old Testament hope. That was Job's hope, was it not?

- **Job 19:26**
And *though* **after my skin** *worms* **destroy this** *body*, **yet in my flesh shall I see God:**

- **Job 19:25**
For I know *that* **my redeemer liveth, and** *that* **he shall stand at the latter** *day* **upon the earth:**

That is a wonderful hope.

- **Titus 2:13**
Looking for that blessed hope, **and the glorious appearing of the great God and our Saviour Jesus Christ;**

There is a *"hope"* for believers. One day, the Lord Jesus Christ will be coming back. That is a *"blessed hope."* This old earth, one day, will pass from those of us who are saved and we will go up yonder to be with Christ which, as Paul wrote, is *"far better"* (Philippians 1:23).

The Three Bible "Heavens"

There are three "heavens" in the Bible:

(1) The aerial heaven of the sky.
(2) The sidereal heaven of the stars.
(3) The third Heaven of God where God's throne is (2 Corinthians 12:2).

"whereof ye heard before in the word of the truth of the gospel." There is much that is *"false gospel."* The Colossian Christians heard the straight and true *"gospel."* One false gospel says that salvation is by our works.

Good Works Can't Save

We cannot be saved by our own good works.

Another false gospel is that we can be saved by water baptism. We had a baptismal service recently, but that water baptism will not save anyone. The Church of Christ teaches this false gospel. It is after we are saved that we are to be baptized in obedience to the Lord Jesus Christ.

Another false gospel is that only the *"elect"* can be saved. The gospel can be received and believed by whoever accepts and trusts the Lord Jesus Christ as their Saviour from sin. All those who receive Christ will be saved. Harold Camping of Family Radio was asked, *"Does God love everybody?"* Mr. Camping said, *"Oh no, he just loves those who are of the elect."* That is contrary to the truth of John 3:16. Family Radio has a tract called, *"Does God Love You?"* It is printed by the hundreds of thousands of copies in many languages of the world and passed out by Family Radio followers. This is refuted by the Bible's clear teachings.

- **John 3:16**
  For God so loved the world, that he gave his only begotten Son, that whosoever believeth in him should not perish, but have everlasting life.

God loved the entire world.

The "Hyper-Calvinist" Heresy

The hyper-Calvinists say that John 3:16 means only that God loved the *"world of the elect."*

No, that means that God loved the whole world. It is up to everyone in the world to trust the Lord Jesus Christ, believe He died for them, and either receive Him, or reject Him. That is their choice. That is their decision. But the gospel message is to be proclaimed and received by the entire world.

False "Lordship Salvation" Gospel

Another false gospel is the gospel of "lordship salvation."

John MacArthur believes in lordship salvation. It is the belief that you must make Christ the Lord of your life, actions, and thoughts. Failing of that, you cannot be saved. That is a salvation by works, and not a salvation by grace.

The gospel is the good news that tells us how we can be delivered by faith in the Lord Jesus Christ from the bad news of going to the Lake of Fire. That is what the gospel is. It is the EUAGGELION. It is the *"good news"* or *"good tidings."* The bad news is that we are lost and bound for Hell. The bad news is that there is no way we can save ourselves.

The Gospel Is Good News

The good news of the gospel is that the Lord Jesus Christ came into this world to die for our sins, the sins of the whole world, so that anyone who trusts Him may be saved and have everlasting life.

That is the good news of the gospel that delivers us from the bad news.

Colossians 1:6

"Which is come unto you, as *it is* in all the world; and bringeth forth fruit, as *it doth* also in you, since this day ye heard of *it*, and knew the grace of God in truth"

"Which is come unto you as *it is* in all the world; and bringeth forth fruit, that as *it doth* also, in you" This gospel has come into *"all the world."* It is wonderful that we can, by the Internet, by the radio, by the television, and by satellite, preach the gospel all over the world. It is amazing. This gospel has come and it bears *"fruit."* Sometimes this *"fruit"* is manifested in saving those who are lost and delivering them from sin. At other times this *"fruit"* is for the believers who are in need of growth and strength in Christ. In this way, they can be strengthened and edified. That is *"fruit."*

We are glad that we can send forth the gospel through the missionaries we support, through the radio ministry, through the Internet **(www.BibleFor Today.org)**, and through our own local church ministry. The gospel makes some people mad when it is preached as light is shed on the darkness of this world. This gospel does go out *"in all the world."* Just imagine the outreach of the shortwave radio station we are on. It might not cover everybody, because it is aimed at certain parts of the world. The Internet can get to all parts of the world who have this capability. Every country of the world has access to the Internet. At various times, our Bible For Today programs can be heard at:

www.Tabernacle Ministries.org. Our own web page carries our messages we preach. It is www.Bible For Today.org.

The "Fruit" of Paul's Labor

The Colossian Christians were *"fruit"* from Paul's labor. We praise the Lord for that *"fruit."*

"since this day ye heard of *it*, and knew the grace of God in truth" They were fruit-bearers from the very day they *"heard"* and *"knew the grace of God in truth."* The Lord Jesus said in John 15:5, *"I am the vine ye are the branches."* He wants us to go and bear *"fruit"* like the Colossians did.

Colossians 1:7

"As ye also learned of Epaphras our dear fellow-servant, who is for you a faithful minister of Christ." Evidently, Epaphras took Paul's message to the Colossians. He probably took the letter from the prison in Rome to the church at Colosse. Paul loved Epaphras. He was a *"faithful minister of Christ."* It is very important to be *"faithful."* The Lord will tell us Christians at the judgment seat of Christ whether or not we are *"faithful."*

- Matthew 25:21

   His lord said unto him, Well done, thou **good and faithful servant**: thou hast been faithful over a few things, I will make thee ruler over many things: enter thou into the joy of thy lord.

I hope that everyone of us who is saved will have service for the Lord which will result in His telling us: *"Well done, thou good and faithful servant."*

- Luke 16:10

   He that is faithful in that which is least is faithful also in much: and he that is unjust in the least is unjust also in much.

Epaphras was a dear and *"faithful"* servant and *"minister of Christ."*

- 1 Corinthians 4:2

   Moreover **it is required in stewards, that a man be found faithful**.

Stewardship demands faithfulness. There are many in the New Testament who were called *"faithful."*

- **1 Corinthians 4:17**
  For this cause have I sent unto **you Timotheus, who is my beloved son, and faithful in the Lord,** who shall bring you into remembrance of my ways which be in Christ, as I teach every where in every church.
- **Ephesians 6:21**
  But that ye also may know my affairs, and how I do, Tychicus, a beloved brother and **faithful minister in the Lord,** shall make known to you all things:
- **Colossians 4:7**
  All my state shall Tychicus declare unto you, who is a beloved brother, and **a faithful minister and fellowservant** in the Lord:
- **2 Timothy 2:2**
  And the things that thou hast heard of me among many witnesses, the same **commit thou to faithful men,** who shall be able to teach others also.

It is important that we have *"faithful"* people. People who are faithful can be trusted and depended upon in all the activities in which they engage.

Are You "Faithful"?

The Greek word for "faithful" is used "of persons who show themselves faithful in the transaction of business, the executions of commands, or the discharge of official duties."

We who are saved must be faithful in reading of the Scriptures, faithful in our prayers, and faithful to the Lord in all areas of our lives. This man showed that these people were faithful. Epaphras was a dear and *"faithful minister of Christ"* for the Colossian believers.

The Greek word for *"minister"* is DIAKONOS. It is the word from which we get *"deacon."* It is also used for anyone who is a *"servant"* of the Lord. It means *"anyone who executes the commands of another."*

If we're saved, our Lord Jesus Christ is our Master. We are His servants. We are to serve Him faithfully. We are to follow His commands and His orders. We are not to invent commands. Many people invent commands that are not in Scripture. God wants us to follow the commands that are in Scripture. There are enough commands in Scripture that we don't have to follow any others. Though not direct commands, there are many applications in Scripture that we can make and follow as well. Certainly, as Epaphras was a *"faithful minister of Christ,"* so should we be.

Colossians 1:8

"Who also declared unto us your love in the Spirit."

There is the second time in this first chapter of Colossians that Paul mentions *"love."* He mentioned that their *"love"* was *"to all the saints."* Here, he says that they have *"love in the Spirit."* These Colossian Christians had a loving disposition. That is an important trait.

One of the parts of the *"fruit of the Spirit"* is *"love."* They had love in their hearts. That is the thing that breaks down hardness and coolness; am I right? It is like the sun that melts the ice.

The Warmth of Love
Love is something that warms like the sun.

There is a story about the three environmental elements, the cold, the wind, and the sun. They wanted to try to take a man's coat off. The cold tried to freeze the coat off, but the man clung closer than ever to his coat. The wind tried to blow the coat off, but again, the man held tightly to his coat. Then the sun tried. The sun made the man so warm that he voluntarily removed his coat.

That is exactly what the Lord does with the love we have for the Lord Jesus Christ. This *"love"* is manifested in our hearts and in our lives by God the Holy Spirit as He fills us. People see the evidences of that Divine love. They feel the warmth. People can feel the coldness in a church. They can also feel the warmth of a church when it is present. You can sense that the Spirit of God is there. It is that love which makes friends, breaks down barriers, and causes people to come to Christ.

Colossians 1:9

"For this cause we also, since the day we heard *it*, do not cease to pray for you, and to desire that ye might be filled with the knowledge of his will in all wisdom and spiritual understanding" Paul kept on praying and desiring continuously (present tense, continuous action in the Greek language) that they might be filled to the brim with the knowledge of God's will. If you know God's will, do you do it? I hope you do. Knowing and doing are two separate things. There are a number of passages about the *"will of God."*

- **Mark 3:35**
  For **whosoever shall do the will of God**, the same is my brother, and my sister, and mother.

We are closely related to the Lord Jesus Christ if we do the *"will of God."*

- **Romans 8:27**
  And he that searcheth the hearts knoweth what is the mind of the Spirit, because he **maketh intercession for the saints according to the will of God**.
- **Romans 12:2**
  And be not conformed to this world: but be ye transformed by the renewing of your mind, that ye may prove what is that good, and acceptable, and **perfect, will of God**.
- **Romans 15:32**
  That **may come unto you with joy by the will of God**, and may with you be refreshed.

Paul wanted to be in the will of God when he comes to a certain place to minister to them.

- **2 Corinthians 1:1**
  Paul, **an apostle of Jesus Christ by the will of God**, and Timothy our brother, unto the church of God which is at Corinth, with all the saints which are in all Achaia:
- **Galatians 1:4**
  Who gave himself for our sins, that he might deliver us from this present evil world, **according to the will of God** and our Father:

Deliverance From The Evil World

It is God's will for believers to be delivered from this *"present evil world."* We are not to be all bound-up in it and captured by its allurements.

- **Ephesians 6:6**
  Not with eyeservice, as menpleasers; but as the servants of Christ, **doing the will of God from the heart**;
- **Colossians 4:12**
  Epaphras, who is one of you, a servant of Christ, saluteth you, always labouring fervently for you in prayers, **that ye may stand perfect and complete in all the will of God**.

- **1 Thessalonians 4:3**
  For this is the will of God, even your sanctification, that ye should abstain from fornication:

That is the *"will of God."* *"Fornication"* usually refers to sexual relations on the part of a single person. The wicked sin of fornication abounds in all the nations of the world, even among professing Christians, both young and old. The *"will of God"* is to abstain from this sin of the flesh and to be sanctified.

- **1 Thessalonians 5:18**
  In every thing give thanks: for this is the will of God in Christ Jesus concerning you.

It is God's will to *"give thanks."* I am glad we sing *"Thank you Jesus for all you've done"* each Sunday in our church. That is one of our themes. We thank Him for His love, His tenderness, His Word, His answers to prayer, and His blood shed at Calvary.

- **Hebrews 10:36**
  For ye have need of patience, that, **after ye have done the will of God, ye might receive the promise.**

When God promises to do something, we are to be patient. He will do it if it is the *"will of God."*

- **1 Peter 3:17**
  For it is **better, if the will of God be so**, that ye suffer for well doing, than for evil doing.

- **1 Peter 4:2**
  That he no longer should live the rest of his time in the flesh to the lusts of men, **but to the will of God.**

- **1 John 2:17**
  And the world passeth away, and the lust thereof: but **he that doeth the will of God abideth for ever.**

Paul wanted these Colossian Christians to stand perfect and complete in all the full *"knowledge"* of God's will.

God's Will and God's Words

As many have said, *"the full knowledge of God's will is to be found in the full knowledge of God's Words."*

There is no getting around it. God's will is to be found from Genesis through Revelation in one way or another. We must stand in that full *"knowledge of God's Words"* so that we can know the *"will of God."*

This was Paul's prayer for these Christians. They probably were baby Christians. They did not know much about the Old Testament. (The New Testament had not yet been written.) Paul prayed unto the Lord that they may be filled with the *"knowledge of the Lord in all wisdom and spiritual understanding."*

We must receive the Word of God in wisdom. It is not enough to have a head knowledge of the Lord. We must use that knowledge with a proper and *"spiritual understanding"* of how to use the Scriptures, when to use the Scriptures, why to use the Scriptures, and in what way to use the Scriptures.

Colossians 1:10

"That ye might walk worthy of the Lord unto all pleasing, being fruitful in every good work, and increasing in the knowledge of God"

"That ye might walk worthy of the Lord unto all pleasing" Paul is praying for a number of things. One prayer Paul makes for the Colossian believers is that they *"might walk worthy of the Lord."* How do you *"walk worthy"*? If you are saved, you follow the prescriptions of the Scripture, the Word of God. That is the only place that tells us how to be *"worthy"* of the Lord. He prays that they would *"walk worthy."* If Paul is praying that they would *"walk worthy,"* could not the possible implication be that they might be walking unworthily?

That is so true in the lives of many Christians. I trust it is not true in our church here. I trust that each of us would *"walk worthy."* If we walk unworthily, that is a bad testimony for the Lord. He will not be pleased. The *"worthy"* walk is one that is suitable and conformable to the directives of God's Words.

"being fruitful in every good work, and increasing in the knowledge of God" There are a few verses on *"worthiness"* and *"being fruitful in every good work and increasing in the knowledge of God."* That is what Paul prayed. It is being *"worthy"* in God's eyes, not in the eyes of men and women of this world. There are many people who are very *"worthy"* in the view of the world, but not in the God's eyes. They are lost and have never trusted Christ.

- **Genesis 32:10**
  I am not worthy of the least of all the mercies, and of all the truth, which thou hast shewed unto thy servant; for with my staff I passed over this Jordan; and now I am become two bands.

Everyone of us can say that with Jacob, and mean it. There is not one of us who is *"worthy."* The Lord Jesus Christ has made us *"worthy"* if we are saved by faith in Him. If He has redeemed us, He has made us worthy, but we must

have humility, realizing that we are *"not worthy"* in and of ourselves.
- **Ephesians 4:1**
  I therefore, the prisoner of the Lord, **beseech you that ye walk worthy of the vocation wherewith ye are called,**
- **1 Thessalonians 2:12**
  That ye would walk worthy of God, who hath called you unto his kingdom and glory.

This is repeated many times in the Bible.
- **Revelation 3:4**
  Thou hast a few names even in Sardis which have not defiled their garments; **and they shall walk with me in white: for they are worthy.**

Those that are walking with the Lord in white are *"worthy"* because Christ has given us a robe of righteousness, and made us *"worthy."* Not that we are *"worthy"* in ourselves. The Greek word for *"worthy"* is AXIOS. It means *"befitting, congruous, corresponding to a thing."* The thing to which it should be *"corresponding"* is the Word of God.
- **Revelation 4:11**
  Thou art worthy, O Lord, to receive glory and honour and power: for thou hast created all things, and for thy pleasure they are and were created.

This is speaking of the Lord Jesus Christ.
- **Revelation 5:12**
  Saying with a loud voice, **Worthy is the Lamb** that was slain to receive power, and riches, and wisdom, and strength, and honour, and glory, and blessing.

Our Worthy Saviour
The Lord Jesus Christ is the only One Who is *"worthy."*

Paul wanted these Christians in Colosse *"to walk worthy"* of the Lord in all things. That was his desire and his prayer.

> ## Consider Him
>
> He alone is worthy of our trusting
> Touched is He with every grief and pain
> He rebukes with perfect, Holy knowledge
> He tries oft' that we might patience gain.
> He alone can make earthly ties grow fainter
> Only He can make world-lure fade away
> He alone--none but Christ consider
> As we journey on this pilgrim way.
>
> **By Gertrude Grace Sanborn**

Somebody might say that they know enough about the Lord and they don't need to increase in *"knowledge."* Then why did Paul ask them to increase? You say, well I've read the Bible once. Some of you might say that you have read a little of the Bible, but not the whole Bible. The Bible is the source of our *"knowledge"* about the Lord.

Noah Amatucci was baptized recently. He read his Bible through from Genesis through Revelation last year. He is reading it again this year. He was 17 years of age at the time. May God continue to encourage him to read that Bible from Genesis through Revelation every year of his life. May everyone of us do the same. You can see a film or a video, but that is not going to do as much for you as reading the Word of God.

The *"increasing in the knowledge of God"* comes about by getting into His Word, and asking Him to lead you, guide you, and give you understanding and spiritual discernment. That is *"increasing in the knowledge of God."* There is no end to this "increase" because God is infinite. Our knowledge is not infinite because we are finite. Therefore, we must continue to increase in the knowledge and power of God.

Colossians 1:11

"Strengthened with all might, according to his glorious power, unto all patience and longsuffering with joyfulness"

"Strengthened with all might" Paul prays that they would not only *"walk worthy,"* but also that they would be *"strengthened with all might."* Many unsaved people are weak. There are some weak Christians as well.

- **Ephesians 3:16**
  That he would grant you, according to the riches of his glory, to be **strengthened with might by his Spirit** in the inner man;
- **2 Timothy 4:17**
  Notwithstanding **the Lord stood with me, and strengthened me**; that by me the preaching might be fully known, and that all the Gentiles might hear: and I was delivered out of the mouth of the lion.
- **Philippians 4:13**
  I can do all things through **Christ which strengtheneth me.**

"according to his glorious power" Paul wanted the source of God's strength to be *"according to His glorious power"* rather than our own. You can go to all the physical fitness places in the world. Your muscles can bulge, and everything else can be fit as a fiddle, but that is not the type of strength that Paul is talking about here. I think he is talking about the Holy Spirit of God Who indwells the body of every single born-again Christian.

"unto all patience and longsuffering with joyfulness" Now notice the goal of the strength of God's power. Three things are involved.

The Meaning of Patience

"Patience" is involved here. What is *"patience"*?
That is *"putting up with things."*

You've heard of the *"patience"* of Job (James 5:11). He had *"patience"* when his goods went, his servants went, his children went--he was still patient. Job put up with the loss of all possessions and people.

The Meaning of Longsuffering

What is *"longsuffering"*? The Greek word for it is MAKROTHUMIA. It means *"putting up with people."*

I think that is even more difficult than putting up with *"things."* People are so different. All of us are different. It is disturbing to you when you think you have mastered what someone believes, and you think they see eye-to-eye with you on things, to have them suddenly go off on some unexpected track. There is nothing you can do but have Biblical *"longsuffering"* and try to recover your close friendship.

As I mentioned before, MAKROTHUMIA is the Greek word translated *"longsuffering."* It comes from two Greek words: MAKROS which means *"far, or a long way off,"* and THUMOS which means *"hot or boiling."* So that word literally means that *"the boiling point is still a far way off."* That is what *"longsuffering"* means. Do you boil over at the first sign of a difference of opinion with someone? If so, you don't have *"longsuffering."* Do you boil over the second time they may assault you or say mean and ugly things about you? If so, you don't have *"longsuffering."* What about the third time? Do you wait until the third time before you boil over? If you don't react, even after this third test, then your *"boiling point is still a long way off."* You indeed have been blessed with that element of the *"fruit of the Spirit"* known as *"longsuffering"* (Galatians 5:22).

We are weak. In the flesh, sometimes our boiling points are not *"far off."* They are very much skin-deep and at the surface. Paul prays that these Colossian Christians, back in the first century of the Christian church, would have this trait of being *"Strengthened with all might according to his glorious power unto all . . . longsuffering . . ."*

Just think of the *"longsuffering"* that Moses needed. Those 600,000 men plus women and children (perhaps two or three million in all) who came out of Egypt, Moses had to deal with for forty years in the wilderness. He finally failed the Lord and got angry (Numbers 20:12). Because of this, the Lord wouldn't let him come into the promised land at that time. We note, however, in the New Testament, he was on the Mount of Transfiguration with Elijah and the Lord Jesus Christ (Matthew 17:1-3). Moses did get to go to that land of promise after the Lord Jesus Christ was born.

A Scarce Commodity

"Longsuffering" is a very important, yet scarce commodity today.

Paul said that he wanted the Colossian believers to have *"longsuffering with joyfulness."* Some individuals put up with people, but they do not do so with *"joyfulness."* Sometimes they seem to have a *"martyr's complex"* about their sufferings, enduring it all with a sad countenance. Paul said he wanted the Christians at Colosse to have *"patience and longsuffering with joyfulness"*--all three.

Let people slap you, or say anything they want about you. Let your money go, your kindred go, your house burn down. Let all four tires go flat. But take all these things with *"joyfulness."* *"Joy"* is another part of the *"fruit of the Spirit"* (Galatians 5:22). You say that is impossible. Yes, it is impossible in your flesh alone. It is not impossible if you have the power of God in your life and the Holy Spirit of God giving you His victory and giving you the *"fruit of the Spirit"* (Galatians 5:22-23). It is not impossible. If it were impossible Paul would never pray that this would be the case for the Colossian Christians that did not have even a tenth as much as we have in our country today. Nor did they have the New Testament like we have.

Colossians 1:12

"Giving thanks unto the Father, which hath made us meet to be partakers of the inheritance of the saints in light" Paul said he was thankful to God Father Who *"hath made us meet."* He is the One who made believers *"meet, fit, or suited"* to be *"partakers of the inheritance of the saints in light."*

God Equips the Saved Ones
If we are saved, God has equipped us.

We have not made ourselves *"meet."* If we could do it ourselves, that would be salvation by works. We could not, by ourselves, make ourselves fit and meet for the Master. God Himself, through our faith in His Son, the Lord Jesus Christ, has made us *"partakers of the inheritance of the saints in light."* There is no command that God has ever given the believers that He has not also equipped us to obey by the power of the Spirit of God within us. The Lord Jesus said, *"I am the light of the world: he that followeth me shall not walk in darkness"* (John 8:12b).

Colossians 1:13

"Who hath delivered us from the power of darkness, and hath translated *us* into the kingdom of His dear Son"

"Who hath delivered us from the power of darkness"
That *"power of darkness"* is Satan's power from which the believer has been *"delivered."* There are many verses on deliverance.

- **2 Corinthians 1:10**
  Who delivered us from so great a death, and doth deliver: in whom we trust that he will yet deliver us

Paul was delivered by the Lord Jesus Christ in all three tenses: past, present, and future.

- **Galatians 1:4**
  Who gave himself for our sins, **that he might deliver us from this present evil world**, according to the will of God and our Father

- **1 Thessalonians 1:10**
  And to wait for his Son from heaven, whom he raised from the dead, even Jesus, **which delivered us from the wrath to come.**

We who are born-again don't have the *"wrath"* of either the Great Tribulation or of Hell facing us. Christ has delivered us and rescued us from these *"wraths."*

- **2 Timothy 3:11**
  Persecutions, afflictions, which came unto me at Antioch, at Iconium, at Lystra; what persecutions I endured: **but out of them all the Lord delivered me.**

Here, Paul talked about the Lord's deliverances from his *"persecutions"* and *"afflictions"* that came upon him.

- **2 Timothy 4:17-18**
  Notwithstanding the Lord stood with me, and strengthened me; that by me the preaching might be fully known, and that all the Gentiles might hear: and **I was delivered out of the mouth of the lion. And the Lord shall deliver me from every evil work**, and will preserve me unto his heavenly kingdom: to whom be glory for ever and ever. Amen.

- **Hebrews 2:14-15**
  Forasmuch then as the children are partakers of flesh and blood, he also himself likewise took part of the same; that **through death he might destroy him that had the power of death, that is, the devil; And deliver them who through fear of death were all their lifetime subject to bondage.**

In this verse it is stated that the Lord Jesus Christ has delivered us from the *"power of death."* If we have trusted Christ and are saved, then darkness, the Devil, and evil do not have any more power over us. If these do have power about us, God's power within us (God the Holy Spirit) is greater than that *"power"* that is outside us. As 1 John 4:4 says: *"Greater is He that is in you, than he that is in the world."* The Spirit of God has transposed us.

"and hath translated *us* into the kingdom of His dear Son" Not only has God delivered us from the *"power of darkness,"* and has made us inheritors with the *"saints in light,"* but He has also *"translated us into the kingdom of His dear Son."* God has given us a change of relationship. He has brought us *"into the kingdom of His dear Son."* If He only took us out of darkness, we would only have *"half a loaf."* That is all! That was the trouble with the man who had an evil spirit (Luke 11:24-26). The spirit left, but when he found the man's *"house"* empty, he returned with *"seven other spirits more evil than himself."* This last estate was *"worse than the first."*

Just to have the evil go from us and be *"delivered"* from it is not enough. We must have God to *"transform us into the image of His dear Son."* It is not enough to quit sinning. It is not enough to stop evil. Every person who is in the coffin today, tomorrow--whenever they are laid out in the coffin (and they are dying at a huge rate every day)--has stopped sinning. They no longer commit evil.

An absence of sin or an absence of evil is not enough. Being delivered from the *"power of darkness"* is not enough. We must be *"translated into the Kingdom of His dear Son."* We must be saved by God's grace. We must be given a righteousness of God through faith. That is what He has done if we've trusted Him and are saved.

Colossians 1:14

"In whom we have redemption through his blood, *even* the forgiveness of sins"

This verse is a reference to the Lord Jesus Christ as He *"translates"* those who are saved from the power of darkness and into the kingdom of His dear Son. He is the beloved Son whom His Father loved and yet sent Him into this world to die for all sinners. He so loved the world that He gave us His only begotten Son (John 3:16). He loved His Son, but He also loved the world with the result that He gave us His Son who was *"made to be sin for us that we might be made the righteousness of God in Him"* (2 Corinthians 5:21). He loved the world, He loved His Son; but He gave His Son because he loved the world equally as much as He loved His Son so that the World, and those who are out in the world, might trust Him, be saved, redeemed, and set free from sin.

It is in the Lord Jesus Christ *"in Whom we have redemption through His blood."* The Greek word for *"redemption"* is APOLUTROSIS. It means *"liberation , procured by the payment of a ransom."*

Free and Redeemed

If you have Christ as your Saviour, your sins have been placed on Him and sent away. You are free and redeemed *"through his blood."*

The *"payment"* for a Christian's *"liberation"* was the *"blood"* of the Saviour in His death on Calvary's cross. That is what *"redemption"* is, *"payment of a ransom."*

By the way, the words, *"through his blood"* are not found in the New International Version. They are not in the New American Standard Version. They are not in the Revised Standard Version or the New Revised Standard Version. They are not in Manuscripts "B" (Vatican) and "Aleph" (Sinai). They are not in the Westcott and Hort false Greek texts (like the Nestle-Aland or the United Bible Society texts). These words are out of there because those heretical Gnostics removed them. They did not like the doctrine of *"redemption through His blood."* But the Bible says that *"without the shedding of the blood"* of the Lord Jesus Christ, there is no redemption (Hebrews 9:22b).

"Even the forgiveness of sins"

Redemption and Forgiveness

Those of us who have *"redemption"* also have God's *"forgiveness of sins."*

The Greek word for "forgiveness" is APHESIS. This comes from two Greek words, APO (*"from or away from"*) and HIEMI (*"to send."*). God's *"redemption"* through personal faith in the Lord Jesus Christ means *"to send away"* our sins.

The *"scapegoat"* which was sent into the wilderness on the day of atonement (Leviticus 16) illustrates this picture of redemption as a *"sending away"* of sins.

- **Leviticus 16:10**
  But **the goat, on which the lot fell to be the scapegoat, shall be presented alive before the LORD**, to make an atonement with him, *and* to let him go for a scapegoat into the wilderness.

On the day of atonement, Aaron offered one goat as a sacrifice. On the live goat, he confessed the sins of Israel and let it go into the wilderness.

- **Leviticus 16:21-22**
  21 And **Aaron shall lay both his hands upon the head of the live goat, and confess over him all the iniquities of the children of Israel**, and all their transgressions in all their sins, **putting them upon the head of the goat**, and shall send *him* away by the hand of a fit man into the wilderness: 22 And **the goat shall bear upon him all their iniquities** unto a land not inhabited: and he shall let go the goat in the wilderness.

This is what *"redemption"* means literally. It is the *"sending away"* of our sins. The Lord Jesus Christ's death on the cross was the sacrifice for the sins of the world. His shed blood was the ransom that was paid to a holy and offended God to gain that redemption for those who receive it by genuine faith in Christ. The blood of Christ is the payment and ransom for the sins of the whole world. It is not only the ransom for the elect. It is the ransom for the whole world.

Release From Bondage

When we receive God's *"forgiveness,"* we have a *"release from bondage or imprisonment."*

That is what the Greek word, APHESIS, means. Further, it means *"forgiveness or pardon, of sins (letting them go as if they had never been committed), remission of the penalty."* That is what *"forgiveness"* is. It is a tremendous gift that God has given to us. Those of us who are saved should praise God that we have been delivered from the power of darkness. We ought to thank God that we have been translated or taken out of that *"darkness"* and put into the *"kingdom of His dear Son."* We are now "Christ's Ones" or Christians, because we have faith in Christ and have been regenerated by God.

Colossians 1:15

"Who is the image of the invisible God, the firstborn of every creature"

This word, *"Who,"* is referring back to the Lord Jesus Christ. He was and is *"the image of the invisible God."* How can you be *"invisible"* and have an image? With the Triune God, this is not a problem, though it is to us who are mortals. How could God the Father, God the Son, and God the Holy Spirit, Who were *"invisible,"* become visible? How could the Trinity permit us humans to see God? How could we, who are ordinary people--sinners, lost, and undone, come to know intimately the *"invisible God"*? That is why God the Father had to send His Son, Who was the *"image,"* the absolute perfection of the image of the *"invisible God."* God *"was made flesh, and dwelt among us"* (John 1:14). It is also true that *"God was manifest in the flesh."* This is a wonderful truth.

- **1 Timothy 3:16**
  And without controversy great is the mystery of godliness: **God was manifest in the flesh**, justified in the Spirit, seen of angels, preached unto the Gentiles, believed on in the world, received up into glory.

The other versions like the *New International Version* (NIV), *Today's New International Version* (TNIV), *New American Standard Version* (NASV), *Revised Standard Version* (RSV), *New Revised Standard Version* (NRSV) and others don't have this verse correctly translated. Their false Greek critical texts, on which these versions are based, omit the word, *"God."* It is essential to make the *"invisible God"* to become "visible" that the living and eternal *"God"* would be *"manifest."* This *"manifestation"* makes Him *"visible."* By His incarnation, the Lord Jesus Christ became the *"image,"* the exact likeness of all that God was. If you want to see who God the Father is, and who God the Holy Spirit is, then look at the Lord Jesus Christ. He is the *"image of the invisible God."*

By the term, *"firstborn,"* Paul is not teaching that Jesus was a creature or a created being. The Greek term, PROTOTOKOS, translated *"firstborn,"* is from two smaller Greek words. The first part is PROTO which means *"first."* The second part is TOKOS which is from the verb, TIKTO, which means *"to be born."* *"Firstborn"* could be taken as being chronologically the *"firstborn."* This is not what is meant here.

The Lord Jesus Was Not Created

The Lord Jesus Christ was not a created Being, but was eternal. He had no beginning. There was never a time when he wasn't here.

It is the second sense which is to be understood here by the word, *"firstborn."* It is *"right of the firstborn"* as mentioned repeatedly in the Old Testament. The *"firstborn"* have greater blessings and rights. This is the sense used here in Colossians.

- **1 Chronicles 5:1**
  Now the sons of Reuben the firstborn of Israel, (**for he was the firstborn**; but, forasmuch as he defiled his father's bed, his birthright was given unto the sons of Joseph the son of Israel: and the genealogy is not to be reckoned after the birthright.

The *"firstborn"* of Israel was Reuben, but because of his sin God passed him over for the privileges of that birthright. Usually, the *"firstborn"* had a double blessing. He received double possessions and inheritance from his father. God passed Reuben over for this double blessing and gave it to the *"sons of Joseph,"* Ephraim and Manasseh.

The Lord Jesus Christ is the head of all the *"firstborn"* because of this title. He is the *"firstborn"* and the privileges and honor resulting from it. That is the idea of the title of the "firstborn." It does not mean that the Lord Jesus Christ was a created Being. He was not a creature. The Jehovah Witnesses falsely teach this. They believe that the Lord Jesus Christ was made or created. This was also what the Gnostics believed and taught. The Gnostics were the ones who corrupted the false Westcott and Hort Greek New Testament upon which the false versions were based. The Jehovah Witness's Bible is changed for instance in the Gospel of John.

- **John 1:1**
  In the beginning was the Word, and the Word was with God, and the Word was God.

They say *"the Word was a God"* instead of *"the Word was God."* They believe that the Lord Jesus Christ was a created being and not *"the image of the invisible God."*

Colossians 1:16

"For by him were all things created, that are in heaven, and that are in earth, visible and invisible, whether *they be* thrones, or dominions, or principalities, or powers: all things were created by him, and for him"

"For by him were all things created that are in heaven, and that are in earth, visible and invisible" As one of the gospel song writers wrote: *"The great Creator became my Saviour."* The Lord Jesus Christ, in this passage of Scripture, is said to be the Creator of *"all things that are in Heaven"* and all things *"that are in earth."* The Heavenly things would include all the holy angels. It would include each and every one of the billions of stars. It would include all the planets. That is quite a feat. The earthly things would include all the fish of the sea, the fowls of the air, and the insects and animals of the earth. This includes both the things that are *"visible"* and can be seen, as well as the things that are *"invisible"* and can't be seen such as the atom. The atom is what everything is made of. The atoms are *"invisible,"* to the naked eye, but Christ created them as well as all things *"visible."*

"whether they be thrones, or dominions, or principalities, or powers all things were created by him, and for him" Those are all words signifying the various authority systems, wherever they may be. It includes Satan's realm of authority which Satan presently controls as well as the authority systems of men on earth.

- Ephesians 6:12
  For **we wrestle not against flesh and blood, but against principalities,** against powers, against the rulers of the darkness of this world, against spiritual wickedness in high places.

One day all these authority systems will be made subject to the Lord Jesus Christ. Not only have *"all things"* been created by the Lord Jesus, but they were also created *"for Him."* He was to be the beneficiary of all of these things that He *"created."*

- Ephesians 2:10
  For **we are his workmanship, created in Christ Jesus** unto good works, which God hath before ordained that we should walk in them.
- Colossians 3:10
  And have put on **the new** *man*, which is renewed in knowledge **after the image of him that created him:**

Created For the Lord Jesus Christ

If you have been *"created"* in Christ Jesus as a *"new creature"* (2 Corinthians 5:17), you have been *"created"* for Him as well, just like the Heavenly things and the earthly things.

If we are *"born again"* (John 3:3), we have a new nature that has been created *"by"* the Lord Jesus Christ and *"for"* His purposes as well. We have been *"created"* for His purpose and for His glory to be used as He sees fit. We are not created for our own purpose but for His. In this way, we have been made *"partakers of the divine nature"* (2 Peter 1:4). This new nature, that is thus *"created,"* is one of the *"invisible"* things made by the Lord Jesus Christ.

There are a number of verses about the Lord Jesus Christ as the Creator.

- **John 1:3**
  All things were made by him; and without him was not any thing made that was made.

This is a clear reference to the Lord Jesus Christ. If He were just a man, as the modernists and liberals believe, how could He create "*all things*"? It would be impossible!

Modernist and Liberal Denials

The modernists and liberals all around the world deny that He was the Creator. They deny His Deity. They teach that He could not be the Creator because He was only a human being like the rest of us. They even deny the Virgin Birth of Christ.

They don't believe in the miraculous birth of the Lord Jesus. They teach that He had a human father, Joseph, and a human mother, Mary. No. He was a born of a virgin without any human father. He is "*the Son of God.*" By the miracle of His incarnation, the Lord Jesus Christ was "<u>God</u> *manifest in the flesh*" (1 Timothy 3:16--**Textus Receptus Greek and KJB English reading**).

- **John 1:10**
  He was in the world, and **the world was made by him**, and the world knew him not.
- **Ephesians 3:9**
  And to make all men see what is the fellowship of the mystery, which from the beginning of the world hath been hid in God, **who created all things <u>by Jesus Christ</u>**

If you have the right Bible it reads correctly. If you have a *New International Version*, you won't find "*by Jesus Christ*" because the "B" and "Aleph" manuscripts from which it was taken, leave off the fact that He was part of the creative power of God. The *New American Standard Version* and *The Revised Standard Version* also leave out this phrase. If you have a *New International Version* you won't understand the gospel song, "*When Christ rent the veil in two.*" Do you know why? Because in the *New International Version* there is no "*veil*" that separated the Holy Place from the Holy of Holies. They make it just a "*curtain.*" The "*veil*" is gone. Many of our hymns have no meaning anymore because of these false perversions of Scripture.

- **Revelation 4:11**
  Thou art worthy, O Lord, to receive glory and honour and power: **for thou hast created all things, and for thy pleasure they are and were created.**
- **Revelation 10:6**
  And sware by him that liveth for ever and ever, **who created heaven, and the things that therein are, and the earth, and the things that therein are, and the sea, and the things which are therein,** that there should be time no longer.

Our Saviour, along with God the Father and God the Holy Spirit, was truly the Creator.

Colossians 1:17

"And he is before all things, and by him all things consist"

"And he is before all things" When it is stated of the Lord Jesus Christ that *"He is before all things,"* this speaks of His eternal preexistence. That is one of the things that Bishop B. F. Westcott denied. You can find this perversion in his commentary on *The Gospel of John* (pp. 2, 13, 248). I make reference to this in my book on the *Theological Heresies of Westcott and Hort* [BFT #595 @ $7 + $3 S&H].

The Lord Jesus was *"before all things,"* because He was the creator of *"all things."* There is no question about that. This is a very important doctrine of Scripture. He was primary. John the Baptist testified of this.

- **John 1:15**
  John bare witness of him, and cried, saying, This was he of whom I spake, **He that cometh after me is preferred before me: for he was before me.**

Even though John the Baptist was born physically before the Lord Jesus Christ, the Lord Jesus was *"before"* Him by virtue of His eternal preexistence.

- **1 John 1:1-2**
  That which was from the beginning, which we have heard, which we have seen with our eyes, which we have looked upon, and our hands have handled, of the Word of life; (For the life was manifested, and we have seen it, and bear witness, and shew unto you that eternal life, which was with the Father, and was manifested unto us;)

He was in the beginning.

- John 8:56-58

  Your father Abraham rejoiced to see my day: and he saw it, and was glad. Then said the Jews unto him, Thou art not yet fifty years old, and hast thou seen Abraham? Jesus said unto them, Verily, verily, I say unto you, **Before Abraham was, I am.**

The Lord Jesus Christ was arguing with the self-righteous and hypocritical Pharisees. The eternal Son of God and God the Son was *"before Abraham"* and before everything in Heaven or in earth.

"and by him all things consist." That Greek word translated "consist," SUNISTAO, means *"to bring or band together."*

Jesus Holds the World Together

The whole universe would fly apart if it weren't for the Lord Jesus Christ. He is not only the Creator of all things, but He is also the One Who holds these created things together.

Another meaning of SUNISTAO is *"to preserve."* The created things are not only held together by Him, but they are also *"preserved"* by Him. One of the important things that have been *"preserved"* by the Lord Jesus Christ are His Hebrew and Greek Words that make up our Bible. This is one more verse to be used to support the Bible preservation of the original Hebrew and Greek Words.

Colossians 1:18

"And he is the head of the body, the church: who is the beginning, the firstborn from the dead; that in all *things* he might have the preeminence"

"And he is the head of the body, the church" The "church" is here called *"the body."* We are a local church, and as such, a part of *"the body."* Can you be a local church if you don't have a special church building? The building you meet in is not the essence of a local church. The Greek term for "church" is ECCLESIA. It comes from two Greek words, EK (*"out or from"*) and KALEO (*"to call or summon"*). It means *"called out ones."*

The Essence of a Local Church

The essence of a local church is a group of saved people who have been *"called out"* of the world and unto the Lord Jesus Christ, their Saviour.

This *"called out"* group of persons assembles together in some place for the purpose of listening to sound Bible preaching, of praying, of singing praises to the Lord, of remembering Christ's two ordinances, and of sending missionaries to the ends of the earth. Christ is the head of our local church. Your pastor is the under-shepherd seeking to care for those who attend.

"Who is the beginning the firstborn from the dead, that in *all things* he might have the preeminence" Again, Paul repeats the truth that the Lord Jesus Christ is *"the beginning,"* the preexistent One from all eternity past. This is the reason that He should have *"preeminence"* in *"all things."* The Greek word for *"preeminence"* is used only here in the New Testament. It is PROTEUO. It means *"to be first, hold the first place."* He should *"hold the first place"* in the lives of whose whom He came to save. Though the Lord wants us to take care of ourselves since our bodies are the *"temple"* of the Holy Spirit (1 Corinthians 6:19-20), we should never put ourselves before the Saviour. The Person we should think about pleasing, more than any others, including ourselves, is the Lord Jesus Christ. At every time, in every place, in every way, the Lord Jesus Christ should have the *"preeminence"* in our lives and in our activities. That is what John the Baptist had decided for himself.

- John 3:30
    He must increase, but I must decrease.

John's wish should be the hearts and minds of every born-again believer. We should not be pompous and puffed up, thinking we're the most important person in the world. The Lord Jesus Christ is the most important Person in the world. *"He must increase"* and we *"must decrease."*

- 3 John 9
    I wrote unto the church: **but Diotrephes, who loveth to have the preeminence among them**, receiveth us not.

> ## Diotrephes and His Relatives
>
> Diotrephes sounds like people we have met in many Baptist churches. He would be considered a *"church boss."* He had a selfish *"preeminence"* in the church. That is the wrong *"preeminence."* Not a single person in the Lord Jesus Christ's local church should be *"preeminent,"* but only He Himself. This includes strict obedience to His Words which He gave us in the Bible. This is putting the *"preeminence"* of the Lord Jesus Christ into action and practice.

- Ephesians 1:22
  And hath put all things under his feet, **and gave him to be the head over all things to the church**
- Ephesians 4:15
  But speaking the truth in love, may grow up into him in all things, **which is the head, even Christ**

The *"head"* determines what we say, what we do, and where we go. When our heads, which house our brains, are out of order, we don't know what we are doing. That is why the head is punched in boxing to knock out the opponent. What a terrible experience that would be. The head is the most important part of our body. It controls the actions of the other members of the body. We have seen people who have brain injuries. They cannot control their bodies. A healthy person, Dr. Atkins (the founder of the Atkins diet), injured his head in a fall on the ice. After that, he could no longer control his body. In fact, he died as a result of that head injury.

- Ephesians 5:23
  For the husband is the head of the wife, **even as Christ is the head of the church**: and he is the saviour of the body.
- Colossians 2:19
  And not holding the Head, from which all the body by joints and bands having nourishment ministered, and knit together, increaseth with the increase of God.

The Lord Jesus Christ is the head of the local church no matter where it meets, whether in a house, in a building, in the catacombs, out in a field, or wherever. Any church which magnifies the Lord Jesus Christ will grow up and *"increase"* in love and in knowledge of the things of the Lord. May God give us His own Divine blessings as a local church while we strive to teach, preach, and practice His Words until the Lord Jesus calls us Home to Heaven.

Colossians 1:19

"For it pleased *the Father* that in him should all fulness dwell." God the Father has placed the *"fullness"* of the Godhead in His Son, the Lord Jesus Christ.
- Colossians 2:9
 For in him **dwelleth all the fulness of the Godhead bodily.**

Heresy by Some "Fundamentalists"

There are even some Fundamentalists today who say our Lord Jesus Christ did not have all of His Divine attributes while here on earth. They say He did not have all the Omniscience, Omnipresence, and Omnipotence of Deity. That is a heretical doctrine which should be forsaken by Fundamentalists.

I have pointed this out to our Fundamentalist brethren, quoting Scriptures to prove what I have said, but with some, it is to no avail. I heard a recent tape from a Pastor who was teaching this falsehood.

The Lord Jesus Christ knew everything while here on earth and He knows everything today as he is seated at the Father's right hand. There was not a particle of Deity that was withheld or left out of the Lord Jesus while He was here upon this earth. There was not a single scintilla absent from His full and complete Deity with all of the *"fullness"* that goes with it.

Colossians 1:20

"And having made peace through the blood of his cross, by him to reconcile all things unto himself; by him, I say, whether *they be* things in earth, or things in heaven"
This is a specific verse that shows the *"peace"* with God comes through the *"blood of His cross."* It was not just the *"blood"* of the Lord Jesus Christ as it was coursing through His veins. It was the *"blood of His cross."* It was the substitutionary shedding of His *"blood"* on Calvary's cross that provided for *"peace"* to the sinner who trusted in Him as Saviour.
- Romans 5:1
 Therefore being justified by faith, **we have peace with God through our Lord Jesus Christ**

That is where the Lord Jesus made *"peace."* It was at the *"cross."* It was by the shedding of His sinless, spotless, precious *"blood"* on that *"cross"* as an atonement for sin. By the Lord Jesus Christ, God the Father could *"reconcile all things unto Himself."* This *"reconciliation"* was also based on the *"blood of His cross."*

- **Romans 5:10**
  For if, when we were enemies, **we were reconciled to God by the death of his Son**, much more, being reconciled, we shall be saved by his life.
- **2 Corinthians 5:18-20**
  And all things are of God, **who hath reconciled us to himself by Jesus Christ**, and hath given to us the ministry of reconciliation; To wit, that God was in Christ, **reconciling the world unto himself**, not imputing their trespasses unto them; **and hath committed unto us the word of reconciliation.** Now then **we are ambassadors for Christ**, as though God did beseech you by us: we pray you in Christ's stead, **be ye reconciled to God.**

This shows the believer's part in *"reconciliation."* That is the ministry we have. We must preach that *"word of reconciliation"* by faith in Christ wherever we go.

We are *"ambassadors for Christ."* An ambassador represents the king, the prince, the governor, or any other high official. Our job is to preach so God can *"reconcile"* men to Himself through His Son. There is a false teaching that God has to be reconciled to us. On the contrary, we must be reconciled to God. He has not moved. We are the one to be *"reconciled."* This verse is very clear about this matter.

It is similar to the couple who has been married for 55 years. The wife, who is driving along with the husband, said she remembered when they were first going together before they were married. She reminded him that they used to sit close together while they were driving. The man replied to her: *"I haven't moved."* If the wife wants to be close to her husband while driving with him, she must move closer to him. So with *"reconciliation."* God hasn't moved either. If we want to be brought back and close to Him we need to be the one to move. That is what *"reconciliation"* means. The Greek word is APOKAT- ALLASSO. It means *"to bring about a peace, to reconcile again, to bring back to a former state of harmony."* This was accomplished through the *"cross"* of Calvary.

The History of the "Cross"

"The cross was a well-known instrument of most cruel and ignominious punishment, borrowed by the Greeks and Romans from the Phoenicians; to it were affixed among the Romans, down to the time of Constantine the Great, the guiltiest criminals, particularly the basest of slaves, robbers, the authors and abaters of insurrections, and occasionally in the provinces, at the arbitrary pleasure of the governors, upright and peaceable men also, and even the Roman citizens themselves."

The Lord Jesus was peaceable, upright, perfect, and sinless; yet the sinners still crucified Him on a *"cross."* It was necessary in the plan of God. It was predicted by the Lord in the Old Testament. The shedding of blood in death by an innocent Substitute was necessary to redeem the lost people in the world. *"Without the shedding of blood is no remission"* (Hebrews 9:22b).

Colossians 1:21

"And you, that were sometime alienated and enemies in your mind by wicked works, yet now hath he reconciled."

"And you that were sometime alienated" Paul is talking about those who were formerly unsaved. If you are unsaved, you are now like these Colossian Christians were, that is, *"alienated."* The Greek word for *"alienated"* is APALLOTRIOO. It refers to someone who is "shut out from one's fellowship and intimacy. We talk about *"aliens"* being from outer space. They are not citizens. They do not relate to us in any way. Paul said that we are *"alienated and enemies in your minds."*

"and enemies in your mind" Not only were these Colossians *"alienated"*, but they were also *"enemies"* in their *"mind."*

Thought-Life Dangers

You can hate the Lord, and be an enemy of the Lord in your *"mind."* The thought life is important. It is internal.

"by wicked works" These *"works"* are outside and can be seen by others. Inside is the *"mind"* and outside are the *"wicked works."* This is the condition of every unsaved, lost sinner in the world. They are dirty and defiled both inside and outside.

"yet now hath he reconciled" Because these Colossians repented of their sins and trusted the Lord Jesus Christ as their Saviour, God *"reconciled"* them to Himself. God has made those who were *"enemies"* into friends. If you are saved, He has reconciled you as well. Praise God for that. If you are not saved, you need to trust the Lord Jesus Christ and receive Him by faith.

Colossians 1:22

"In the body of his flesh through death, to present you holy and unblamable and unreproveable in his sight."

"In the body of his flesh through death" God did this Divine act of *"reconciliation"* in the *"body"* of Christ's flesh *"through death."*

The Only Antidote for Sins

The *"peace by the blood of His cross"* was accomplished by means of the sinless *"body"* of the Lord Jesus Christ as He shed His blood and died on the cross for the sins of the world. That was the only thing that God could use as an antidote for the sins of mankind.

God's own Son had to come from Heaven. Through the incarnation, by means of Christ's virgin birth, God took upon Himself a perfect human body. Through His willing sacrifice in His crucifixion death, the death by the shedding of His precious blood, the Lord Jesus Christ accomplished this *"reconciliation"* for the Colossians and for all who have trusted in the Saviour since that awful day.

"to present you holy and unblamable and unreproveable in his sight" This gives the purpose of God's *"reconciliation."* The purpose is to *"present"* these believers in Colosse (and all believers) qualified in three areas. The first area is that they be *"holy."* Once we have been saved, we are no longer considered by the Lord as unholy, filthy or wicked like we used to be in the world. On the other hand, God sees us as *"holy and unblamable and unreproveable in His sight."*

Though positionally before God, the Christian is looked on in all these three ways, He also wants us to work out this positional truth in practical ways while we're on earth.

God Wants Us Holy
God wants us to be "*holy*" in our lives.

God wants us to be "*unblamable.*" God wants us to be "*unreproveable.*" Men and women might want to let these things slide, but God wants us to pay attention to these areas in a practical way every day of our lives.

God Lets No Sin Slide
Man's sight is not God's sight. God doesn't let anything slide. If He lets a single sin slide He will not be God. That is why every sin of all of us in the whole world had to be placed on the Lord Jesus Christ, the sacrificial Lamb Who came to seek and to save that which was lost.

Through that sacrifice of the Saviour, the shedding of His blood, we who have trusted and received Him can be redeemed from those sins. We can be made "*holy and unblameable and unreproveable in His sight.*" That is what is known as justification.

Justification is the sovereign declaration by a Holy God that those who have repented of their sins and trusted by faith the Lord Jesus Christ are, "*in His sight,*" absolutely holy, absolutely righteous, and absolutely perfect. That is "*in His sight.*" That is recorded in God's records in Heaven.

I've mentioned before that there are two important words beginning with "S" that we must understand. One is "*standing.*" The other is "*state.*" Our "*standing*" before God is perfect, holy, and unblamable. The "*state*" is our condition on earth day by day. That is not like the "*standing*" before God. We trust that our "*standing*" up in Heaven and our "*state*" down here will become more equal day by day as we walk closely with the Lord. We hope that our "*state*" here below will approach our "*standing*" with God and we may be "*holy.*"

That is the purpose of Christ's finished work on Calvary--to make us holy. He did not save us merely to get us out of Hell. He wants to get us out of Hell, but He also wants us to be a "*holy*" people separated unto Himself.

Colossians 1:23

"If ye continue in the faith grounded and settled, and *be* not moved away from the hope of the gospel, which ye have heard, *and* which was preached to every creature which is under heaven; whereof I Paul am made a minister."

"If ye continue in the faith" If you who are saved *"continue"* in *"the faith,"* then you can be in a practical and down to earth sense, *"holy"* and *"unblameable"* and *"unreproveable,"* not only in the sight of God, but also in the sight of men. Since the Greek word for *"faith,"* PISTIS, has the Greek article, it is referring to the body of truth and belief taught in the Scripture. What if you don't continue? Peter did not continue. He said after the crucifixion and resurrection of the Lord Jesus Christ, *"I go a fishing"* (John 21:3b). He just went back to his old profession. Only later did Peter return to a bold stand for His Lord and Saviour.

We Must Continue in the Faith

I hope all of us who are saved will continue on with the Lord. You might think you are just as perfect as you can possibly be. No, you are not. No, I am not. We should want to *"continue in the faith"* of the Scripture, in all of its sound doctrines.

"grounded and settled" That Greek verb for *"grounded"* is a perfect tense. That tense describes something that has been put on a foundation in the past, is resting on that foundation in the present, and will continue to rest on that foundation in the future. That *"Foundation"* is the Lord Jesus Christ as Paul has mentioned (1 Corinthians 3:11). You cannot move. You are *"settled"* in the sense of sitting on that foundation without moving away from it.

"and *be* not moved away from the hope of the gospel which ye have heard *and* which was preached to every creature which is under heaven" We must not be *"moved away"* from the *"hope"* of the true *"gospel"* of God's grace. This is what has saved us and this is what we must proclaim to the lost world around us. By radio, by television, by shortwave, and by the Internet, the gospel can be preached today to every creature under Heaven. It is amazing that we can have our church ministry go out by radio and by the Internet all over the world *"to every creature which is under Heaven."* This is literally possible in the day in which we live.

"whereof I Paul am made a minister" Paul wanted the Colossian Christians to *"continue"* in their *"faith."* This *"continuing"* is still needed today.

- John 8:31
  Then said Jesus to those Jews which believed on him, **If ye continue in my word, then are ye my disciples indeed**

If you don't *"continue"* you are not Christ's *"disciple."*

- John 15:9
  As the Father hath loved me, so have I loved you: **continue ye in my love.**
- Acts 13:43
  Now when the congregation was broken up, many of the Jews and religious proselytes followed Paul and Barnabas: who, speaking to them, **persuaded them to continue in the grace of God.**

We must "continue" in our following the Lord Jesus Christ.

- Acts 14:22
  Confirming the souls of the disciples, and **exhorting them to continue in the faith**, and that we must through much tribulation enter into the kingdom of God.
- Colossians 4:2
  Continue in prayer, and watch in the same with thanksgiving
- 1 Timothy 4:16
  Take heed unto thyself, and unto the doctrine; **continue in them**: for in doing this thou shalt both save thyself, and them that hear thee.

Notice you are not only to *"continue"* in the *"doctrine"* but also in areas that concern yourself. You and I can go astray in our personal lives. This would be a terrible catastrophe.

- 2 Timothy 3:14
  But continue thou in the things which thou hast learned and hast been assured of, knowing of whom thou hast learned them
- Hebrews 13:1
  Let brotherly love continue.

We must *"continue"* in all these areas, including Christian love, or *"brotherly love."* We should not stop.

- 2 Peter 3:18
  But grow in grace, and in the knowledge of our Lord and Saviour Jesus Christ. To him be glory both now and for ever. Amen.

> ## Dedicated Christians Must Grow
> There is no other proper way for the dedicated Christian but to *"grow in grace and in the knowledge of our Lord and Saviour Jesus Christ."*

Paul was made a servant or a *"minister"* of the *"gospel."* The Greek word, DIAKONOS, for *"minister"* is *"one who executes the command of another, especially a master."* Paul was *"made a minister"* by the Lord Jesus Christ Himself. If we are servants of Christ and helpers of the Lord Jesus Christ, He must *"make"* us such. We can't be *"made"* His servants all by ourselves.

Colossians 1:24

"Who now rejoice in my sufferings for you, and fill up that which is behind of the afflictions of Christ in my flesh for his body's sake, which is the church"

"Who now rejoice in my sufferings for you" When writing this, Paul was in prison, but he *"now rejoices."* He was *"rejoicing"* even though he was in prison. He was also *"rejoicing"* because he was *"suffering"* for the Colossian Christians. He was paying the price for them in a sense, because he was in prison for preaching Christ. If he was not able to preach Christ, these people in Colosse would never have heard of Christ and would never have received Him as their Saviour and Lord.

"and fill up that which is behind of the afflictions of Christ in my flesh for his body's sake which is the church" The Lord Jesus Christ was not any longer on earth as Paul wrote this letter. He was raised bodily from the dead and He then ascended up to His Father in Heaven forty days after His resurrection. He was, and is today, seated at the Father's right hand (Hebrews 10:12). Paul was still being *"afflicted"* for the sake of His Saviour the Lord Jesus Christ. He was continuing in that suffering there in prison. It was also for the sake of the Colossians as well. He was suffering so that they do not have to suffer.

The Need for Strong Standards
Preachers and those who are practicing the Word of God must have strong standards. They pave the way for others so that they do not have to suffer.

Just like in the home-schooling situation. My son Dan and his wife Tamie, went to a home school conference in Pennsylvania just yesterday. We took care of Anna so they could go. They said some changes in the law were made so that the home schoolers would not be criticized and condemned. In making these changes, some of the home-school leaders suffered so that others could continue to have the freedoms they deserve to teach their own children in the home. Paul as a prisoner was doing that very thing in prison so that the Colossian people would not have to suffer and be put into prison.

Colossians 1:25

"Whereof I am made a minister, according to the dispensation of God which is given to me for you, to fulfill the word of God"

"Whereof I am made a minister" Paul was *"made a minister"* for the gospel and the church, which is His *"body."* Paul repeats this twice that he was *"made a minister."* He did not make himself a *"minister."* The Lord Jesus Christ did that. Paul says he was *"made a minister"* in verse twenty-three and here again in verse twenty-five. Paul was not a *"minister"* or DIAKONOS of Christ to start with; we all know that. This Greek word means *"one who executes the commands of another, especially of a master."* He was anything but. He had been a *"minister"* of Satan. He was one who wanted to kill the Christians. He wanted to put them in prison and to torture as many of these Christians as he could. He officiated at the death of Stephen (Acts 7:58). As those men that hated Stephen and hated Christ stoned him to death, they placed their clothes at the feet of Saul who later became Paul.

"according to the dispensation of God which is given to me for you, to fulfill the word of God" Paul was made a minister according to the dispensation of God. *"Dispensation"* is a good word. The Greek word for it is OIKONOMIA, which means literally, *"the law or management of a house, or household affairs."* God made *"a special rule or law"* for Paul when He made him a *"minister."* This was *"given"* unto him for the Colossians' benefit. It was for all of us also who are believers today in order that we might *"fulfill the word of God."*

Paul Wanted to Obey Completely

Paul wanted to *"fulfill"* God's Word. He wanted to tell it and to obey it completely. He did not want to leave anything out. He wanted to be *"obedient unto death."*

He was obedient in prison. In the book of Philippians, Paul said, *"For unto you it is given on the behalf of Christ, not only to believe on him, but also to suffer for his sake."* So, Paul was suffering and fulfilling the Word of God by his suffering there in the Roman prison.

Colossians 1:26

"*Even*the mystery which hath been hid from ages and from generations, but now is made manifest to his saints"

"*Even*the mystery" This *"mystery"* is a *"sacred secret."* The Old Testament people did not know of Calvary's cross specifically. They knew about it only in picture form. In Psalm 22, for example, the cross was there in picture and illustration form. In the book of Genesis, the cross was pictured there in Abraham's offering of his son, Isaac (Genesis 22). In the book of Galatians, it tells us that the gospel was preached to Abraham (Galatians 3:8).

"which hath been hid from ages and from generations, but now is made manifest to his saints" The mystery of the church, the mystery of the believers, the mystery of salvation by grace through faith in the shed blood of Christ was *"hid from ages and from generations"* in the past. Now, in Paul's days, this *"mystery"* has been *"made manifest to his saints."*

Again, I say that the Roman Catholic church does not have a corner on *"saints."* Every born-again believer is called a *"saint"* in the Word of God. The Greek word for it is HAGIOS. We become a *"saint"* by the Lord Jesus giving us new birth.

This *"mystery"* is now manifested to us who are believers who are called here, *"saints of God."* You might ask how about the unsaved people who are not *"saints."* Is it manifested unto them? They have the gospel message, but they cannot understand the deep things of God. They cannot understand the deep things of Christ.

- 1 Corinthians 2:14
    But the natural man receiveth not the things of the Spirit of God: for they are foolishness unto him: neither can he know them, because **they are spiritually discerned**.

I am glad that we have a King James Bible and the Hebrew and Greek texts which underlie it whereby we can know what has been revealed unto us. God has given us His revelation.

Christ Preserved His OT & NT Words

As we have said before, by Christ all things *"consist,"* hold together or are preserved. I believe very strongly that God has preserved through the Lord Jesus Christ His Hebrew and Greek Words. That battle is a battle shaping up and has been shaping up for a few decades.

Not only from the Roman Catholics, not only from the modernist apostates, not only from the unbelievers, not only from the new evangelicals, but also from the separatist Fundamentalists.

There is a battle royal being fought today as to what Old Testament Hebrew Words and what New Testament Greek Words have been preserved. What text should our English Bibles be founded upon? Which English version is the best? I believe strongly that the King James Bible is the best. Other versions are not built upon the proper Hebrew and Greek texts The translators are inferior to our King James translators. The technique of translation is inferior to our King James Bible. The theology and doctrine is inferior to our King James Bible.

Do You Have All of God's Words?

If you have another version of the English Bible, you do not have all of God's Words.

The New Testament Greek text of these false versions such as the *New International Version*, the *Today's New International Version*, the *New American Standard Version*, the *Revised Standard Version*, the *New Revised Standard Version*, and most of the others, is 2,886 Greek words shorter than the Textus Receptus on which our King James Bible is based. If you leave out 2,886 Greek words, you're short-changed in what God has *"now made manifest to His saints."* You not only have 2,886 Greek words left out, but you also have other Greek words subtracted or changed in some other way. By my actual count, there are a total of 5,604 places where these changes are made in the Textus Receptus Greek text underlying our King James Bible. According to Dr. Jack Moorman's excellent study, these changes in the Greek text involve 356 doctrinal passages. We must stand for His Words that He has given to us. Only in that way can we know all things that are *"made manifest."*

Colossians 1:27

"in whom God would make known what *is* the riches of the glory of this mystery among the Gentiles; which is Christ in you, the hope of glory"

"In whom God would make known what *is* the riches of the glory of this mystery among the Gentiles" In phrase, *"in whom,"* goes back to the *"saints"* in the previous verse. To these *"saints,"* God wanted to *"make known"* some things. God has no lack of *"riches."* We may lack *"riches,"* but God the Father and the Lord Jesus Christ have no lack of *"riches."* In this case, it is the *"riches of the glory of this mystery"* of which Paul is speaking. The Lord Jesus Christ was *"rich"* but became *"poor"* in order that the saved ones might be *"rich."*

- **2 Corinthians 8:9**
  For ye know the grace of our Lord Jesus Christ, that, **though he was rich, yet for your sakes he became poor, that ye through his poverty might be rich**.

The Lord Jesus Christ was poor in this world because He took upon Himself a perfect human body. He had a perfect human nature. He was poor because He surrendered that body to the will of His Father and died the death of the Cross of Calvary, bearing the sins of the entire world, in order that those who received Him as their Saviour might be saved, be forgiven of their sins, and go to Heaven. That is God's grace! After Calvary, the Lord Jesus Christ was raised bodily from the dead and ascended to Heaven that *"at the name of Jesus every knee shall bow"* and *"every tongue should confess that Jesus Christ is Lord to the glory of God the Father"* (Philippians 2:10-11). That is how He could give the believers the *"riches of the glory of this mystery."* Notice that it was *"among the Gentiles"* that this *"sacred secret"* or *"mystery"* was made known. It was not to the Jews.

"which is Christ in you, the hope of glory" The Lord Jesus is now basking in the glory of His Father. The Father is in Heaven with all the glory of His saints that are there. The Old Testament saints who were raised after His resurrection are there. The New Testament believers who have gone Home to be with Christ are there also. The *"mystery"* Paul was talking about in this chapter related to the Gentiles. It is *"Christ in you, the hope of glory."* The only *"hope of glory"* is to have Christ indwelling us. It is true that He indwells the saved ones just as the Holy Spirit does. *"Glory"* is another name for Heaven in this context. We know that in the New Testament the Holy Spirit indwells us, but in John 14:23, we also see that both the Father and Christ promised to make their "*abode*" with those who love Him. What if Christ is not "*in you*"? Then you have no "*hope of glory.*" It is just like when you go up to a motel and you see a big sign reading "NO VACANCY." That is the sign that is held before anyone who does not have Christ in them and has not accepted Him as their Saviour from sin. For them, there will be "NO VACANCY" in Heaven.

The Lord Jesus went "*to prepare a place*" for those who have trusted Him. There is all sorts of room. "*In my Father's house are many mansions: if it were not so, I would have told you. I go to prepare a place for you*" (John 14:2). The apostle Paul is talking about those who have trusted Christ as Saviour and Redeemer.

We don't have this "*glory*" yet; but as the gospel song writer has written, for the Christian, there will be "Only Glory By and By." If you have Christ in you there is hope for "*glory.*" When does that take place? Just as soon as your spirit and soul leave this old body. For some of us it might be tomorrow. For others it might be this month, or this year. For yet others, it might not be for two or three decades. Who knows? We must say with the Psalmist, "*My times are in Thy hand*" (Psalm 31:15). The Lord Jesus could return and all of us who are saved would be caught up to be with Him "*which is far better*" (Philippians 1:23) than going through the veil of the shadow of death. If we are born-again, we all have the hope that when the spirit and soul leave the body, we do not have to suffer in "*purgatory.*" We go straight on to "*glory*" immediately. We praise God for that.

The benefits of "*glory*" are not restricted to those living in our United States of America. Every believer of all nations, if they are "*in Christ,*" has a tremendously precious "*hope*" in glory. We live so well and so high on the hog, you might say in this country, that many of us in this country may say I am so well-off or well-fixed I don't want to go Home to "*glory.*" Just leave me here. I hope God never blesses us to that extent where we don't long for the "*Father's house*" and for the "*glory*" that He has gone to prepare for us.

Colossians 1:28

"Whom we preach, warning every man, and teaching every man in all wisdom; that we may present every man perfect in Christ Jesus."

Paul said "*Whom we preach.*" This "*Whom*" goes back to "*Christ*" Who is in these believers as the "*hope of glory.*" He did not preach politics. He did not preach book reviews. He did not tell jokes. He did not tell one tall story after another. He preached Christ.

In Paul's preaching, he "*warns every man.*" He also "*taught every man in all wisdom.*" The purpose of all of Paul's warning and teaching is that he "*may present every man perfect (*'mature, or grown up'*) in Christ Jesus.*"

- **Acts 20:29-30**
  For I know this, that **after my departing shall grievous wolves enter in among you, not sparing the flock. Also of your own selves shall men arise,** speaking perverse things, to draw away disciples after them.

Paul warned the believers. He is talking about outer enemies and inner enemies. That was the apostle's purpose. It should also be every preacher's purpose. In addition to preaching and teaching, there must be a warning against evil things. As I have recently heard, *"teaching"* is to inform, *"preaching"* is to transform.

- **1 Corinthians 4:14**
  I write not these things to shame you, but as my beloved sons **I warn you.**

Paul led them to Christ. They were like his sons. He was their spiritual Father.

- **1 Thessalonians 5:14**
  Now we exhort you, brethren, **warn them that are unruly,** comfort the feebleminded, support the weak, be patient toward all men.

God wants us to be teachers of the Word. That is why this *Bible For Today Baptist Church* believes in expository preaching and teaching of God's Words. This includes warnings against evil. That is what God expects of us. Jesus said:

- **Matthew 28:19**
  Go ye therefore, and **teach all nations,** baptizing them in the name of the Father, and of the Son, and of the Holy Ghost:

- **Luke 11:1**
  And it came to pass, that, as he was praying in a certain place, when he ceased, one of his disciples said unto him, Lord, **teach us to pray,** as John also taught his disciples.

- **Acts 5:42**
  And daily in the temple, and in every house, **they ceased not to teach and preach Jesus Christ.**

- **Acts 18:11**
  And he continued there a year and six months, **teaching the word of God among them.**

Paul taught the Word of God. On one occasion, Paul preached until midnight. While Paul was preaching, a man named Eutychus fell asleep (Acts 20:7, 9) and fell down from the third loft. He was taken up dead. Paul brought him back to life. In the early New Testament church, the apostles preached long, like preachers do in foreign countries. Today, people here in the United States would be horrified if preachers preached that long, would they not? It is a sad fact that many preachers today have very little of any importance to say from their pulpits on Sunday mornings.

- Acts 28:31
  Preaching the kingdom of God, and teaching those things which concern the Lord Jesus Christ, with all confidence, no man forbidding him.
- Ephesians 4:11
  And he gave some, apostles; and some, prophets; and some, evangelists; and **some, pastors and teachers**;
- Colossians 3:16
  Let the word of Christ dwell in you richly in all wisdom; **teaching** and admonishing one another in psalms and hymns and spiritual songs, singing with grace in your hearts to the Lord.
- Hebrews 5:12
  For when for the time **ye ought to be teachers**, ye have need that one teach you again which be the first principles of the oracles of God; and are become such as have need of milk, and not of strong meat.

We hope that everyone, by reading God's Word daily year by year, can be teachers as well as followers of God's Word.

Colossians 1:29

"Whereunto I also labour, striving according to his working, which worketh in me mightily"

"Whereunto I also labour" For what was Paul laboring? His *"labour"* was preaching Christ and *"warning and teaching every man."* That Greek word for *"labour"* is KOPIAO. It means *"to grow weary, tired, exhausted [with toil or burdens or grief]; to labour with wearisome effort, to toil."* It was not just *"white-collar"* work at a desk, although desk work can be exhausting. Paul was speaking here of *"blue-collar"* work, as we call it.

"striving according to his working which worketh in me mightily" That word translated "striving" comes from the Greek word, AGONIZOMAI. It means *"to contend with adversaries, fight; metaphorically, to contend, struggle, with difficulties and dangers; to endeavour with strenuous zeal, strive: to obtain something."* It is not a pink-tea party. This *"striving"* was in accord to *"His working"* which worked in Paul *"mightily."*

We Need God's Working Power

God must be "*working*" in us if we are to work the works of Christ and of God. He will bless us if we let Him work through us with His power and His might.

Colossians
Chapter Two

Colossians 2:1

"For I would that ye knew what great conflict I have for you, and *for* them at Laodicea, and *for* as many as have not seen my face in the flesh" Remember, Paul was a prisoner in Rome. He was writing to the church at Colosse. He mentioned Laodicea, which is a city close to Colosse. You can find Laodicea on the map found on page one. It is right above Colosse. Since the two cities are neighbors, Paul has a sentiment for both of them. Paul had a *"conflict"* for them. The Greek word is AGON. It refers to *"any struggle or context."* It is used for an athletic battle or anything similar to that. He had a contest and a struggle in his heart for those Christians in both churches. There was apparent fighting between those two churches and that is why Paul had a *"conflict."* Paul had a way about him. They said of him that he was very strong in his letters (2 Corinthians 10:10); but when he came in person, *"his bodily presence was weak"* and his *"speech was contemptible."*

Colossians 2:2

"That their hearts might be comforted, being knit together in love, and unto all riches of the full assurance of understanding, to the acknowledgement of the mystery of God, and the Father, and of Christ"

"That their hearts might be comforted" The first part of Paul's prayer and the conflict that he had was, *"That their hearts might be comforted."* There are a number of verses on *"comfort."* Let us look at a few of them.

- **Acts 9:31**
  Then had the churches rest throughout all Judaea and Galilee and Samaria, and were edified; and walking in the fear of the Lord, **and in the comfort of the Holy Ghost**, were multiplied.

The churches had "*comfort*" of the Holy Spirit. They did not have much money in the early church, but they had "*comfort*" of the Holy Spirit.

- **Acts 16:40**
  And they went out of the prison, and entered into the house of Lydia: and when they had seen the brethren, **they comforted them**, and departed.

The Ministry of Comfort

There is a ministry of "*comfort.*" Do you have that ministry in your life? There are others who are perhaps in need of "*comfort*"; but, you and I, if we know Christ as our Saviour and are walking by the Spirit of God, can bring "*comfort*" to those who are in need.

- **Romans 1:12**
  That is, **that I may be comforted together with you by the mutual faith both of you and me.**

Here is "*comfort*" that can be brought by other people. "*Comforting*" one another works both ways, to the one who "*comforts*" and to the one who is "*comforted.*"

- **Romans 15:4**
  For whatsoever things were written aforetime were written for our learning, **that we through patience and comfort of the scriptures might have hope.**

The Scriptures bring us "*comfort.*"

- **2 Corinthians 1:3-4**
  Blessed be God, even the Father of our Lord Jesus Christ, the Father of mercies, **and the God of all comfort; Who comforteth us in all our tribulation, that we may be able to comfort them which are in any trouble, by the comfort wherewith we ourselves are comforted of God.**

The word "*comfort*" is used five times in this section. God "*comforts*" us so that we can "*comfort*" someone else. That is the wonderful thing that God gives to us.

- **2 Corinthians 7:6**
  Nevertheless God, **that comforteth those that are cast down, comforted us by the coming of Titus**;
- **2 Corinthians 13:11**
  Finally, brethren, farewell. Be perfect, **be of good comfort**, be of one mind, live in peace; and the God of love and peace shall be with you.
- **Ephesians 6:22**
  Whom I have sent unto you for the same purpose, that ye might know our affairs, **and that he might comfort your hearts**.
- **1 Thessalonians 3:2**
  And sent Timotheus, our brother, and minister of God, and our fellowlabourer in the gospel of Christ, to establish you, **and to comfort you concerning your faith**:

Hearts Need Comfort

Broken hearts need *"comfort."* Breaking hearts need *"comfort."* Hearts that are about to be broken need *"comfort."*

We know that this consolation which is Godly comes from the Lord.

"being knit together in love" It would seem like if Paul's prayer was that *"their hearts"* would be *"knit together in love,"* then, perhaps, due to this *"conflict"* their hearts were not *"knitted together"* in love. You can't be *"knitted together"* if you have hatred, anymore then you can mix together oil and water. They are unmixable.

Knit Together

The Greek word for *"knit together"* is SUMBIBAZO. It means *"to cause to coalesce, to join together, to put together, to unite in affection and in love."*

This is what Paul wanted to have happen to the Christians at Colosse.

"and unto all riches of the full assurance of understanding" The *"mystery of God"* is *"Christ in you the hope of glory."* This *"mystery"* was not revealed in the Old Testament. It was a *"secret."* *"Mystery"* is the Greek word meaning *"secret."* This was God's *"sacred secret"* that He did not reveal. He said he wanted them to have a *"full assurance"* of a certain confidence in this *"understanding"* that is *"Christ in you the hope of glory"* and *"knit together in love"* in this full knowledge that they might have. **"to the acknowledgement of the mystery of God, and the Father, and of Christ"**

The Trinity

Notice, there is no distinction between God the Father, God the Son, and God the Holy Spirit, as far as equality. They are co-equal, they are co-Sovereign, they have the same attributes, they are all perfect.

Colossians 2:3

"In whom are hid all the treasures of wisdom and knowledge" In the Lord Jesus Christ, in hidden form, are *"all the treasures of wisdom and knowledge."*

Heresy on Christ's Omniscience

Some Fundamentalists have wrongly said that the Lord Jesus Christ was not Omniscient while He was on earth.

Omniscience is one of the attributes of God and Deity. God is Omniscient. He is all-knowing. The Lord Jesus Christ did know all things. He may have disused that attribute of Omniscience at times, but all the other times He used the attribute of omniscience. He knew Philip while he was under the fig tree (John 1:48). He knew how many husbands the woman at the well had, before the present man she was living with, which was not her husband (John 4:18).

The Lord Jesus Christ did not want to reveal Himself to people in John 2:24-25 because He knew all men. He knew what was in men. He knew the hearts of the disciples. He knew them when they were complaining who was going to be the first (Mark 9:33-34). It says in the book of 1 Corinthians, if the rulers of this world had known Him they would not have crucified the Lord of glory (1 Corinthians 2:8).

The Lord Jesus' Treasures

The Lord Jesus has hidden in Himself all the *"treasures of wisdom and knowledge."*

What is a *"treasure"*?
- **Matthew 6:19-21**
  Lay not up for yourselves treasures upon earth, where moth and rust doth corrupt, and where thieves break through and steal: But **lay up for yourselves treasures in heaven**, where neither moth nor rust doth corrupt, and where thieves do not break through nor steal: For **where your treasure is, there will your heart be also.**

In this passage, the Lord Jesus Christ mentioned *"treasures."* He taught his disciples about how *"moths and rust"* corrupt. Rust corrupts cars and other steel or iron products.

"Thieves" do *"break through and steal"* treasures. The temple in Jerusalem with all of its gold and hundreds of talents of treasures was a place where thieves broke into and stole. In the recent war in Iraq, many valuables were stolen from the museum in the capital city. But there are no thieves in Heaven. If you look at a used car lot you will see a fence all the way around the cars with barbed wire at the top to keep the thieves from stealing the cars. I don't know how many cars are stolen everyday, but many I am sure.

The Bible says that *"where your treasure is there will your heart be also."* If your *"treasure"* is in Heaven that is where your heart will be.
- **2 Corinthians 4:7**
  But we have this treasure in earthen vessels, that the excellency of the power may be of God, and not of us.

The Believer's Treasure

Believers have a *"treasure."* This *"treasure"* is God the Holy Spirit Who indwells the saved ones.

He indwells the *"earthen vessels"* of our bodies. Our bodies are like imperfect pots with cracks in them. If we had excellency of ourselves we would say, *"Look at me how beautiful I am."* The excellency is of God, and that is why He has given us these *"earthen vessels"* which are cracked in different places because the glory or the excellency is to be of God and not of us.

In the Lord Jesus Christ is the *"treasures"* of all the *"wisdom and knowledge"* that this universe has. We human beings think we are so smart. We have repeatedly sent men into outer space. That is nothing when compared to the Lord Jesus Christ's creation of all the host of Heaven and the earth. Man has built complicated computers, but who do you think gave us our minds to construct them? It was the Lord Jesus Christ, *"in Whom are hid all the treasures of wisdom and knowledge."*

Is there anything the Lord Jesus Christ doesn't know? No! He knows everything. It says in Psalm 139:4, 23 that the Lord even knows our thoughts afar off--even before the words are in our mouths. The Lord Jesus Christ has within His power, *"all the treasures of wisdom and knowledge."*

Colossians 2:4

"And this I say, less any man should beguile you with enticing words" Paul said that the Lord Jesus Christ has all the "wisdom" we need. No one should *"beguile"* us with *"enticing words."*

The Meaning of "Beguile"

The word, *"beguile"* comes from the Greek word, PARALOGIZOMAI. It means *"to cheat by false reckoning, or to miscount."*

Sometimes the ushers in a church miscount the offering. Then you have the wrong total. This is a *"beguiling"* situation. This also occurs when you buy what is supposed a pound of meat; yet the salesperson's finger is on the scale to make it seem like a pound, though it is not a full pound. That is *"beguiling"* or false reckoning.

Paul said he did not want the believers at Colosse to be *"beguiled"* and to be led astray with *"enticing words."*

"Enticing Words"

The Greek word translated *"enticing words,"* is PITHANOLOGIA. It means *"in a bad sense, persuasiveness of speech, specious discourse leading others into error."*

This is like the cults who use "enticing words" to bring people into their errors. Paul was very concerned that the Colossian believers should neither be *"beguiled"* nor *"enticed."* The first mention of *"beguiling"* is in Genesis.

- **Genesis 3:13**
  And the LORD God said unto the woman, What is this that thou hast done? And the woman said, **The serpent beguiled me**, and I did eat.

Eve was saying that the serpent sold her a *"bill of goods,"* as we say. He made this sin seem so sweet, so nice, so tempting, so wonderful. In 2 Corinthians, the Lord referred back to the Garden of Eden.

- **2 Corinthians 11:3**
  But I fear, lest by any means, **as the serpent beguiled Eve through his subtilty**, so your minds should be corrupted from the simplicity that is in Christ.

This is the *"beguiling"* by the Devil that takes away the *"simplicity"* that is in Christ. There is an example of *"enticing words"* in the Old Testament in the book of Judges.

- **Judges 14:15**
  And it came to pass on the seventh day, that they said unto Samson's wife, **Entice thy husband**, that he may declare unto us the riddle, lest we burn thee and thy father's house with fire: have ye called us to take that we have? is it not so?

The Philistines wanted to find out the source of Samson's strength. Samson yielded to that wicked woman, Delilah, and told the source of his strength. He got weak. The Philistine's captured him. They put out both of his eyes thus blinding him. They made him serve in a granary like an ox, treading out the corn. Samson's wife *"beguiled"* her husband with *"enticing words,"* but the Philistines still burned her house and her father's house with fire. So much for the word of people who don't keep it. You can't trust them.

We have to be careful of *"beguiling"* and *"enticing words."* I believe there are *"beguiling"* and *"enticing words'* in the false Bible versions of our days. The *New International Version* has many *"beguiling"* and *"enticing words."* They might look good and nice, but we must be careful that we are not *"beguiled."* When false cultists knock at our doors and want entrance, they have a *"beguiling"* and *"enticing"* way about them, too. False doctrine of all kinds comes to us in this way, and Paul was rightfully and certainly concerned.

Colossians 2:5

"For though I be absent in the flesh, yet am I with you in the spirit, joying and beholding your order, and the stedfastness of your faith in Christ"

"For though I be absent in the flesh, yet am I with you in the spirit" Paul was *"absent in the flesh"* because he was in prison and could not be there. From a distance he says *"I am with you in the spirit."* When some people don't come to church they say, *"I am with you in spirit."* I am glad that they are praying for us. Everyone can't come to the house of the Lord wherever that may be. Paul was with them *"in spirit."*

"joying and beholding your order" Notice what Paul was doing while in the Roman prison. He was rejoicing with them, even in prison with all the adverse conditions, in their *"order."* The Greek word for *"order"* is TAXIS. It has a number of meanings such as: *"due or right order, orderly condition; the post, rank, or position which one holds in civic or other affairs; since this position generally depends on one's talents, experience, resources; character, fashion, quality, style."*

The *"order"* here was, no doubt, a reference to their *"orderly"* conditions in the Colossian church. In our case, it would include sitting in our seats in an orderly manner so that late-comers would be able to sit in the aisle seats rather than having to make people stand up so they could get by. When there is a serious meeting to discuss a serious problem, it is good to have an agenda so that the meeting can proceed in an orderly manner. In 1 Corinthians 14:40, Paul said, *"Let all things be done decently and in order."* We must have *"order"* in our services of worship rather than chaos.

"and the stedfastness of your faith in Christ" Though absent from the believers in Colosse, through accurate first-hand reports probably, Paul also beheld their *"stedfastness"* in their *"faith in Christ."* There is something about *"stedfastness"* of which we must understand and be aware.

- 1 Corinthians 15:58
   Therefore, my beloved brethren, **be ye stedfast**, unmoveable, always abounding in the work of the Lord, forasmuch as ye know that your labour is not in vain in the Lord.

Colossians 2:5

> ## The Meaning of "Stedfast"
> That word *"stedfast"* is a very interesting word. It comes from the Greek word, STEREOMA. It means *"that which furnishes a foundation; on which a thing rests firmly; firmness."* That is *"stedfastness."*

- **1 Peter 5:9**
  Whom resist stedfast in the faith, knowing that the same afflictions are accomplished in your brethren that are in the world.

The *"stedfastness in the faith"* is important. It is important for you. It is important for me.

You might ask why did modernistic churches take over the United Methodist Church? Why did modernist, apostate churches take over the churches in the Northern Baptist Convention? Why are apostate churches coming into and taking over some of the Southern Baptist Churches, or the Episcopal Churches, or whatever the denomination? Why are the apostates coming in and taking over many of these mainline denominations? It is because the saved members of those churches in time past were not *"stedfast"* and firmly grounded in their faith.

If their local churches had the opportunity (and most of these mainline denominations do not make this provision), they might not have known what they should ask when a would-be preacher came to be interviewed and to candidate for the pulpit. When the preacher comes for an interview with the church, the people ask him certain questions and he gives certain answers. The people might say, *"Oh, I guess he is all right,"* because they don't know anything about the Word of God. They are not *"stedfast in their faith."* They don't even know what their *"faith"* is. Sad to admit, this visiting preacher is able to pull the wool over their eyes, as we say. He might talk sweetly. He sounds great. The church might vote him in as their pastor because his answers have beguiled them. He comes into the church, and all of a sudden, there is a big and unexpected change, whether gradually or overnight.

One of the men in a church in our area was talking to me recently. He said that he had trouble in his church. He said his church had a visiting young preacher who did not believe in the rapture of the church. His church had a pulpit committee who wanted to call a preacher. I hope that they get a good one who believes in sound doctrine. This man said that this preacher is even changing the doxology. This young man talked to the pastor and told him of his concerns about how he was changing everything in the church. He told the pastor that *"The next thing you know you will be changing the Bible."* That pastor said that was what he was thinking of doing. The people in that church were not grounded and *"stablished in the faith"* (Colossians 2:7). They should have been. If they had been, they would not have allowed that minister to come into their church.

Colossians 2:6

"As ye have therefore received Christ Jesus the Lord, so walk ye in him" If you have *"received"* the Lord Jesus Christ as your Saviour, how did you receive Him? God's only way of receiving Christ in salvation is by faith. God's salvation is based on God's grace. He sent His Son to die for the sins of the world that through faith in the Lord Jesus Christ, we can *"receive"* Him as our Saviour and be saved.

- John 1:12-13

    But as many as received him, to them gave he power to become the sons of God, even to them that believe on his name: Which were born, not of blood, nor of the will of the flesh, nor of the will of man, but of God.

We *"receive"* Christ by faith. We don't receive Christ by works or anything we can do. We don't receive Christ by our mind or intelligence. We only receive Christ by faith, and trusting in Him. If we *"received"* Christ by faith, then we should *"walk"* in the same way, by faith. That *"walk"* should be in consistency and in the very same way that we receive Christ. We *"walk by faith, not by sight"* as Paul says in 2 Corinthians 5:7. That is exactly how our *"walk"* should be. We must stay on the same faith upon which we were founded. Don't change your faith. As you have received the Lord Jesus Christ by faith, and were founded on Him, continue to walk in Him with the same doctrines built on the same Words of God.

Colossians 2:7

"Rooted and built up in him, and stablished in the faith, as ye have been taught, abounding therein with thanksgiving"

"Rooted and built up in him" We are to be *"rooted"* and to *"walk"* as we have received Christ. That big tree out in our yard is *"rooted."* In fact it is so *"rooted,"* it goes under the walk, and it pulls the walk up. A big tree has big roots. If you go down Park Avenue, you will see sidewalks pulled up all around it. You can't escape it. Trees have roots. They need roots in order to live. We who are saved must also be *"rooted."*

Our roots must go to the Lord Jesus Christ Himself. We are the branches, He is the true Vine. We need to be *"rooted"* in Him to have strong roots. Once we are *"rooted"* in the Lord Jesus Christ, we are to be *"built up in Him."* It is not enough to be *"rooted."* You should not say, *"Oh, I am saved and that is all*

I need to know. I don't need to read my Bible. I don't need to pray. I don't need to come to the house of God to have fellowship with believers. I am rooted!" That is a very poor attitude.

The Meaning of "Build Up"

Paul says, in addition to being *"rooted,"* you have to be *"built up in Him."* The Greek word for *"build up"* is APOIKODOMEO. To be built up means: *"To finish the structure of which the foundation has already been laid, to give constant increase in Christian knowledge and in a life conformed thereto."*

You start with the foundation first, then you build up the building on that foundation. We must be strengthened in our faith. To do that, we must read and study the Words of God. We must believe the Words of God. We must obey the Words of God.

"and stablished in the faith, as ye have been taught, abounding therein with thanksgiving" The word, *"stablished,"* comes from the Greek word, BEBAIOO. It means: *"to make firm, establish, confirm, make sure."*

Weak As Water, or Strong?

Are you weak as water in your faith? Or are you *"firm"*? If somebody asked you some questions about your faith, would you tell them clearly and straight out what you believed, and why you believed it? If they asked you if you were a Christian and going to Heaven, can you give them a straight answer?

Could you say, *"No, I am not going to Heaven"* or *"Yes, I am going to Heaven"*? Why are you going to Heaven? What makes you think that you are good enough to go to Heaven? Do you know that you are not good enough to go to Heaven? Do you know that I am not good enough to go to Heaven, but that the Lord Jesus is good enough to take us to Heaven when we trust Him by faith and accept Him?

We must be *"stablished in the faith."* The word for *"faith"* in Greek has an article before it, meaning that it is *"the faith"* or body of doctrine which is taught in the Bible. Can people shake you? Can they shake me? Can they come with their false doctrine and their false theories, and move us from that solid rock which is the Lord Jesus Christ and the faith taught in the Bible? I hope not. Many different people have various theories and much sweet talk. Paul said he wanted the Colossian believers to be firmly and solidly *"stablished in the faith."* He also wanted them to be *"abounding therein with thanksgiving."*

There is an expression that Dr. George Dollar used in his book, *The History of Fundamentalism in America.* I used his book in the course I taught in the Bible Baptist Institute in Philadelphia on Monday nights. Dr. Dollar uses the term for some compromising Christians who are really wishy-washy. He calls them *"jelly on the wall Christians."*

What happens when you throw jelly on the wall? Does it stay firm? No, it droops and falls. That is exactly how some Christians are. They are drooping Christians. Paul tells us to be firm, to be established, and to make sure what we believe. We sang that gospel song this morning, *"In Times Like These, We Need a Saviour."* One of the stanzas mentions, *"This Rock is Jesus."* We need to be *"firm"* as a rock and *"stablished in the faith"* so that nobody can move us or shake us.

Colossians 2:8

"Beware lest any man spoil you through philosophy and vain deceit, after the tradition of men, after the rudiments of the world, and not after Christ."

"Beware lest any man spoil you through philosophy and vain deceit"

Beware!

Paul told the believers to *"beware."* It is the usual Greek word for see, BLEPO, but it also means, as in this case, *"to turn the thoughts or direct the mind to a thing, to consider, contemplate, to look at, to weigh carefully, examine, beware."*

That is a warning to us, is it not? God gives us warnings. We have to be *"rooted and built up"* in Christ, but we must also be watchful *"lest any man spoil us."* By putting this caution in this verse, Paul indicated that it is possible for Christian believers to be *"spoiled"* through various things mentioned here. The word, *"spoil,"* comes from the Greek word, SULAGOGEO, which means various things: *"to carry off booty; to carry one off as a captive (and slave); to lead away from the truth and subject to one's sway."* We speak of the *"spoils"* of war. When someone is *"spoiled,"* he or she becomes a captive or a slave. In the case of the false cults, we could be *"spoiled"* or enslaved to their erroneous doctrines. Some people have been in physical slavery. There are prostitutes who are still in slavery.

The word, *"philosophy,"* means literally *"the love of wisdom."* It was also used in more specific senses in Paul's day:

"Used either of zeal for or skill in any art or science, any branch of knowledge. Used once in the NT of the theology, or rather theosophy, of certain Jewish Christian ascetics, which busied itself with refined and speculative enquiries into the nature and classes of angels, into the ritual of the Mosaic law and the regulations of Jewish tradition respecting practical life; used either of zeal for or skill in any art or science, any branch of knowledge."

The Dangers of Philosophy

"Philosophy" has to do with the thinking of men. It is a result of what goes on in the brain, the mind, and the thoughts. That is where liberalism, modernism, apostasy, and all forms of false thinking comes from. These dangerous systems and doctrines come from the mind of men.

"Vain deceit" is also a dangerous force that could *"spoil"* believers and make them ineffective for the Lord Jesus Christ. Empty *"deceit"* and deceitfulness that could take us away and trick us.

"after the tradition of men, after the rudiments of the world, and not after Christ" Paul has given us *"traditions"* in the Word of God which we should follow (2 Thessalonians 3:6). We are supposed to obey and to use Paul's teachings or *"traditions."* We are not, however, to follow the *"tradition of men"* or the *"rudiments of the world."*

Rome's False Authorities

The Roman Catholic Church illustrates what not to do.
They follow three things as their authorities:
(1) corrupt versions of the Bible,
(2) church traditions, and
(3) decrees of the Pope.

Our course of action must be *"after Christ"* and Him alone. His Words, that we must follow, are to be found in the most accurate form in the English language in our King James Bible. These English words are founded upon the most accurate Hebrew and Greek texts that underlie the King James Bible.

Colossians 2:9

"For in him dwelleth all the fulness of the Godhead bodily" We must not be *"spoiled"* by the *"tradition of men"* or the *"rudiments of the world."* We must follow the Lord Jesus Christ because *"in him dwelleth all the fulness of the Godhead bodily."* He is the only member of the Trinity who has a perfect human body. Somebody might ask if born-again people will be able to see the resurrected body of the Lord Jesus Christ when they go to Heaven. Yes, I believe we will be able to behold the glorified body of the Lord Jesus Christ. Will we be able to see the Holy Spirit? No! Will we be able to see God the Father? No, but we will be able to see our Saviour because *"in Him dwelleth all the fulness of the Godhead bodily."*

The Error of "Oneness" Teaching

I don't believe in the so-called *"oneness"* teaching. We had some people in our Bible study a few years ago who believed in that heresy. They don't believe that we have one God in three Persons, God the Father, God the Son, and God the Holy Spirit. They believe that God is one and only in one Person rather than three. They believe that Christ is the Father, Christ is the Holy Spirit, and Christ is the Son. No! We will be able to see in bodily form the Lord Jesus Christ when we get to Heaven.

That is why God the Father sent His Son and made His Son incarnated, God in flesh (1 Timothy 3:16). Perfect Deity was put in a perfect body. Then the Lord Jesus Christ died for the sins of all of us so that we might, by faith, trust in Him, and be saved for all eternity. Truly, *"God was manifest in the flesh"* (1 Timothy 3:16)

"In Him dwelleth all the fulness of the Godhead bodily." This means that there is nothing that the Lord Jesus Christ does not possess in *"fulness."*

Every Attribute of Deity

There is not a single attribute of Deity that is absent from the Lord Jesus Christ. We see, in the Lord Jesus Christ, every attribute of God, even while He was on this earth.

We see His omnipresence, His omnipotence, His omniscience, His love, His power, His righteousness, His perfection, His impeccability or sinlessness, and every other attribute of Deity was in Christ in all of its *"fulness."* The Unitarians, the Christian Scientists, the Jews, the Muslims, the apostate Modernists and others demote and denigrate the Lord Jesus Christ, teaching that He is only human. This is the doctrine of Antichrist and is serious blasphemy.

These groups, and others like them, admit that they deny that in the Lord Jesus Christ dwells *"all the fullness of the godhead bodily."* They teach otherwise, and they are in error to do so. The Lord Jesus is not simply a man in human form as the false cults teach.

Heresy Among Fundamentalists

There are even some Fundamental Bible-believing Christian people who teach that Christ renounced the attributes of Deity when He came to this earth. This is serious error and, indeed, is heresy.

Christ did not give up anything except His form and His status as a perfect Spirit. He took upon Himself and combined His perfect Deity with a perfect human body and became flesh. Truly, *"God* [with 100% of His attributes] *was manifest in the flesh"* (1 Timothy 3:16). He gave up none of the attributes of Deity. He left His Home above to inhabit this wicked world for a short length of time in order to save sinners like we are, but He did not give up any of the attributes of Deity to accomplish this.

Some Fundamentalists who say that Christ gave up the attributes of Deity are wrong. They are teaching heresy at this point. I am thinking of a man who is a preacher and has been a teacher in Fundamentalist Bible schools. Both he, his son, and his brother proudly teach that Christ gave up some or all of the attributes of Deity. They teach that He did not perform any miracles while He was on this earth. They believe that God the Father performed those miracles through Him, but that He personally did not perform any miracles while on earth.

They do not believe He knew everything and was therefore not omniscient. To me this teaching is heresy. When I point this out to my fellow Fundamentalists and fellow believers they think I am *"wacky."* The *"fullness of the Godhead bodily"* was true before the Lord Jesus Christ came to earth, was true while He was on earth, and it is still true while He is in Heaven.

Christ Could Not Have Sinned

There are even some Fundamentalist preachers who think that the Lord Jesus Christ could have sinned. They don't think that Christ <u>did</u> sin, but they think Christ <u>could</u> have sinned. How can perfect Deity commit sin?

If this were true, He wouldn't be perfect Deity. Think this through another way. If the Lord Jesus Christ could have sinned while He was on this earth, could He sin now that He is in Heaven? It is the same Jesus. He is resurrected, but the same Jesus. If the Lord Jesus Christ could sin in Heaven, departing from all His Holiness and glory, of what value is our salvation?

No, He not only did not sin, but He could not sin. Here are two Latin phrases that give the two possibilities-- *"no posse pecare"* and *"posse no pecare."* The translation of the first phrase is *"not able to sin."* This teaching is the true position regarding the Lord Jesus Christ. The translation of the second phrase is *"able not to sin."* This second phrase is heresy because it implies that the Lord Jesus Christ could have sinned, but he was able not to sin. It leaves Christ's sinlessness in doubt not only while He was on earth, but also while He is in Heaven now.

Colossians 2:10

"And ye are complete in him, which is the head of all principality and power" There is nothing that can be added to *"completeness"* for the saved ones in the Lord Jesus Christ. You can't add your works to this. You can't add anything the church can give you. There is nothing to be added to *"completeness."* Can you add anything to 100%? No, you cannot.

What Is "Completeness"?

The Greek word for *"complete"* is PLEROO. It means *"to render full, i.e. to complete; to fill to the top: so that nothing shall be wanting to full measure, fill to the brim."*

The above Greek word for *"complete"* is related to the Greek word for *"fullness"* (PLEROMA) used in the phrase, *"the fulness of the Godhead bodily."*

The Lord Jesus Christ is the one Who has saved us, if we are saved. He is the One who keeps us. He is the One building a Home in Heaven for us. He has gone to prepare a Place for us like He says in John 14:2. He is the *"head of all principality and power."* As the *"head"* all is His. He is in charge of it. Nobody can overrule Him. There is no need for anybody to do anything else to take us to Heaven and to fill our lives. Christ has done it all.

We who are saved are *"complete"* in the Lord Jesus Christ. That is why Paul could say in Philippians 1:21, *"For me to live is Christ."* For us, perhaps, to live is a home or the next meal. But Paul had one Person in mind--the Lord Jesus Christ. I am sorry to say, this is not our mind-set. If we were to have one Person in mind, the Lord Jesus Christ, as Paul did, people would call us fanatics. Sometimes people call some of us fanatics if we put our Saviour first much of the time. Oh, that we would put Him first all of the time.

Colossians 2:11

"In whom also ye are circumcised with the circumcision made without hands, in putting off the body of the sins of the flesh by the circumcision of Christ"

This is a difficult verse to understand. This is not speaking of physical *"circumcision"* but of Spiritual *"circumcision."* The Lord Jesus Christ *"circumcised"* us in a Spiritual sense. Circumcision was the rite of the Jewish males to be set apart as a nation, by a *"covenant"* as a special chosen people of God (Genesis 17:11).

Spiritually, when the Lord Jesus circumcises us, He sets us apart from the world, from the judgment of the world, from the wickedness of the world. The *"sins of the flesh"* should not be a part of a believer's life. The Lord Jesus Christ has made us one of His own. That is a special thing.

We don't believe, as the Presbyterians, that circumcision of the Old Testament is related to baptism in the New Testament. They sprinkle their babies, calling it *"baptism."* I don't go along with that. This is a spiritual setting apart that the Lord does. We will never lose our Salvation. Once we are saved we are always saved. The Lord Jesus said in John:

- John 10:27-30

My sheep hear my voice, **and I know them**, and they follow me: And **I give unto them eternal life; and they shall never perish**, neither shall any man pluck them out of my hand. My Father, which gave them me, is greater than all; and no man is able to pluck them out of my Father's hand. I and my Father are one.

By this spiritual "*circumcision*" the saved people have received salvation. They have also been sanctified by the Spirit of God. God has put the Holy Spirit inside our bodies and made us His own. We are one of His.

We Must Be "Stablished"

I hope, through the agency of the Spirit of God, if you are saved, that you will be "*stablished in the faith*." I hope that you will have nothing push you down, hold you down, or in anyway keep you back from what the Lord will have for you as His very best.

I would hope that you would not be shaken or moved around, but that you would remain firm. Remember the expression of "*jelly on the wall*." This depicts certain people who are wishy-washy and not stabilized. They move, droop, and fall down. I trust that the Lord would give each one of us stability, firmness and make us rooted, built up, and stablished in the "*faith which was once delivered unto the saints*" (Jude 3b).

Colossians 2:12

"Buried with *him* in baptism, wherein also ye are risen with him through the faith of the operation of God, who hath raised him from the dead" Paul is speaking to believers there in Colosse. This is not talking about the unsaved world. He is talking to believers. Saved people not only have been "*crucified with Christ*" (Galatians 2:20), but also, as this verse declares, have been "*buried*" with Christ. We have also been "*raised*" with Christ, and we are "*seated*" with Christ (Ephesians 2:6). These are blessings that believers have in Christ.

Obviously, you are sitting on earth, but, according to this verse, positionally, if you are saved, you are "*risen with Him*" through "*baptism*." This is a spiritual "*baptism*." It is true of every believer. What is the meaning of the word, "*baptism*," mentioned here?

Two Primary Baptisms

I believe there are two primary baptisms in the New Testament.

1. There is the baptism by the Holy Spirit as we will see in 1 Corinthians 12:13 which is referred to here; and,

2. There is baptism in water for believers after they have been saved through faith in Christ (Matthew 28:19).

There is a false *"baptism"* of the Pentecostals and Charismatics. We do not agree with this teaching. They claim that the baptism of the Holy Spirit is manifested by the speaking in tongues. We do not believe that is Scriptural. The speaking in tongues are foreign languages in Acts 2 so that those who were gathered at that special feast of Pentecost would be able to hear the gospel in their own language. It was not some kind of "prayer language" that no one could understand.

- 1 Corinthians 12:13
  For **by one Spirit are we all baptized into one body**, whether we be Jews or Gentiles, whether we be bond or free; and have been all made to drink into one Spirit.

This is for believers.

Baptized By the Spirit When Saved

As soon as we are saved we are baptized by the Holy Spirit into one body of the saved ones. The Lord Jesus is the head of that body. Other believers are members of that body. This is a spiritual baptism, a spiritual fact, and a spiritual truth.

So, this Spirit baptism joins every believer to Christ the Head and to every other saved person as members of a body. It is not something that happens subsequent to salvation. It is not something that happens when you speak in tongues. That is not the baptism spoken about here. It occurs as soon as we trust Christ, are joined to Christ, and are joined to the other members of the body. That is called the baptism of the Holy Spirit.

- **Romans 6:3-4**
  Know ye not, that so many of us as were baptized into Jesus Christ were baptized into his death? Therefore **we are buried with him by baptism into death**: that like as Christ was raised up from the dead by the glory of the Father, even so we also should walk in newness of life.

The baptism of the Holy Spirit is pictured by water baptism. That is, the baptism by water is an emblem, or a symbol, of the Spirit baptism of the Holy Spirit. The figure of spiritual burial and resurrection is pictured in water baptism by the immersion of believers.

We also *"should walk in newness of life."*

What Baptism Pictures

The picture of baptism by water is a picture of the death, the burial, and the resurrection of Christ as the believers are joined in picture form with these events. That is why we, as Baptists, believe the Scriptures that baptism is by the immersion of believers.

That word for *"baptism"* means *"to immerse, to dip, and to put under some influence of a liquid."*

- **Romans 6:6**
  Knowing this, that **our old man is crucified with him**, that the body of sin might be destroyed, that henceforth we should not serve sin.

God reckons that positionally the old nature was crucified when the Lord Jesus was crucified. We were not physically there, but our old nature is reckoned to be *"crucified with Him."* We ought to reckon our bodies and old natures as dead so we wouldn't be a slave to sin. Dead men and dead women don't practice sin. This whole idea of the baptism with Christ by the Holy Spirit and reckoning ourselves dead unto sin is very important.

- **Ephesians 2:6**
  And **hath raised us up together, and made us sit together in heavenly places in Christ Jesus:**

> ## The Believers' Position in Christ
> In a spiritual and positional sense, the believers not only died with Christ, were buried with Christ, were raised with Christ, but also have been seated in *"heavenly places"* with Christ.

That is exactly how God sees the saved Christians.
- Colossians 3:1
  If ye then be risen with Christ, seek those things which are above, where Christ sitteth on the right hand of God.

Here is another verse speaking of our being raised with Christ. The ordinance of the believer's water baptism is very important. In the Muslim countries, as soon as any believer is baptized, the Muslims have nothing to do with them. That is when the persecution of the Christian starts--at the time of his or her baptism as a believer.

Colossians 2:13
"And you, being dead in your sins and the uncircumcision of your flesh, hath he quickened together with him, having forgiven you all trespasses"

Our condition was being *"dead"* in our sins before we were saved. These Colossian believers, before they were saved, were also *"dead"* in sins. But now, they are *"quickened"* or made alive.
- Ephesians 2:1
  And you hath he quickened, who **were dead in trespasses and sins;**
- Ephesians 2:5
  Even **when we were dead in sins**, hath quickened us together with Christ, (by grace ye are saved;)

It is important to realize, as these Colossian Christians realized, that before they were saved they were *"dead"* in sins. It is also important to realize that God the Father has *"forgiven us all trespasses."* Those *"trespasses"* are past, present, and future. They are sins of the mind, heart, body, and mouth.
- 1 John 1:9
  If we confess our sins, **he is faithful and just to forgive us our sins**, and to cleanse us from all unrighteousness.

In this verse, upon genuine confession of our sins, God forgives us those sins for fellowship. He has already forgiven our sins past, present, and future for salvation. But for fellowship we must confess our sins and be renewed and restored again to fellowship with Him.

- **Acts 26:18**
  To open their eyes, and to turn them from darkness to light, and from the power of Satan unto God, **that they may receive forgiveness of sins,** and inheritance among them which are sanctified by faith that is in me.

That is why he was ordained as an apostle of the Lord Jesus Christ.

- **Romans 4:7**
  Saying, **Blessed are they whose iniquities are forgiven,** and whose sins are covered.

I am sure, if you are trusting Christ as your Saviour you can be *"blessed"* and be happy that your sins are forgiven and covered by the blood of Christ.

- **Ephesians 1:7**
  In whom we have redemption through his blood, **the forgiveness of sins,** according to the riches of his grace;

By faith in Christ, He has forgiven us all trespasses. It is a tremendous truth.

- **1 John 1:9**
  If we confess our sins, **he is faithful and just to forgive us our sins,** and to cleanse us from all unrighteousness.

What is Confession?

If we who are believers *"confess"* the *"sins"* we commit with our thoughts, with our words, and with our bodies, we must agree with God that it is sin. That is what confession is.

If we do this, *"He is faithful"* and He is *"just to forgive us"* and *"to cleanse us"* from those *"sins."*

Colossians 2:14

"Blotting out the handwriting of ordinances that was against us, which was contrary to us, and took it out of the way, nailing it to his cross."

All the sins that you and I have committed, before we came to Christ, were facing us until Christ redeemed us. Now, God says that *"He has blotted out the handwriting of ordinances that was against us."* He has taken them *"out of the way, nailing it to his cross."* That Greek word for *"blotted out"* is EXALEIPHO. It means *"to wipe off, wipe away; to obliterate, erase, wipe out, blot out."*

- **Psalm 51:1**
  Have mercy upon me, O God, according to thy lovingkindness: according unto the multitude of thy tender mercies **blot out my transgressions.**

That is what God has done at Calvary. That is what He has done when we trust the Lord Jesus Christ as our Redeemer. He has blotted out our transgressions.

- **Psalm 51:9**
  Hide thy face from my sins, and **blot out all mine iniquities.**
- **Isaiah 43:25**
  I, even I, am he that **blotteth out thy transgressions** for mine own sake, and will not remember thy sins.

That is an important fact for every believer to know. God has *"blotted out"* our transgressions.

- **Isaiah 44:22**
  I have blotted out, as a thick cloud, thy transgressions, and, as a cloud, thy sins: return unto me; for I have redeemed thee.

You can't see through *"thick clouds"*. That is why planes using "visual flight rules" must have so many miles of visibility in order to land. If we're in Christ and redeemed by faith in Him, God has *"blotted out as a thick cloud"* our *"transgressions."* Not just an ordinary cloud, but a *"thick cloud."* God does a thorough job of *"blotting out"* our sins. John the Baptist said, *"Behold the Lamb of God which taketh away the sin of the world."*

The "Handwriting of Ordinances"

This *"handwriting of ordinances"* is a note in handwriting. The Greek word is CHEIROGRAPHON. It means

"a note of hand or writing in which one acknowledges that money has either been deposited with him or lent to him by another, to be returned at the appointed time in which one acknowledges that money has either been deposited with him or lent to him by another to be returned at the appointed time."

If you have loaned money to someone he has your I.O.U. in your own handwriting. It has to be repaid at a certain time.

The Lord Jesus repaid all the debt that was due to us. That is what this *"handwriting of ordinances"* is that has been *"blotted out."* There is no more need for us to repay anything. We can't repay anything because we are sinners lost and bound for Hell. He nailed everything that the sinners owe to the cross.

At the cross the debt was paid in full. Jesus paid it all. Our sins were nailed to that cross, and there they were *"blotted out."*

> ## The History of the "Cross"
> "The cross was a well-known instrument of most cruel and ignominious punishment, borrowed by the Greeks and Romans from the Phoenicians; to it were affixed among the Romans, down to the time of Constantine the Great, the guiltiest criminals, particularly the basest of slaves, robbers, the authors and abaters of insurrections, and occasionally in the provinces, at the arbitrary pleasure of the governors, upright and peaceable men also, and even the Roman citizens themselves."

The dying on a cross was a most shameful way for the Lord Jesus Christ to suffer, to bleed, and to die. That was what God the Father had in mind for Him. In the Garden of Gethsemane, He prayed, *"Nevertheless not my will, but thine, be done"* (Luke 22:42). In Philippians 2:8, it says that the Lord Jesus Christ died *"even the death of the cross."*

So forgiveness is possible because He nailed all our sins to His cross on Calvary. *As far as the East is from the West so far hath He removed our transgression from us* (Psalm 103:12).

Colossians 2:15

"And having spoiled principalities and powers, he made a shew of them openly, triumphing over them in it"
The Greek word for "spoiled" is APEKDUOMAI. It means *"wholly to strip off for one's self (for one's own advantage); despoil, disarm."* Who are these "*principalities and powers*"? I believe they include all the Satanic evil angels, the evil spirits and demons. The Lord Jesus Christ spoiled them. He stripped them. He took away from them their former authority. He completely robbed them of all their power. Satan no longer has any power over us if we are trusting Christ. We plead the blood of Christ and use God's methods of keeping clean and holy. The display of Christ's triumph was made *"openly"* for all to see. Satan has no more power over the saved ones.

- **Hebrews 2:14**
  Forasmuch then as the children are partakers of flesh and blood, he also himself likewise took part of the same; **that through death he might destroy him that had the power of death, that is, the devil;**

Satan was the one who had the *"power of death."* At Calvary, the Lord Jesus Christ *"destroyed"* the Devil in the sense that he rendered him powerless to control death any more.

- **Hebrews 2:15**
And deliver them who through fear of death were all their lifetime subject to bondage.

The Lord Jesus Christ *"delivered"* us from Satan's *"bondage."*

The Lord Jesus, through the power of His death, burial, and bodily resurrection, *"spoiled"* Satan's power that he had over the believers. He *"triumphed"* over the Satanic powers and celebrated that triumph at the cross by *"nailing"* these *"ordinances"* and sins to it. If we're saved, this is our status and our standing before God.

Colossians 2:16

"Let no man therefore judge you in meat, or in drink, or in respect of an holyday, or of the new moon, or of the Sabbath days" These believers were no longer under the Law of Moses. These meats, drinks, holy days, new moons, and Sabbath days were all old remnants of the Law of Moses. They are no longer binding on the child of God in this age of grace.

Negative Commands In Greek

There are two ways to construct a negative command or prohibition in the Greek language. One way is to use a prohibition in the aorist tense which means *"Don't even begin to do some action."* The other way is to use a prohibition in the present tense which means *"Stop doing an action already in progress."* The words, *"Let no man judge"* constitute a present tense prohibition. It means to *"stop having anyone judge you"* in regard to meat or drink or the various days mentioned. This means that some of them were judging them in these areas, but should cease from doing it.

These Christians at Colosse apparently did not want to go along with the Mosaic Law. They did not want to have special dietary laws as far as their eating of meats, or drinking, or in respect of holy days, or new moons, or Sabbath days. They did not keep all these things. Paul said for them to stop letting people judge them about these things. They were being judged wrongly for this. These believers had no obligation to keep any part of the Law of

Moses.

I was talking to a gentleman on the phone a couple of days ago. He said that he believed the whole Bible is for us. Well, it is for us, but it is not all **to** us. Did God ask us to build an ark? No, He did not. There are certain things that are not to us. Did He ask us to sacrifice animals on the altars? No! So, though the Bible is all for our learning that we *"through patience and comfort of the scriptures might have hope"* (Romans 15:4), we are not under any obligation to keep the Law of Moses.

The Bible is not all written to us, so the dispensational understanding of Scripture is very vital.

The Three Major Bible Dispensations

In addition to four others, the three major Bible dispensations are:

(1) the Law of Moses,

(2) the Age of Grace (what we are in right now), and

(3) the Kingdom Age (which is the thousand-year reign of our Saviour upon this earth.)

Paul says you Colossians have no business having people judge you because of some of the Old Testament dietary restrictions and laws. *"Ye are not under the law, but under grace"* (Romans 6:14). You don't have to keep the Sabbath, the holy days, or any other part of the Mosaic Law.

Colossians 2:17

"Which are a shadow of things to come; but the body is of Christ" These parts of the Law were simply a *"shadow of things to come."* Remember when God told Moses to make the Tabernacle? He was very specific. He said how many cubits long, how many cubits wide, and how many cubits high each of the articles was to be. He told Moses every article of furniture that was to go inside the ark. Some have said the Law of Moses was micro-managed. Moses was given every detail of the Tabernacle, but that was a *"shadow of things to come"* because God said He was going to make the earthly tabernacle after the pattern of the *"heavenly things"* (Hebrews 8:5), that is, a heavenly tabernacle.

So, there is a heavenly tabernacle. The Lord Jesus Christ is there in Heaven. The Bible speaks about a *"temple"* and an *"altar"* in Heaven (Revelation 11:1). It speaks about the *"ark of His testament"* in Heaven

(Revelation 11:19). It speaks of the *"testimony"* in Heaven, probably a reference to the Word of God (Revelation 15:5). It speaks of the *"smoke"* from the *"glory of God"* in Heaven, which is the Shekinah glory.

Christ's Blood Is In Heaven

I believe the blood of Christ is on the Mercy Seat on the *"altar"* of Heaven because the Tabernacle is simply a shadow of that which is true up in the Heavens themselves. Christ did not enter into Heaven *"by the blood of goats and calves, but by His own blood He entered in once into the Holy place having obtained eternal redemption for us"* (Hebrews 9:12).

One day, Lord willing, if the Lord spares us, we will be studying the book of Hebrews. It is a tremendous book indeed to study.

All of these things were a *"shadow"* of things to come, but the body is of Christ. The Lord Jesus is a fulfillment of all the Mosaic Law. The Greek word for *"shadow"* is SKIA. It means *"shade caused by the interception of light; an image cast by an object and representing the form of that object"* If I put my hand over the light, I have a shadow on the page. If you want to see what you look like, just put a light behind you and you can see your shadow. You can hop around and your shadow moves with you. It is also a *"sketch or an outline."* That is all the Law of Moses was. The *"body"* and fulfillment of all of it was the Lord Jesus Christ.

As it says in John 1:17: *"The law was given by Moses, but grace and truth came by Jesus Christ."* There is a vast difference between law and grace. We are not under the law; and no one should beguile anybody by teaching that we, who are saved, should be brought back under the law of Moses, including all of the blood offerings. This is unscriptural.

- **Hebrews 10:1**
  Forthe law having a shadow of good things to come, and not the very image of the things, can never with those sacrifices which they offered year by year continually make the comers thereunto perfect.

Christ can make us perfect, not the law.

Colossians 2:18

"Let no man beguile you of your reward in a voluntary humility and worshipping of angels, intruding into those things which he hath not seen, vainly puffed up by his fleshly mind"

"Let no man beguile you of your reward in a voluntary humility." Here is another what we call a stop sign. In Verse 16, we saw a prohibition in the present tense. It was *"stop letting people judge you,"* according to all these Jewish days on the calendar. Here is a second stop sign in this present verse. Again, we see the present tense, negative command, which means to stop an action already begun. Some people were *"beguiling"* the Colossian Christians. They were muddying the waters. Paul told them to stop it. We don't want anyone to defraud or *"beguile"* you from your victory in Christ and your obedience to His Words.

What were people in Colosse doing as far as beguiling the Colossian believers? First, there was a *"voluntary humility."*

"Voluntary Humility"

This condition is observed when a person says or acts like he or she is extremely humble. Because of their seeming *"humility,"* they may try to *"beguile"* or fool you into doing something for them that is not Scriptural.

Recently we saw, on one of the TV news shows, something about a witch. She had some Tarot Cards. The TV people were trying to show that she was a fake. She was an old lady, but very skilled in collecting money. Apparently those Tarot Card people make up to $100,000 dollars a year. This woman seemed very humble. She asked her customers for a little bit of money and then a little bit more each time. Pretty soon she was getting a lot of money from each customer. Then she tells the fortune which is *"off the wall,"* as far as I am concerned.

Stop Letting People "Beguile" You

Stop letting anybody *"beguile"* you even though they seem to do it with a *"voluntary humility."* Just because somebody is humble doesn't mean they are going to teach you proper doctrine. They must teach the Word of God. We must be careful that someone does not fool us with their piety, spirituality, or seeming *"humility."*

"and worshipping of angels" The TV show, "Touched by an Angel," was very popular. The world seemed to have gone crazy over *"angels."* There are books written about *"angels."* People say an angel told me to do this or that. They have revelations from supposed *"angels."* God says to stop all such *"worship"* of *"angels."* These are fallen demon *"angels."* They are evil spirits. They are not God's holy *"angels."* God's holy *"angels"* would never think of deceiving people in this way. They know that all true worship must be directed only to the Lord God of Heaven and earth and to His Son the Lord Jesus Christ, not to themselves.

"intruding into those things which he hath not seen"
When you worship the *"angels"* and people draw you away with *"beguiling"* things, like Satan did Eve at the Garden of Eden, there is an *"intruding into those things which"* we have not seen. That Greek word for *"intruding"* is EMBATEUO. It means *"to invade, make hostile incursion into; or to investigate, search into, scrutinize minutely."* To *"invade"* would be like a robber coming into your home. That robber is an invader to your safety and your security. To *"search into"* would be like people who seek wizards (like Harry Potter), tea leaf readers, spiritualists, occult leaders and others connected with Satan.

"No man hath seen God at anytime" (John 1:18; 1 John 4:12). Somebody may come to you and tell you that they have seen God and He told them to do this or that and it is contrary to Scripture. Don't listen to that person. That is an intrusion into the things *"not seen."* We have the Word of God to go by, and that is our guide and our map. *"Thy Word is a lamp unto my feet and a light unto my path"* (Psalm 119:105). God's Words are the *"lamp"* and the *"light"* we must use. We find these Words in our King James Bible and the Hebrew and Greek texts underlying it.

"vainly puffed up by his fleshly mind" These false teachers are *"vainly puffed up"* because of their *"fleshly mind."* One of the many kinds of fish is the blow fish. When danger comes near, this fish puffs himself up to frighten away his enemies. There are blow fish kind of people who are *"vainly puffed up."*

> ## "Puffed Up"
> The Greek word for *"puffed up"* is PHUSIOO. It means *"to inflate, blow up, to cause to swell up; to puff up, make proud; to be puffed up, to bear one's self loftily, be proud."*

That is why sometimes people's noses go up a little bit when they speak with you. There is pride. There is a *"bearing of one's self loftily."* They don't really see the people around them. They are looking up in the sky because they think they are so superior. This is what these false teachers do. They are *"puffed up"* in a vain manner in their *"fleshly mind."* It is a mind that is depraved. It is a mind that is off. It is a mind that is "dead in trespasses and sins" (Ephesians 2:1). It is a mind that has been judged by the Lord at the cross of Calvary.

Paul warns these Colossians to watch out for these false teachers who worship angels, who have false humility, who intrude and go into things with their fleshly mind. There are many people who think that intelligence is all there is. I am not against intelligence, but faith in the Words of God supersedes all the intelligence that we have in our fleshly minds.

God has not given us in our minds His revelation of things to come, or the revelation of sin, or the revelation of Heaven and Hell, and many other things. He has given us these things in His Word. May God give us the minds to read His Word, to understand His Word, and to discern His Word. We must **"LEARN TO DISCERN."**

Colossians 2:19

"And not holding the Head, from which all the body by joints and bands having nourishment ministered, and knit together, increaseth with the increase of God"

"And not holding the Head" These who are intruding into things they have not seen and these who are puffed up in their fleshly mind, are not holding the Head. The Head is our Saviour, the Lord Jesus Christ. If they have puffed up minds they are not holding fast to the Saviour, the Head.

Holding Fast

The Greek word for "hold" is KRATEO. It means *"to hold fast, i.e. not discard or let go; to keep carefully and faithfully."* These false teachers are *"discarding"* the Lord Jesus Christ. They are not *"keeping Him carefully and faithfully."*

The Lord Jesus wants us to continue to hold and to retain Him in all of His glory and attributes. The Lord Jesus Christ is the *"Head"* of the church. The pastor is the under-shepherd of the church. The Lord Jesus Christ is the *"Head"* of the church. He is the Head of the husband. He is the one who is the master. He is the One to whom we're to look. These false teachers do not hold, cling to, and retain the Lord Jesus Christ as their *"Head."* The human body is controlled by the head. We have many uncontrolled churches who are "brain dead," so to speak, because they ignore their *"Head,"* the Lord Jesus Christ.

"from which all the body by joints and bands having nourishment ministered, and knit together, increaseth with the increase of God" It is important for believers to hold to the *"Head,"* the Lord Jesus Christ. From Him *"all the body"* hangs together. It has *"nourishment ministered"* and it is *"knit together."* Because of this, it *"increaseth with the increase of God."* God says here we are in a body. Through the ministry of the Holy Spirit and God's Word, saved people have *"joints and bands."* We are bound together with Christian love. Since that is the case, as I believe that it is, our *Bible For Today Baptist Church*, is also *"knit together"* one with another.

One of the uses of the Greek word, SUMBIBAZO, which is translated *"knit together"* is: *"to cause a person to unite with one in a conclusion or come to the same opinion, to prove, demonstrate."* On the basic doctrines of the Word of God and the faith, we should be bound together and *"knit together"* in affection, love, and unanimity. If this be true, there will be a continual spiritual increase in the *"increase of God."*

The *"increase"* is either qualitative, quantitative, or both. Which is more important for you as a person: to grow quantitatively by means of growing taller and heavier; or to grow qualitatively by means of having a healthy body? I trust that you are able to be healthy in all that you can do. It is the same way with Christian things.

Numbers Mania

Quantity rather than quality is the measure of many churches. Quantity or numbers is all that is important in some churches. Some have called it numbers mania. They will do anything.

These churches sometimes have two services. One service for the contemporary with all the rock music and modern versions, and the other for the old "fuddy duddies" who like the traditional services, the traditional Christian music, and the traditional King James Bible. This is so they won't miss out on anyone's preferences, regardless of whether or not they are based upon the Bible.

We were at a Fanny Crosby meeting a few years ago. The pastor told us proudly about his two services. My wife asked him why he had the contemporary service. Now, we were told, both of that church's services are contemporary. Also, it seems like that pastor's morals turned "*contemporary*," as well. He went off with his secretary and committed adultery. I don't know if adultery and contemporary go hand-in-hand, but it is a horrible thing. You have to stay traditional in every way, including music, church services, the Bible, doctrines, marriage, and fidelity to your mate.

Importance of Qualitative "Increase"

In my considered opinion, the qualitative "*increase*" in a church is much more important than the quantitative "*increase*." God commands believers to "*grow in grace and the knowledge of our Lord and Saviour Jesus Christ*." That is genuine "*increase*" which God expects. As we grow in the things of the Lord spiritually we must be established in the faith.

If the Lord prospers us, we can grow in other ways as well; but the quality is more important then the quantity. If you don't believe it, look at the size of your wife's diamond. You can buy a large box filled with groceries or something much more costly, and that wouldn't be worth a fraction of what a diamond is worth. God wants quality in His saints.

Colossians 2:20

"Wherefore if ye be dead with Christ from the rudiments of the world, why, as though living in the world, are ye subject to ordinances" It is fact that, positionally, the believers are *"dead with Christ."* From God's standpoint, we who are saved took our place with the Lord Jesus Christ when He died on the cross of Calvary. This death was from the *"rudiments of the world."* The Greek word for *"rudiments"* is STOICHEION. It means *"any first thing, from which the others belonging to some series or composite whole take their rise, an element, first principal."* Because of this positional death with Christ, various *"ordinances"* of the law of Moses or of the Pharisees who defiled the law of Moses do not apply. This is discussed in the next verse.

Colossians 2:21

"(Touch not; taste not; handle not" These three things are some of the Jewish *"ordinances."* The Pharisees were good at this. The Pharisees *"made the Word of God of none effect through their tradition"* (Mark 7:13) and their ordinances.

- **Matthew 15:1-3**
  Then came to Jesus scribes and Pharisees, which were of Jerusalem, saying, Why do thy disciples transgress the tradition of the elders? for they wash not their hands when they eat bread. But he answered and said unto them, **Why do ye also transgress the commandment of God by your tradition?**

The scribes and Pharisees asked a question and the Lord Jesus answered them with a question. Sometimes that is a good idea. If someone asks you a question you might ask them one right back.

- **Mark 7:9**
  And he said unto them, Full well **ye reject the commandment of God, that ye may keep your own tradition**.

We must make sure our practices are in line with the Word of God and not our own made up *"tradition."*

- **Mark 7:13**
  Making the word of God of none effect through your tradition, which ye have delivered: and many such like things do ye.

I think that the *"ordinances"* mentioned in these verses here are rules that are superimposed by the world rather than being specifically or in principal mentioned in the Bible. There are commands and *"ordinances"* that are in

Scripture. We are to obey every one of them. I think the reference here in this context is to *"ordinances"* and rules given to the Jews that are used to trying to make Gentile Christians act as if they were Jews.

These *"ordinances"* may be rules found in the MISHNA or other books of Jewish traditions. The Jews might have been trying to encourage the believers to go along with these rules. Paul says no, this is not what is to be done. We must follow the Word of God. Many people sometimes use the words in Verse 21 to lambaste, criticize, and crucify those of us who believe in Biblical standards. They think that Paul is making a mockery when he says, *"Touch not; taste not; handle not."* These people accuse some of us as being *"negative."* Listen, did you know that the Bible is *"negative"* in many areas.

These negatives that the Jews had imported into the Scripture are superficial. They have nothing to do with the Bible.

Only Two Positive Commandments

Do you know how many of the Ten Commandments are negative? Eight of the ten are negative. There are only two positive commandments which are:
1. "Remember the Sabbath day, to keep it holy" (Exodus 20:8)
2. "Honour thy father and thy mother" (Exodus 20:12a).

All the other eight commandments are negative.

When I was a member of a church in association with the General Association of Regular Baptists Churches (GARBC), I remember one of the State meetings of that group. It was at a meeting of what they call the Garden State Fellowship of Regular Baptist Churches. This group traditionally passed some good resolutions at their meetings. It is fine to have some good resolutions. One pastor jumped up and said, *"I don't like these resolutions."* He wondered why they should have any resolutions. The resolutions stood up for the Bible and stood against the sins of the world. He said that the churches were getting too negative. I began to search the Bible and went through several Bible books and found many, many *"negatives."*

The Bible is full of negatives. Make sure the negatives are negatives from the Word of God rather than things some man has imposed upon the Word of God. That is the issue. So, keep being positive where the Bible is positive and negative where the Word of God is negative. Ours is a call to obedience to God's Words, regardless of what people might say, or what they might think about us.

Colossians 2:22

"Which all are to perish with the using;) after the commandments and doctrines of men?"

All of these things mentioned in the previous verse, whether it is eating, or drinking, or whatever it might be will *"perish with the using."* Touching, tasting, and handling are all things that have to do with our senses. These Christians at Colosse were *"subject to ordinances"* (v. 20) *"after the commandments and doctrines of men."* Instead of looking at these things which will *"perish with the using,"* they should be looking at things that won't perish.

- 1 John 2:15-17

  Love not the world, neither the things that are in the world. If any man love the world, the love of the Father is not in him. For all that is in the world, the lust of the flesh, and the lust of the eyes, and the pride of life, is not of the Father, but is of the world. And **the world passeth away, and the lust thereof: but he that doeth the will of God abideth for ever**.

These *"things"* of the *"world"* will pass, but *"he that doeth the will of God abideth for ever"* and will never perish. The Lord Jesus promised us this, if we are saved.

- John 10:27-30

  My sheep hear my voice, and I know them, and they follow me: And **I give unto them eternal life; and they shall never perish**, neither shall any man pluck them out of my hand. My Father, which gave them me, is greater than all; and no man is able to pluck them out of my Father's hand. I and my Father are one.

I am totally opposed to the phony kind of alleged *"salvation"* whose visible effects seem to last only for a second, or a minute, or a day, or a week, or a month, or a year, or a decade. God's salvation by His grace, through personal faith in the Lord Jesus Christ--if it is genuine--is eternal. Those who are saved *"shall never perish."*

Once we come to the Lord Jesus Christ and are genuinely saved, we are in our Saviour's hand. Our Heavenly Father's hand is surrounding the Saviour's hand, and *"no man is able to pluck them out of the Father's hand."* So we have *"things"* that will *"never perish."* God's Words will *"never perish."* The born-again people will never perish. *"He that doeth the will of God"* will never perish.

Colossians 2:23

"Which things have indeed a shew of wisdom in will worship, and humility, and neglecting of the body; not in any honour to the satisfying of the flesh"

"Which things have indeed a shew of wisdom in will worship, and humility" In the best way he could, Paul was pointing out some of the things that these Judaizers were trying to impose on these Colossian Christians. When someone has a *"shew of wisdom in will worship,"* many people tend to follow that *"someone."* That is why students follow the professors and the teachers in colleges and universities. The professors are not always right. Sometimes they are wrong.

I remember one professor at the *University of Michigan*, when I was a student there, many years ago. He was in Sociology. He was talking about gullies all over this country, and how terrible the free enterprise system was. He was probably a communist. He got me thinking along those lines. I did not have the discernment. Later, when I learned the truth of our Constitutional government, I threw this false communistic thinking overboard. Finally, I could see how wrong that professor was.

The false cults quite often show *"wisdom."* The leaders seem to be very wise, very sharp, and very intelligent. They make *"error"* appear to be so reasonable and logical. It is *"will worship."*

"Will Worship"

The Greek word for *"will worship"* is ETHELOTHRESKEIA. It means: *"worship which one prescribes and devises for himself, contrary to the contents and nature of faith which ought to be directed to Christ."*

That is the difference. The false teacher makes worship directed to himself rather then directing his love and loyalty to Christ. It is a *"shew of wisdom in will worship."* Notice, there is *"humility"* connected with this heresy. The Greek word is TAPEINOPHROSUNE. It means *"having a humble opinion of one's self."* So it is really a false *"humility."*

"and neglecting of the body" Many people look at someone who is physically fit and think they look good. He or she is *"neglecting"* the comforts of the body. If they are runners, they run even in the rain. When I see them, I wonder why they are out in the rain. I am not against that, if this is what they want to do. Don't look up to and admire those people who neglect their bodies. Other people starve themselves until they become toothpick-thin. Some of them don't get much sleep. Some overeat, not caring what they are doing to their bodies.

Some of the early monks neglected their bodies by punishing themselves, thinking that in that way, they might gain salvation, or at least more favor with the Lord. This is the wrong reason for *"neglecting of the body."* That is the thing that found its way into the asceticism of the medieval church. Asceticism means *"the religious doctrine that one can reach a higher spiritual state by rigorous self-discipline and self-denial."* It is a *"neglecting of the body"* as mentioned in this verse. If you are an ascetic you might stay up later each night, get less sleep, eat a bit less, walk more, work harder, and wear uncomfortable hair shirts to punish your flesh.

Martin Luther thought that the way to please God was to ascend the steps of a cathedral in Rome on his knees. With bleeding knees he would reach the top of the stairs. Finally he came to the realization of the truth in God's Word in the book of Romans, *"The just shall live by faith"* (Romans 1:17). He came to see and understand that salvation was not by works, not by *"neglecting of the body,"* but by faith.

In this regard, I think of our good friends, Dr. Richard and Rose Durham, who were for many years missionaries in the Philippines. Rose is with the Lord now. Richard, who has remarried, is back in the United States. He taught for many years at Cedarville University in Cedarville, Ohio. He told me about the *"flagellants"* in the Philippines that came out during the Easter season. Those individuals used to go up the road with large crosses in huge processions. As they went, they were beaten severely with whips. Those men had bloody backs as they moved along the road. They were doing this in order to be saved and gain favor with God. That is not God's way for salvation. It was the Lord Jesus Christ, Who was flagellated in our place.

The Suffering Saviour

It was the Lord Jesus who suffered a crucifixion with thorns on His brow, nails in his hands and feet. He was scourged on His back, and the spear pierced His side. He is the One Who, for us, neglected His body, as it were. He suffered the pain so that we did not have to suffer for our sins.

The prophet Isaiah talked clearly about this.
- **Isaiah 53:3-6**
  ³"**He is despised and rejected of men; a man of sorrows, and acquainted with grief**: and we hid as it were *our* faces from him; he was despised, and we esteemed him not. ⁴Surely he hath borne our griefs, and carried our sorrows: **yet we did esteem him stricken, smitten of God, and afflicted.** ⁵But **he** *was* **wounded for our transgressions,** *he was* **bruised for our iniquities**: the chastisement of our peace *was* upon him; and **with his stripes we are healed.** ⁶All we like sheep have gone astray; we have turned every one to his own way; and the LORD hath laid on him the iniquity of us all."

You say, if I suffer and my body suffers is that going to be pleasing to God? No, not necessarily. The things that please the Lord are the things which are spiritual. It is not the external things which please the Lord, but sometimes (not always) the external things reveal our inner heart. *"Man looketh on the outward appearance, but the LORD looketh on the heart"* (1 Samuel 16:7c).

"not in any honor to the satisfying of the flesh" Anything goes, when there is a *"satisfying of the flesh."* This is self-gratification. God is against this. Many people today say, *"Why not do this?"* Self gratification is the way they live their lives. They think any and all illicit sex is all right. They see nothing wrong with smoking, using alcohol, using drugs, gambling or anything else that pleases them. This is what the *"satisfying of the flesh"* means. Let me ask you a question. Do you really think that your old wicked flesh can ever be satisfied with anything? The flesh always says *"I want more."* That is the only thing the flesh knows. Do you think that the flesh of millionaires are satisfied with their millions? No, they always want more millions. The *"flesh"* is the thing which is against God.
- **Romans 8:8-9**
  So then **they that are in the flesh cannot please God.** ⁹But ye are not in the flesh, but in the Spirit, if so be that the Spirit of God dwell in you. Now if any man have not the Spirit of Christ, he is none of his."

If we are saved, the Lord Jesus Christ is the One that we should please. He is the One Who has redeemed us.

Forgiven All Trespasses

The Lord Jesus Christ is the One who has forgiven us all trespasses. He is the One Who has nailed these trespasses to His cross blotting them out, never to be remembered anymore forever.

We praise God for this substitutionary sacrifice of the Lamb of God. May we continue to love Him and serve Him.

Colossians
Chapter Three

Colossians 3:1

"If ye then be risen with Christ, seek those things which are above, where Christ sitteth on the right hand of God."

"If ye then be risen with Christ" That *"if"* has the meaning here of *"since."* It is in the Greek indicative mood. This mood always indicates a positive action. The saved people have been positionally *"risen with Christ."* We are here on earth, how can we be *"risen with Christ."* This is a positional truth. In God's eyes, the saved person has been raised with the Lord Jesus Christ.

The Believers' Position in Christ

The Apostle Paul, through the Holy Spirit, has given us many such positional truths. First of all the Bible teaches us that the born-again Christian is *"dead with Christ"* (Romans 6:8). Then the Bible teaches us we've been *"buried with Him"* (Romans 6:4; Colossians 2:12). Then it says Christ has *"raised us up together"* with Him (Ephesians 2:6). Then He has made us *"sit together in Heavenly places"* (Ephesians 2:6). This is positional truth. If we are saved, we have been *"risen with Christ"* even though we are here on earth.

"seek those things which are above" If it is the case that we have been *"risen with Christ,"* we should *"seek those things which are above"* where we have been positionally *"risen."*

- **Romans 8:34**
  Who is he that condemneth? **It is Christ that died, yea rather, that is risen again, who is even at the right hand of God,** who also maketh intercession for us.
- **1 Corinthians 15:20**
  But **now is Christ risen from the dead,** and become the firstfruits of them that slept.
- **Colossians 2:12**
  Buried with him in baptism, wherein also **ye are risen with him through the faith of the operation of God, who hath raised him from the dead.**
- **Colossians 3:1**
  If ye then be risen with Christ, seek those things which are above, **where Christ sitteth on the right hand of God.**

"where Christ sitteth on the right hand of God" There are a number verses where the Lord Jesus Christ is said to be on *"the right hand of God."* The *"right hand"* is the place of authority and power.

- **Acts 2:32-33**
  This Jesus hath God raised up, whereof we all are witnesses. Therefore **being by the right hand of God exalted,** and having received of the Father the promise of the Holy Ghost, he hath shed forth this, which ye now see and hear.
- **Acts 5:31**
  Him hath God exalted with his right hand to be a Prince and a Saviour, for to give repentance to Israel, and forgiveness of sins.

The *"right hand"* is always a place of honor. That is why we husbands should have our wives walk on our *"right."* That is where we should place them. I realize that, because there could be water which might splash on the wife if she were on the street-side, sometimes they allow exceptions to this rule and permit the husband to walk street-side to take any splashing that might come about on a rainy day. In the military, the senior officer is always to be on the right, the junior officer is always to be on the left.

- **Acts 7:55-56**
  But he [Stephen], being full of the Holy Ghost, looked up stedfastly into heaven, and saw the glory of God, and **Jesus standing on the right hand of God,** And said, Behold, I see the heavens opened, and **the Son of man standing on the right hand of God.**

Colossians 3:1

- **Romans 8:34**
  Who is he that condemneth? It is **Christ that died, yea rather, that is risen again, who is even at the right hand of God**, who also maketh intercession for us.
- **Ephesians 1:20**
  Which he wrought in **Christ, when he raised him from the dead, and set him at his own right hand in the heavenly places,**

Have you ever wondered why God the Father put God the Son at His right hand after His resurrection from the dead and ascension to Heaven? The Lord Jesus Christ was rejected of men on this earth, crucified, and condemned to a terrible, ignominious death, yet the Father was pleased with the sacrifice of His Son and put Him at His right hand. He is exalted.

- **Hebrews 1:3**
  Who being the brightness of his glory, and the express image of his person, and upholding all things by the word of his power, when he had by himself purged our sins, **sat down on the right hand of the Majesty on high**;

The Lord Jesus Christ "*sat down*" on the "*right hand of the Majesty on high*" as our Great High Priest. Why was He standing while the first martyr, Stephen, was slain? The Lord Jesus Christ was waiting for the first martyr to come Home to Glory. Now, he is seated as our great High Priest.

- **Hebrews 8:1**
  Now of the things which we have spoken this is the sum: We have such an high priest, **who is set on the right hand of the throne of the Majesty in the heavens**;
- **Hebrews 10:12**
  But this man, after he had offered one sacrifice for sins for ever, **sat down on the right hand of God**;
- **Hebrews 12:2**
  Looking unto Jesus the author and finisher of our faith; who for the joy that was set before him endured the cross, despising the shame, and **is set down at the right hand of the throne of God.**
- **1 Peter 3:22**
  Who is gone into heaven, and **is on the right hand of God**; angels and authorities and powers being made subject unto him.

Colossians 3:2

"Set your affection on things above, not on things on the earth" We who are saved and are *"risen with Christ"* must *"set our affection"* continuously on the *"things above"* rather than on the *"things on earth."* PHRONEO is the Greek word for *"set your affection."* It means *"to direct our minds"* to something. We are to seek and to strive for things in Heaven.

Who is *"above,"* that is, in Heaven? The Lord Jesus Christ is in Heaven. God the Father is in Heaven. The Holy Spirit is in Heaven. All of the Trinity is everywhere present. We are primarily to think about things that are in Heaven and things that are blessed by the Lord rather than *"things on the earth."* Why do so many Christians think so much on earthly things?

Of course, we must take care of our earthly needs. But why then do we spend so much time as Christians with things of this life and worry, and worry, and worry? The stocks go up. The stocks go down. We lose a job. We gain a job. We get a raise in pay. We get a reduction in pay. We have to pay the income taxes. All of these *"things on earth"* can bring worry to our souls.

Set Your Affections Above

God says we are to *"set our affection on things above."* If all of our *"affection"* and things we are looking at are in Heaven, the *"things on earth,"* with their trials and troubles, have a way of not being so difficult for us. They are there. You can't whisk them away. You can't play *"Christian Science"* and say that the physical things aren't there. Our sicknesses are there. Our tiredness is there. Our deaths are there. Our hard work and aches and pains are there. But if our affections are up in the Heavens above, then the things down here won't be quite so hard to take.

Colossians 3:3

"For ye are dead and your life is hid with Christ in God" Again Paul tells these believers that they are *"dead"* physically, yet they are alive. Again, it is a spiritual position. Believers who are living, God considers to be *"dead."* That is a difficult thing for us to understand. How can God consider us to be *"dead"*? God wants Christians *"dead"* because He doesn't want them to do the works of our flesh. If we consider ourselves really *"dead,"* we discover that dead people don't talk back, argue, steal, lie, commit adultery, use narcotics, engage in fornication, homosexuality, have hurt feelings, or any of

Colossians 3:3-4

the sins of the flesh. Believers are to reckon themselves to be *"dead"* because our *"life is hid with Christ in God."*

- **Romans 6:2**
  God forbid. How shall **we, that are dead to sin**, live any longer therein?

Saved people are considered by God as *"dead to sin"* as far as the sin nature is concerned. We are to reckon ourselves *"dead to sin"* so it won't have any attraction for us anymore. You can't pick wooden objects up with a magnet because there is no attraction. There must be a metal object in order for a magnet to lift it up. So, if we are *"dead,"* sin should exercise no magnetic attraction for us.

- **Romans 6:8**
  Now **if we be dead with Christ**, we believe that we shall also live with him:
- **Romans 6:11**
  Likewise **reckon ye also yourselves to be dead indeed unto sin**, but alive unto God through Jesus Christ our Lord.

In nautical terms there is a term known as *"dead reckoning."* You don't know exactly where you are in that ocean or lake, but by *"dead reckoning"* you can observe the stars. From these, you can determine exactly what longitude and latitude you are in. You know exactly where your position is, not because someone tells you, but because of *"dead reckoning,"* figuring it out yourself.

Reckoning Ourselves Dead

God wants us to *"reckon"* ourselves *"dead indeed unto sin."* We should consider it to be true. If this be true, sin won't have any power over us. When temptation comes for the old sinful-nature that we all have-- none of us are sinlessly perfect until Christ changes us and we get our new bodies--we are not attracted to it. Sin can't touch us. Try to tell somebody who is trying to get you into a fight, *"Sorry, I can't fight with you, I am dead."* That is our position in the Lord Jesus Christ that we are to *"reckon"* on.

Colossians 3:4

"When Christ *who is* our life shall appear then shall ye also appear with him in glory"

"When Christ *who is* our life shall appear" The first thing we must understand is that the Lord Jesus Christ *"is our life."* Many verses bear this out.

- **John 1:4**
  In him was life; and the life was the light of men.
- **John 3:16**
  For God so loved the world, that he gave his only begotten Son, that whosoever believeth in him should not perish, but **have everlasting life**.

He is life.

- **John 3:36**
  He that believeth on the Son hath everlasting life: and he that believeth not the Son shall not see life; but the wrath of God abideth on him.
- **John 5:26**
  For as the Father hath life in himself; **so hath he given to the Son to have life in himself**;
- **John 5:40**
  And ye will not come to me, **that ye might have life**.

The Pharisees needed life eternal and they wouldn't come to Christ.

- **John 6:33**
  For the bread of God is he which cometh down from heaven, and **giveth life unto the world**.

That "*Bread*" is the Lord Jesus Christ.

- **John 6:35**
  And Jesus said unto them, **I am the bread of life**: he that cometh to me shall never hunger; and he that believeth on me shall never thirst.

The Lord Jesus Christ is life eternal.

- **John 6:47-48**
  Verily, verily, I say unto you, **He that believeth on me hath everlasting life. I am that bread of life**.
- **John 10:10**
  The thief cometh not, but for to steal, and to kill, and to destroy: **I am come that they might have life**, and that they might have it more abundantly.

The Lord Jesus Christ is the life-giver.

- **John 10:28**
  And **I give unto them eternal life**; and they shall never perish, neither shall any man pluck them out of my hand.
- **John 11:25**
  Jesus said unto her, **I am the resurrection, and the life**: he that believeth in me, though he were dead, yet shall he live:

This is what the Lord Jesus Christ told the sorrowing Martha and Mary at the tomb of Lazarus.

- **John 14:6**
  Jesus saith unto him, **I am the way, the truth, and the life**: no man cometh unto the Father, but by me.
- **Romans 6:23**
  For the wages of sin is death; but **the gift of God is eternal life** through Jesus Christ our Lord.

There is a gospel song that begins, "*Some golden daybreak Jesus will come.*" The Lord Jesus Christ one day "*shall appear.*" He is coming again. Paul, who was writing from prison, said that one day our Saviour is going to "*appear.*" That is at the rapture. We call it the rapture or the snatching away of those who are saved by God's grace through genuine saving faith in His Son.

"then shall ye also appear with him in glory" What if the Lord Jesus Christ comes while we are here on earth? If you are born-again and the Lord Jesus should appear in air at the Rapture, your body and my body will be changed from "*mortal,*" subject to death, into "*immortality,*" not subject to death (1 Corinthians 15:53-54). We would go Home to be with Christ. That is called the Rapture or the "*snatching away by force*" by our Saviour.

No Choice in the Rapture

By the way, if you are saved, you have no choice about being taken to Heaven at this time. It is a mission to Heaven that is absolutely required of us. When our Saviour requests our presence with Him in Glory, we shall "*appear with Him in Glory.*" He will not take "No" for an answer. That is a command performance. The King of Kings will summon us to Himself. We will be raised with Him and changed immediately. The dead in Christ which have gone before us will be raised and, together, we will meet the Lord in the air.

Those believers who have died are called "*corruptible.*" They will "*put on incorruption*" (1 Corinthians 15:53-54). We will go Home and be with our Saviour in Glory for all eternity to come. We shall appear, not with our old tattered garments of this earth, and not with our weaknesses. We will have "*Glory*" because we will have new resurrected bodies.

Colossians 3:5

"Mortify therefore your members which are upon the earth, fornication, *uncleanness*, inordinate affection, evil concupiscence, and covetousness, which is idolatry"

"Mortify therefore your members" Let us bring on the mortician. Let us bring on the one who deals with dead bodies. That is what *"mortify"* means. It means *"to put to death."* You see, if we Christians have died with Christ positionally (and we have), let us put it into practice. Let us kill off the desires and lusts of the old flesh and its attraction to sin.

The *"members"* of our body can be thought of as having *"ten strings."* Dr. William Pettingill wrote a book many years called, *An Instrument of Ten Strings*. That title was taken from Psalms 33:2: *"Praise the LORD with harp: sing unto him with the psaltery and an **instrument of ten strings**."* Dr. Pettingill likened these *"ten strings"* to our two eyes, our two ears, our mouth, our two hands, our two feet, and our heart. These *"ten strings"* are our instruments by which we can praise the Lord.

If our *"members"* are put to death and rendered, like the illustration of the wood and the magnet, sin cannot attract them. Steel can be magnetized. If you have a powerful enough magnet, a steel poker could be lifted up; but not with wood, because there is no attraction. If we *"mortify"* our *"members,"* (our old nature), these five sins will not bother us. We should treat them as if we were dead. Then they could not attract us.

"fornication"

The sin of *"fornication"* (PORNEIA) is rampant all over the world. There are *"shack-ups"* everywhere. Many young people, as well as older people, don't want marriage anymore. There is even fornication among born-again believers. It is still grievous sin. Fornication is usually defined as sexual relations on the part of an unmarried person.

"uncleanness"

"Uncleanness" (AKATHARSIA) is a grave situation indeed. It is *"the impurity of lustful, luxurious, profligate living."* That is what that word means. If we *"mortify"* our *"members,"* we will not be so attracted.

"inordinate affection"

"Inordinate affection" (PATHOS), means *"in the NT in a bad sense, depraved passion, vile passions."*

"evil concupiscence"

"Concupiscence" (EPITHUMIA) means *"desire, craving, longing, desire for what is forbidden, lust."* When the word, *"evil,"* (KAKOS) is added to this expression, it means that this *"concupiscence,"* is *"injurious, pernicious, destructive, and baneful."*

"covetousness"

"*Covetousness*" (PLEONEXIA) simply means a "*greedy desire to have more.*" When we are hungry don't we want more food? This "*more*" is natural and is not "*covetousness.*" When we have money sufficient to care for our needs and want "*more,*" this is "*covetousness.*" "*Covetousness*" has been defined as "*the itch for more.*" It is when a person is never satisfied. When a person covets someone else's wife or husband, that is covetousness. It is the wanting of something that is not proper. It is to want something and then to steal from someone else to get it. One of the commandments is, "*Thou shalt not covet*" (Exodus 20:17). In a very real sense, "*covetousness*" is called here "*idolatry.*"

The definition of "*covetousness*" is wanting more and more. God does not call it "*covetousness*" in the evil sense when we are instructed to "*covet*" the best gifts as it says in the book of 1 Corinthians 12:31. That is the desire to have the best spiritual gifts we can possibly have. That is not the evil covetousness. Paul and God wants us to be the best Christians we can be.

Colossians 3:6

"**For which things' sake the wrath of God cometh on the children of disobedience**" For these five things mentioned in the previous verse, and many other things, God's wrath is poured out upon the "*children of disobedience.*" This is the gravity of it.

Beware Of These Five Sins!

All five of these sins (fornication, uncleanness, inordinate affection, evil concupiscence, and covetousness, which is idolatry) are committed by unsaved people all the time. Unfortunately, some professing Christians who are out of fellowship with the Lord might also practice these things . I would hope that this is rare, but I cannot be sure.

Paul said that, the "*wrath of God*" will come on the "*children of disobedience*" for these sins. The modernists deny this aspect of God's character. They teach that God is only a God of love. God also has "*wrath*" against sin.

- John 3:36
  He that believeth on the Son hath everlasting life: and he that believeth not the Son shall not see life; but **the wrath of God abideth on him.**

"*The wrath of God*" sits right on those who refuse to accept Christ as their Saviour.

- Romans 5:9
  Much more then, being now justified by his blood, **we shall be saved from wrath through him.**
  God is not only a God of love. He is also a God of wrath and justice as well.
- 1 Thessalonians 1:10
  And to wait for his Son from heaven, whom he raised from the dead, even Jesus, **which delivered us from the wrath to come.**

The Fires of Hell Are Real

This verse speaks of the *"wrath"* of Hell. It is the *"lake of fire"* (Revelation 19:20; 20:10, 14, 15). It is the *"lake which burneth with fire and brimstone"* (Revelation 21:8). It is *"everlasting fire"* (Matthew 25:41). It is *"where the worm dieth not and the fire is not quenched"* (Mark 9:44, 46, 48). That is the *"wrath to come"* from which God has delivered us (1 Thessalonians 1:10). If you have come to the Saviour, the Ark of Refuge, and said, "Yes, Lord, I trust you as Saviour and Redeemer. I trust you as my own," you will escape this wrathful judgment.

- Revelation 6:16-17
  And said to the mountains and rocks, Fall on us, and **hide us from the face of him that sitteth on the throne, and from the wrath of the Lamb:** For **the great day of his wrath is come**; and who shall be able to stand?

This speaks of the judgment of unbelievers after the saved people have been raptured out of this world. These unbelievers want to be hidden from the face of the Lord Jesus Christ. It is true that, while here on earth, the Saviour had a sweet face, a kind face, a forgiving face. But these people in the Tribulation period have rejected the Lord Jesus Christ. For this reason they want to hide from His face and *"the wrath of the Lamb."* When the *"Lamb"* comes for judgment, it will be with *"wrath."* When the Lord Jesus Christ came the first time, He came in grace. He invited all to: *"Come unto me all ye that labour and are heavy laden, and I will give you rest"* (Matthew 11:28).

In this verse, the time is during the Tribulation period when these people have rejected Him. They have worshiped the Antichrist and Satan. They are asking to be hidden from the *"face"* of the One sitting on the throne and from the *"wrath of the lamb."*

- **Revelation 19:15**
  And out of his mouth goeth a sharp sword, that with it he should smite the nations: and he shall rule them with a rod of iron: and he treadeth the winepress of the **fierceness and wrath of Almighty God.**

> ## God Is Both Wrathful and Loving
> This speaks of the Lord Jesus Christ in judgment. God is both a wrathful Being as well as a loving Being.

Wouldn't it be better to accept and receive the Lord Jesus Christ now, by faith, and not have to face the wrath of the almighty God and be sent to Hell. The Lord sends no man, woman, or child to Hell. People send themselves to Hell by rejecting His free gift and offer of salvation through genuine faith in the Lord Jesus Christ.

Colossians 3:7

"In the which ye also walked some time when ye lived in them" The *"wrath of God"* comes because of the nature and practice of sin in the lives of the disobedient. These five sins mentioned in verse 5 were formerly practiced by those in Colosse. That city was a part of Asia Minor, now known as Turkey. The sin of fornication was theirs. The sin of uncleanness was theirs. The sin of inordinate affection was theirs. The sin of evil concupiscence was theirs. The sin of covetousness was theirs. Notice that the past tense is used. In the past life they *"walked"* and they *"lived."*

> ## Stop Walking in These Sins!
> The believer has no business walking in these sins anymore. Our life, if we're saved, should be living for Christ. It should be a life that pleases Him. Christ lives in the saved people to give them strength and help.

- **Galatians 2:20**
  I am crucified with Christ: nevertheless I live; yet not I, but **Christ liveth in me**: and the life which I now live in the flesh I live by the faith of the Son of God, who loved me, and gave himself for me.

There are some Christians who, perhaps, never lived in any of the five sins that were mentioned. On the other hand, there are some who have lived in some or all of them. But by the wonderful and saving grace of our God, these sins can be in the past of our lives. We do not any longer have to live or walk that way after we have been redeemed by genuine faith in our Saviour. God has freed us from these things. He commands us to "*mortify*" or put to death these sins. Our old flesh should not anymore be tempted by the evil around us and by the sins that are there.

Do you think that these Colossians were happy when they lived in these sins? I don't believe they were happy. I don't believe any man, woman, or child is happy living in sin. They say they are happy. I think they are a little "*slap-happy*" myself. I think they are a little foolish and giddy. They drink and use dope, and all of these things, to deaden the pain of their lonely and wicked hearts.

Colossians 3:8

"But now ye also put off these: anger, wrath, malice, blasphemy, filthy communication out of your mouth" Paul said that these Colossian Christians once lived in the sins mentioned in verse 5. Now, in verse 8, there are five more sins that are mentioned. These are believers who are to "*mortify*" the "*members*" of their bodies. They were to "*put them off*" just like taking "*off*" a coat, a shirt, or some other garment.

"anger"

Here, the thing to "*put off*" is "*anger*." The Greek word, ORGE, means "*movement or agitation of the soul, impulse, desire, any violent emotion, but esp. anger.*" Righteous "*anger*" is one thing, but "*anger*" in general has no purpose and is wrong.

"wrath"

We are to put off "*wrath*." The Greek word, THUMOS, means "*passion, angry, heat, anger forthwith boiling up and soon subsiding again.*" This is a stronger emotion than simple "*anger*." There is a distinction.

- Ephesians 4:26

   Be ye angry, and sin not: **let not the sun go down upon your wrath:**

"malice"

We are to put off "*malice*." The Greek word, KAKIA, means "*malignity, malice, ill-will, desire to injure; wickedness, depravity; wickedness that is not ashamed to break laws.*" It is ill will. If you are going to win a libel suit, you must prove that there was "*malice*" involved in the written material. The legal elements of libel include: (1) Someone has written something about you. (2) It has been published to others. (3) It harmed you in some way. (4) It is false. (5) It must have been written with "*malice*" or hatred. If you cannot prove there was

was *"malice"* involved, you cannot win the case. *"Malice"* is evil intent. This is what God has told the believers to put off.

"blasphemy"

We are to put off *"blasphemy."* The Greek word, BLASPHEMIA, means *"slander, detraction, speech injurious to another's good name; impious and reproachful speech injurious to divine majesty."* This sin looks two ways. *"Blasphemy"* against God is taking His Name in vain and not honoring Him, loving Him, and serving Him. *"Blasphemy"* against people would refer to *"speech that is injurious to another's good name."* That is also *"blasphemy."* We can blaspheme a person and we can blaspheme God. God wants us to put those things off.

"filthy communication"

We are to put off *"filthy communication"* out of our mouth. The Greek word, AISCHROLOGIA, means *"foul speaking, low and obscene speech."* Why did Paul have to tell the Colossian Christians to watch their mouths, and to put off this low, foul obscene speech? Evidently because some of them were practicing such foul speech. I believe this includes so-called "minced oaths" which also should be out-of-bounds for believers in Christ.

There are some who profess to be Christians and use foul language. I doubt that they are Christians if they use foul language. I can think of one preacher in Pensacola, Florida who has been married three times. He uses all kinds of foul and obscene language. He swears as he preaches. He is a Baptist preacher.

I don't like the foul mouth of various TV personalities who profess to be Christians. They may be saved, but I will tell you, God says to put away foul, obscene, and low speech which God calls *"filthy communication."*

Before I came to Christ as a High School senior, I used to swear on the football field in the huddle. I was a tackle. After I was saved, I caught myself using Jesus' name in vain and asked the Lord to forgive me immediately because I was now different. I was saved. I don't take the Lord Jesus my Saviour's name in vain anymore. That is the end of it. I remember in high jumping, before I was saved, every time I knocked that bar off I would swear and curse all kinds of swear words. When I became saved the Lord got hold of my mouth. He must get hold of our mouths. The Lord must get hold of our hearts. He must get hold of our entire selves so that we can *"put off"* all these evil things. God wants us who are born-again to be new persons. God says those of us who are called Christians should *"put"* these things *"off"* and straighten up.

Colossians 3:9

"Lie not one to another, seeing that ye have put off the old man with his deeds" The words, *"lie not,"* represent a prohibition in the Greek present tense. As I have said many times before, there are two types of prohibitions in the Greek language. One uses the aorist tense. This means not even to begin to do a certain action. The present tense prohibition, on the other hand, means to stop an action already in progress. Since this is in the Greek present tense, here is another *"stop sign"* as I call it. It means *"stop lying one to another."* You mean these Christians at Colosse were liars? That seems to be right. Why else would Paul have to mention it? Paul said to quit this practice. Are we liars? If so, we should also *"stop lying one to another."* Somebody might ask you how you are. You might say, *"Fine."* In reality, you have all kinds of aches and pains. You are trying to be pleasant. Is that lying? We might not want to have an *"organ recital,"* telling how every organ in your body is worn out and hurting. Whether this is lying or not, we must be careful to *"stop lying one to another."*

The Greek Meaning of "Lie"

When we try to tell something that is not true, that is lying. That is falsification. The Greek term for that is PSEUDOMAI. This Greek verb comes from the root noun, PSEUDOS. This word means a falsehood. It doesn't matter whether you meant it to be false or not. When we say *"lie"* in English, it usually implies a purposeful intent of deceiving someone. This is not so with the Greek word, PSEUDOS.

Who is the father of lies?
- **John 8:44**
  Ye are of your father the devil, and the lusts of your father ye will do. He was a murderer from the beginning, and abode not in the truth, because there is no truth in him. When he speaketh a lie, he speaketh of his own: for he is a liar, and the father of it.

When Paul told the Colossian Christians to *"stop lying,"* he is telling them to stop doing the work of the Devil.
- **Acts 5:3**
  But Peter said, Ananias, why hath **Satan filled thine heart to lie** to the Holy Ghost, and to keep back part of the price of the land?

Ananias and Sapphira gave the wrong amount for what they sold their land. They did not want to tell the truth. Let us say they said they sold it for $10,000 but they really sold it for $15,000. They presented the $10,000 and said it was the whole price. That was a lie. They did not have to give the whole amount to the Lord, but they deceived the apostles. Because of this, the Lord slew both husband and wife for the sin of lying. The Lord is strongly against lying especially if it is to the Lord or the Holy Spirit. Christians should be more attuned to the truth versus a lie. We should "**LEARN TO DISCERN.**"

- 2 Thessalonians 2:11
And for this cause God shall send them **strong delusion, that they should believe a lie**:

After the true believers are raptured to Heaven, the Antichrist is going to send *"strong delusion"* on this earth so that the people will *"believe a lie."* They will believe lying spirits. They will believe those things that are wrong and those things that are false.

Colossians 3:10

"And have put on the new man, which is renewed in knowledge after the image of him that created him"

"And have put on the new *man*" We who are saved must *"put on"* the *"new man."* God has given us who are saved a new nature. The minute we trust in the Lord Jesus Christ, the Holy Spirit comes into our bodies. We are regenerated by the Spirit of God. We are sealed by the Spirit of God. We are baptized by the Spirit of God (this is not speaking in tongues). We are a new person. *"Old things are passed away"* (2 Corinthians 5:17).

"which is renewed in knowledge after the image of him that created him" The new nature is not a man-made thing. In our modern era, there is much talk about what is called *"make-overs."* People on TV often *"make-over"* funny-looking people so that they are a little less funny-looking. I frankly do not see that it does much good, but that is only my opinion.

Christians Are Not "Make-Overs"

When God saves us He does not *"make us over."* We are not *"make-overs."* God makes Christians into whole new persons inside. He gives the saved ones the Holy Spirit of God. He gives them a new nature. We are called by the name of a *"new creature."* We are to put on this *"new man"* and not follow the works of the flesh. The Lord Jesus Christ creates a new person inside of us when we are saved.

- **2 Corinthians 5:17**
    Therefore if any man be in Christ, **he is a new creature:** old things are passed away; behold, **all things are become new.**

It is the *"new man"* that we are to *"put on."* It is to be *"after the image of the Lord Jesus who created us."* That is the new dress and the new life that we are to live before people. What about a Christian who still lives after the flesh? Will anybody believe him? I don't think so. The unsaved person just will not believe a person is saved if they are living after the flesh. Maybe they are just living a carnal life. That might be the case, but the world will not believe that man or woman.

If you live for the things of Christ, and you live with the new nature *"created in Christ Jesus"* (Ephesians 2:10) as a *"new creature,"* it is a good testimony. That will help both the saved and the unsaved. They will look at your life, and wonder if they can follow your example. This is an uplifting thing--an excellent testimony for the Lord Jesus Christ.

Colossians 3:11

"Where there is neither Greek nor Jew, circumcision nor uncircumcision, Barbarian, Scythian, bond *nor* free: but Christ *is* all, and in all"

With this *"new man,"* this *"new creation,"* this new spiritual nature inside of the believer, there is no distinction in Christ. The lesbian, Virginia Molenkott, used this verse in her books to say that a woman can be a lesbian. She implies a person does not have to be a husband or a wife. She says there is no distinction between males and females. That is absolutely false. This verse has nothing to say about physical reality. It is speaking of spiritual realities of those who are *"in Christ"* and are saved.

"Where there is neither Greek nor Jew circumcision or uncircumcision" Again, this is in the spiritual realm. In the realm of the *"new creation,"* there is no difference between the *"Greek"* or the *"Jew."* Physically there still is Greek and Jew. There are still males and females, but this is not a spiritual distinction when we are *"in Christ."* Though in the flesh, these things apply, God does not see us in these various distinctions in the Lord.

"Barbarian, Scythian, bond *nor* free" A *"barbarian"* is *"one whose speech is rude, rough and harsh; one who speaks a foreign or strange language which is not understood by another."* The word, *"barbarian,"* is an onomatopoeia. This means a *"formation of a word by imitating the natural sound associated with the object or action involved; echoism (Ex.: tinkle, buzz, chickadee, etc.)"* The word comes from two Greek words, ONOMA (meaning a *"name or a noun"*) and POIEO (meaning *"to do or to make"*). In other words, it is a noun that sounds like what it is. If you say "BAR BAR BAR BAR," this is what another person's language might sound like to you, if you did not understand it. The word, BARBAROS, sounds like what it is.

Another sense of the word, *"barbarian,"* is one: *"used by the Greeks of any foreigner ignorant of the Greek language, whether mental or moral, with the added notion after the Persian war, of rudeness and brutality. The word is used in the N.T. without the idea of reproachfulness."* I hope we don't consider people who don't know our language to be *"barbarians."*

The word, *"Scythians"* means *"an inhabitant of Scythia or modern day Russia. By the more civilized nations of antiquity the Scythians were regarded as the wildest of barbarians."* Barbarians were wild enough, but Scythians were even worse. The top of the heap as far as evil is concerned.

"but Christ *is* all and in all" When we trust the Lord Jesus Christ as our Saviour, all these distinctions are passed away spiritually. In Paul's day there was slavery. We used to have slavery in this country. It is gone now, but we do have some people who are enslaved to alcohol, drugs, or something else. There is prostitutional slavery. In Paul's day there were slaves. They had masters. If you were a master and somebody else was a slave, and you are both Christians, you are still master and slave, but *"in Christ"* there is no difference. If you are saved, you have a new nature. God treats you in the same way one with the other. This is a great thing that the gospel can do.

Colossians 3:12

"Put on therefore, as the elect of God, holy and beloved, bowels of mercies, kindness, humbleness of mind, meekness, longsuffering"

"Put on therefore as the elect of God, holy and beloved
Here is a quintet of things God wants the Colossian Christians to *"put on."* If you know the Lord Jesus Christ as your Saviour, you should do the same. The reason these things were expected of this church was because they were the *"elect of God."* They were called *"holy"* and *"beloved."* They were to *"put on"* these virtues just like they would *"put on"* a garment. What are they to *"put on"*?

"bowels of mercies" The Greek word, *"bowels,"* is SPLANGNON. It indicates *"the bowels were regarded as the seat of the more violent passions, such as anger and love; but by the Hebrews as the seat of the tenderer affections, esp. kindness, benevolence, compassion; hence our heart (tender mercies, affections, etc.)."* When you see some person down and out, you should have some manifestation of compassion, mercy, and pity on that person.

"kindness" These are emotions that make us to be kind and compassionate rather than coarse and rough when people are in pain and in trouble. This kindness is a Christian virtue.

"humbleness of mind" The Greek word for this is TAPEINO-PHROSUNE. It comes from two Greek words, one for *"humility"* and the other for *"mind."* It therefore means: *"having a humble opinion of one's self; a deep sense of one's (moral) littleness; modesty, humility, lowliness of mind."* How little are you? How little am I? If we have this quality, we won't be fakes. We won't be puffed up.

"meekness" As it implies, meekness is a mildness and a gentleness quality. It is the opposite of bragging and boastfulness.

"longsuffering" The Greek word for this is MAKROTHUMIA. It is made up of two Greek words, MAKROS and THUMOS. MAKROS is a word that means *"long."* When used of place, it means *"remote, distant, far off."* When used of time, it means *"long, long lasting."* THUMOS means *"passion, angry, heat, anger forthwith boiling up and soon subsiding again."* Putting the two terms together in the same word, you get the meaning of having your boiling point still remote, distant, or far off. That is, nothing makes you boil over. This is what *"longsuffering"* means literally. This has to do with people. It means putting up with people. The related word, *"patience,"* has to do with putting up with things and circumstances.

We who are saved should *"put on"* the *"new man"* in all five of these areas. We must *"put off"* the *"old man."* Just mortify that old flesh. Which is easier, to have *"patience"* or *"longsuffering"*? You can take your pick. I think it is easier to have *"patience "*because things don't talk back to you. They don't slap your face. They just sit there. People can be rough with you. Dealing with people is what takes *"longsuffering."*

People have a way of knowing how to provoke us, especially our mates. They live with us many years and they know which buttons to push. We must show our mates that we are *"longsuffering."* We must show them that our *"boiling point"* has not yet been reached. It is still a long way off. Believe me, there is a point beyond which we will boil over. People have to realize that we do have a boiling point. There is a time and a place for the boil over. Make sure it is not quite as early as some people think. Try to make that point still a long way off in the distance. That is truly *"longsuffering."*

Colossians 3:13

"Forbearing one another, and forgiving one another, if any man have a quarrel against any: even as Christ forgave you, so also *do* ye"

"Forbearing one another" Believers must also have a *"forebearing."* The Greek word for this is ANECHOMAI. One of the meanings is *"to sustain, to bear, to endure"* Believers are to hold up one another. That is what *"forebearing"* means. When some believers are falling down, are rather limp, and don't have their footing, we are to hold them up. We are to show them *"forbearing."*

"and forgiving one another"

- **Matthew 18:21**
  Then came Peter to him, and said, Lord, **how oft shall my brother sin against me, and I forgive him?** till seven times?

There is no end to *"forgiveness."* Is there any end to the *"forgiveness"* of the Lord Jesus Christ? No! If this is so, then there should be no end to believers in the Lord Jesus Christ in *"forgiving"* others.

- **Luke 17:3-4**
  Take heed to yourselves: If thy brother trespass against thee, rebuke him; and if he repent, **forgive him**. And if he trespass against thee seven times in a day, and seven times in a day turn again to thee, saying, I repent; **thou shalt forgive him**.

That is tough to do sometimes. You might wonder if that is a little bit insincere. God says to *"forgive"* those who genuinely repent.

- **Ephesians 4:32**
  And be ye kind one to another, tenderhearted, **forgiving one another**, even as God for Christ's sake hath forgiven you.

Unforgiving Members Frost a Church

This is for believers. There is nothing that will frost up a church as much as having unforgiving members. There is nothing that will quench the Spirit of God quicker in a church than for the members to have an unforgiving spirit. There is nothing that will grieve the Spirit of God quicker than to have the members in a church who are trying to worship when there is friction and unforgiveness among them.

God says that Christians are to *"forgive"* one another. If somebody doesn't like us I hope they tell us what is wrong. But they should not store up their hurts until they begin to boil up. They should take care of them promptly. Then we might be able to patch it up. Let me ask you this. How do we know if someone doesn't like you unless they tell you? Am I right? Sometimes, when you purposely offend somebody, you know you offended them, but many times you are in the dark about it. So, if someone has been offended please come to that Christian and tell them what they did to hurt your feelings. Then is the time to say I am sorry. Three little words, *"I am sorry,"* or two little words, *"forgive me,"* or five little words, *"I am sorry, forgive me,"* and that might take care of it.

- **1 John 1:9**
  If we confess our sins, **he is faithful and just to forgive us our sins**, and to cleanse us from all unrighteousness.

We who are saved can be cleansed from unrighteousness if we honestly confess our sins. We can then get back into fellowship with Him.

Colossians 3:14

"And above all these things *put on* charity, which is the bond of perfectness" Of greater importance than all the things mentioned before is this last virtue that Christians need to put on which is *"charity."* This is called a *"bond."* The Greek word for *"bond"* is SUNDESMOS. It is used *"of ligaments by which the members of the human body are united together."* This is the *"bond"* that *"charity."* Another word for *"charity"* is *"love."*

The Greek word for *"perfectness"* is TELEIOTES. It means: *"moral and spiritual perfection"* or maturity. *"The bond of perfectness"* that *"charity"* makes is the *"bond"* of maturity, and the *"bond"* of full growth. There are two verses especially that talk about love or *"charity"* and what it does to us. There are other verses such as in 1 Corinthians 13 where the whole chapter is on love or *"charity."*

- **Proverbs 10:12**
  Hatred stirreth up strifes: **but love covereth all sins**.

That is true. When you hate somebody, you just strive. There is no end to it. *"Love"* covers all sins. That does not mean that *"love"* forgives all sins. God forgives if we confess and repent of our sins. When we cover sins it makes it so it is not an issue. When we have *"love"* for the person who is a sinner, *"love"* covers. That is what this is. *"Love"* is the *"bond of perfectness."*

Another verse in the New Testament is in 1 Peter.

- **1 Peter 4:8**
  And above all things **have fervent charity among yourselves**: for charity shall cover the multitude of sins.

"Charity" or *"love"* is the oil that greases the squeaking joints in a church family. When you have a squeak in your car, you might take it to the garage to get a grease and oil job. If you have squeaky joints in your body, there are certain vitamins that will take care of that. When you have a squeaky door you can squirt a little WD-40 on that squeak. So *"love"* or *"charity"* is the oil that will stop the squeakiness, the bitterness, the backbiting, and all the other confusion of various people in our churches.

God says to put on *"love"* or *"charity"* just like a coat because it is the *"bond of perfectness."* If you know a person who has a limp or only one leg, you may not like the limp or the missing leg, but you can still love that person with Christian love.

The Love that Bonds

Love *"covers"* and is the *"bond of perfectness."* It is the thing that sees through the imperfections that all of us have. There is not a one of us who is perfect. We are all waiting for the perfect body that the Lord is going to give us at the resurrection if we are saved. In the meantime, the *"love"* is that which just glosses over things that we know are wrong. We can see it straight out. You can see it in your preacher, but that is all right, *"love"* him anyway. Love *"covers"* and is the *"bond"* that glues us together.

Colossians 3:15

"And let the peace of God rule in your hearts, to the which also ye are called in one body; and be ye thankful"

"And let the peace of God rule in your hearts" Paul, from prison, is writing to the Christians at Colosse and he says, *"let the peace of God rule in your hearts"* It is God's peace. There are five different passages concerning peace that I would like to call to your attention.

- **Romans 5:1**
  Therefore being justified by faith, **we have peace with God** through our Lord Jesus Christ:

Justification by faith in Christ gives us *"peace with God."* That is the important starting place. You can't have the *"peace of God"* until you have *"peace with God."*

- **Romans 15:13**
  Now **the God of hope fill you with all joy and peace in believing**, that ye may abound in hope, through the power of the Holy Ghost.

God wants us to be filled with this *"peace"* because of our *"believing"* in the Lord Jesus Christ.

- **Galatians 5:22**
  But the fruit of the Spirit is love, joy, **peace**, longsuffering, gentleness, goodness, faith,

If we are saved, God's Holy Spirit lives in our bodies. Our bodies are the temple of the Holy Spirit of God. Because of this, God wants us to be controlled by His Spirit. When we are controlled, we manifest *"the fruit of the Spirit."* The third part of the Holy Spirit's fruit is *"peace."*

- **Ephesians 2:14**
  For he is our peace, who hath made both one, and hath broken down the middle wall of partition between us;

- **Philippians 4:7**
    And **the peace of God**, which passeth all understanding, shall keep your hearts and minds through Christ Jesus.

"*Peace with God*" is one thing. Trusting in the Lord Jesus Christ as our Saviour gives us "*peace with God.*" No longer are we at war with God. After we are saved, after we are reading the Word of God, after we are in fellowship with the Lord, after we are walking in the power of the Holy Spirit, then the "*peace of God*" can "*keep our hearts and minds through Christ Jesus.*"

God's Peace

One definition of "*peace*" is: "*of Christianity, the tranquil state of a soul assured of its salvation through Christ, and so fearing nothing from God and content with its earthly lot, of whatsoever sort that is.*" That is God's peace.

When it says that the "*peace of God*" can "*rule*" in the hearts, the Greek word for "*rule*" is BRABEUO. It means: "*to be an umpire; to decide, determine; to direct, control, rule.*" May the "*peace of God*" decide and determine what we are to do. We only like an umpire if he rules for us. If he is against us, then we are against him. We remember the shouts from some of the people in the stands when the umpire's ruling goes against them, "*kill the ump!*" Let the "*peace of God*" be the umpire of your heart. Let God's "*peace*" decide. Don't go against God's "*rule*" or umpire in our hearts!

If you have no peace about something, don't do it. If you have no peace about saying something, don't say it. If you have no '*peace*' about thinking about it, don't think it. Let the "*peace of God*" decide and rule. It is in the present tense so it is a continuous action. Let God's peace continue to rule. That will keep the joybells ringing with the "*peace of God*" ruling in your heart.

"to the which also ye are called in one body" This "*peace*" which was to be "*ruling*" in our hearts was the thing to which we were "*called in one body.*" When we are saved by faith in Christ, there is no longer the division of Jews and Gentiles. Both Jew and Gentile have been, through conversion to Christ, made into "*one body.*"

"and be ye thankful" The thankfulness of our hearts should be manifest. Thanksgiving should be one of the manifest traits of the believers. It is one of the things that believers need and should possess. That is why I love to sing every Lord's Day here in our church, "*Thank you Jesus for all you've done, thank you Lord.*"

To be "*thankful*" is a trait sometimes lost by many believers today. God has done so much for us who are saved. He has given us eternal life. He has given us His *"peace."* He has given us eternal salvation. He has given us justification. He has given us a Home in Heaven. He has given us everything that we could possibly need. Yet, sometimes, like the ten lepers, we forget that we were cleansed. Only one of them came back and said thank you. The leper who came back was a Samaritan, a half-breed. God wants us to be *"thankful"* in this *"peace"* that He has given to us.

Colossians 3:16

"Let the word of Christ dwell in you richly in all wisdom; teaching and admonishing one another in psalms and hymns and spiritual songs, singing with grace in your hearts to the Lord"

"Let the word of Christ dwell in you richly" What is the *"Word of Christ"*? The answer to this question is the very essence of the present Bible Version issue. We can't escape it in the Scriptures. It is there. What is the *"Word of Christ"*? What are the Old Testament *"Words"*? What is the Hebrew text? It is the text, I believe, that underlies our King James Bible. It is the *Masoretic Hebrew Text*. What is the text in the New Testament? I believe it is also the text that underlies our King James Bible. It is the *Textus Receptus* or the *Traditional Text*. Those are the Words that God wants to *"dwell"* in us *"richly."* What is the best and only accurate English translation of these two preserved texts of Hebrew and Greek? I believe it is our King James Bible. If we are English-speaking people, I believe we must bathe ourselves in the Words of the King James Bible. It is the *"Word of Christ"* for the English speaking people. God wants us to have those *"Words"* to *"dwell in us richly."*

Defend the True Words of God!

Some people tell me that I am making too much of my standing up for the King James Bible and its underlying Hebrew and Greek texts. They don't think people care about the Bible. They tell me I may have my own views, but I shouldn't care about what Version of the Bible other people use. I disagree. If I believe I have the truth, the opposite of that truth is falsehood. God wants us not only to proclaim and manifest the truth, but also to expose all that is false.

"in all wisdom" The *"Word of Christ"* must *"dwell"* in us *"in all wisdom."* This means that we cannot read just a little bit of the Bible. We must read it from Genesis through Revelation. I urge all of our church people to read

85 verses each day. This takes them through the entire Bible once each year. We must read the Words of God daily. We must study the Words of God daily. We must know the Words of God in order to do them. We have to have the wisdom of the Word and the wisdom of Christ. What are you supposed to do with that Word?

"teaching and admonishing one another" The Christians in Colosse, and Christians today are to be *"teaching and admonishing one another."* But this *"teaching and admonishing"* must be *"in all wisdom."* It must be in the *"wisdom"* that comes from letting the *"Word of Christ dwell in us richly."* How can you teach someone if you do not know anything? You cannot do it. I could not begin to teach piano. I studied piano, but I do not know enough to teach it. I could not teach drafting. I could not teach anybody flying. But every one of us who are saved should know the Word of God clearly enough to be able to teach others also. This should be true of everyone of us, not just the preacher. Every believer must let the *"Word of Christ"* dwell in them *"richly in all wisdom."* In this way, they can teach *"one another"* about the Scriptures.

Then the second thing which is so hard for us to take is *"admonishing."* That is a no-no in so many quarters. The Greek word for *"admonishing"* is NOUTHETEO. This word is made up of two Greek words, NOUS (*"mind"*) and TITHEMI (*"to put or place."*) It means, literally, *"to put in mind."* The resultant meaning is: *"to admonish, warn, or exhort."* It means to warn people, however kindly, about things they should not be doing, saying, or thinking. If we have the *"Word of Christ dwelling in us richly,"* we can give someone a Scripture verse that *"admonishes"* them. All of us need to be *"admonished"* when we are out of line with the Scriptures. We must be brought back to the right way. We must be told we are not doing right. It is often true that this does not go over very well with the people we are trying to help in this way.

"in psalms, and hymns, and spiritual songs" The *"teaching"* and *"admonishing"* of one another can be done in these three areas.

The first word here is *"psalms."* The Greek word for *"psalms"* is PSALMOS. It means: *"a striking, twanging; of a striking the chords of a musical instrument; of a pious song, a psalm."* There is an entire book of Psalms, as we know, in the Old Testament. The Psalms were the song book of the Jews as they sung to the Lord. It would probably involve the use of more formal or worshipful songs in church services today. Some churches even sing the psalms today.

The second word is *"hymns."* The Greek word for *"hymns"* is HYMNOS. It means: *"a song in tithe praise of gods, heroes, conquerors; or a sacred song, hymn."* *"Hymns"* would be godly songs which we have in our hymn book. They would be worshipful songs of praise and worship.

The third word is *"spiritual songs."* They would be what we term today as *"gospel songs."* This is music of the highest class. By no means, however, could any of these three terms be used for the so-called *"Contemporary Christian Music"* or CCM. Nor could it refer under any circumstances for either so-called *"Christian Rock"* or secular *"Rock music"* in general.

"singing with grace in your hearts to the Lord" We are to sing *"with grace in our hearts to the Lord."* The Greek word for *"grace"* is CHARIS. It means: *"that which affords joy, pleasure, delight, sweetness, charm, loveliness: grace of speech."* When we sing in our church, I get the feeling that it *"affords"* all of those qualities of *"grace."* Your voice may not be too good. It may be a little bit flat, or a little bit sharp, but in your *"heart"* you can sing *"with grace"* to the glory of God. That is what God wants us to do in our *"singing."* Our *"singing"* should not be in the cacophony of the "contemporary Christian music" (CCM), the rock music, or all the other things that are popular today. It should be *"in psalms and hymns and spiritual songs."*

Colossians 3:17

"And whatsoever we do in word or deed, do all in the name of the Lord Jesus, giving thanks to God and the Father by him" Whatever we do, either in our *"words"* or in our *"deeds,"* it should be done *"all in the Name of the Lord Jesus."* Our *"words"* must be checked out first with the Lord and His Words. We must be sure that our *"words"* are congruent with His Word. If it is not, don't say it. The same is true about our *"deeds."* Our *"deeds"* must also be in the *"Name of the Lord Jesus"* rather than for ourselves.

During these *"words"* and *"deeds,"* we must *"give thanks to God and the Father by Him."* *"Thanksgiving"* was mentioned in verse 15. It will be mentioned again in verse 17. We can't give *"thanks"* to the Father except through the Son. It is the only basis by which we can thank the Father. We must come to Him by faith. We must accept Him through faith and receive Him by genuine, saving faith. *"Whatsoever"* we say or do, we must ask if it is right as measured by the Word of God. Should I do or say this or do that? Notice that God said *"whatsoever."* That includes everything said or done. Is Christianity to be practiced only one day a week on Sunday? No-no, it is a constant life. For us who are redeemed by faith in Christ, it is a *"whatsoever"* kind of faith that must be active at all times and in all places. We must seek to please the Lord Jesus Christ. That should be our goal if we are saved. We should give *"thanks"* to Him in everything we say or do.

Colossians 3:18

"Wives, submit yourselves unto your own husbands, as it is fit in the Lord." This is similar to the words in Ephesians.

- **Ephesians 5:22**
  Wives, submit yourselves unto your own husbands, as unto the Lord.

This is the second time we have talked about *"submission."* Why does God repeat Himself? Because God thinks it is important. Some of the new versions remove things if they are repeated more than once, but not our King James Bible. God wants what He has said to be repeated wherever it should be.

Submission

"Submission" on the part of *"wives"* to their *"own husbands"* is something contrary to the standards of the world. The Greek word for "submit" is HYPOTASSO. It means: *"1) to arrange under, to subordinate; 2) to subject, put in subjection; 3) to subject one's self, obey; 4) to submit to one's control; 5) to yield to one's admonition or advice; or 6) to obey, be subject."* As to its usage, it is *"A Greek military term meaning 'to arrange [troop divisions] in a miliary fashion under the command of a leader.' In non-military use, it was 'a voluntary attitude of giving in, cooperating, assuming responsibility, and carrying a burden."*

In this verse, the verb is in the present tense. As such, it means for the *"wives"* to *"submit themselves continuously, all the time."* The only exception to this submission would be if the husband were to require something that is contrary to the Word of God. If this is the case, wives are not under that obligation. If the husband wants his wife to kill or steal, or something else that is contrary to the Bible, she must not *"submit."* As Acts 5:29b says, *"We ought to obey God rather than men."*

In the ordinary course of things, *"wives"* are to *"submit themselves"* to their *"own husbands."* That is godly. That is Christian. That is Biblical. But that is also against all the teachings of the world. Many *"wives"* of today (and some who claim to be Christians) say that *"submission"* to their *"own husbands"* is crazy. They say that they are just as powerful as a man. They interpret the Scripture in a perverted manner. Some even teach that the husbands must submit to their wives. This is totally unscriptural and wrong. Yet this is the teaching of the women's liberationists.

God says wives' *"submission"* to their own husbands is *"fit in the Lord."* The *"fitness"* of this means that it is a duty of the wives. You might say *"I don't want to or don't care about submitting unto my husband."* Women, if this is your attitude, I have a suggestion for you. I say it as kindly as I can. Don't get married. Stay single. That is all right. You don't have to get hitched up with a husband, if you don't intend to obey God's Words regarding marriage. But if you are a woman and do get married, then *"submit yourself"* unto *"your own husband."* That is God's command to wives. If your husband doesn't know the Lord Jesus Christ, submit anyway, just as long as there is no conflict with the Scriptures. There are so many things husbands tell wives to do that have nothing to do with the Bible.

Colossians 3:19

"Husbands, love *your* wives, and be not bitter against them" If you think the *"wives"* have a problem *"submitting"* to the *husbands,"* the *"husbands"* also have a problem *"loving"* their wives. Men, if you don't want to *"love"* your wife, stay single. Don't get married. This *"loving"* of your wives is a continuous action command. Since it is in the present tense, it means *"continue to love your wife."*

There are two prohibitions, or negative commands, in the Greek language. One is in the aorist tense which means don't even begin to do something. The other one is with the present tense which means to stop an action already in process.

When this verse says *"be not bitter against them,"* the verb used is in the present tense. As such, it means to stop an action already in progress. These Colossian men, apparently, were being *"bitter"* against their wives. Paul told them to stop it. The Greek word for *"bitter"* is PIKRAINO. It means: *"to make bitter; to produce a bitter taste in the stomach; to embitter. exasperate; render angry, indignant; to be embittered, irritated."* This is the word from which we get the term *"picric"* acid. These *"husbands"* were to *"stop being bitter against their wives."* That is an important thing. These husbands were not only to continue to *"love their wives,"* but also to *"stop being bitter against them."* Sometimes, when *"wives"* don't do what the *"husbands"* want them to do, they get a little bitterness in their hearts. God says quit it! Stop it!

> ## Loving Even Though Unlovely
> This admonition was written for husbands today as well as for the Colossian Christians. We who are "*husbands*" are to "*love*" our wives even if they're unlovely.

Sometimes wives are unlovely. I have only had one wife since our marriage in 1948. I have found that most of the time she is lovely, but sometimes she is not. My job as a husband is to "*love*" her even if I think she might be unlovely. She may not be in reality, but in my eyes she seems a little bit unlovely. Even if this is the case, I, as her husband, am to have a continuous love for her anyway. I must stop being "*bitter*" in any way if I am "*bitter*."

Husbands, keep sweet. Don't have the "*bitterness*" and acid that will make your life miserable. A wife that is sweet will make you sweet. Even if a wife is sour once in a while, we husbands must keep sweet anyway. May there be no sour wives and may there be no husbands who are bitter against their wives. It is so easy to be "*bitter*" when the going gets tough. But let's face it, men, this is a very, very, difficult task to fulfil, and we fail many times at this point!

THE HOUSE OF BITTERNESS

I have been to thy house,
I have seen thy face,
I have yielded myself
To thy strong embrace.

I have sat at thy table
Eaten course by course
Of anger and wrath
Which was garnished by force.

I rose up to leave
But I found that my hands
Were shackled to thine
With carnality's bands.

The more that I struggled,
The stronger thy clasp
Until I was forced
To cry out with a gasp.

Oh, Lord, how I need Thee!
Come take me away!
I am weak and so helpless;
Oh, hear me, I pray!

He spoke e'er I ceased,
"Child, this need not be
For so long ago
I gave thee the key.

To unlock every fetter
And vanquish each foe;
It's God's Holy Word,
Put away and let go!"

By Gertrude Grace Sanborn

Colossians 3:20

"Children, obey *your* parents in all things: for this is well pleasing unto the Lord"

"Children obey *your* parents in all things" The scene is now shifted from *"wives"* and *"husbands"* to the *"children."*

Obedience by Children

What is God's command to them? It is *"obey their parents in all things."* The Greek word for *"obey"* is HYPAKOUO. It means: *"to listen, to harken; of one who on the knock at the door comes to listen who it is, (the duty of a porter); to harken to a command; to obey, be obedient to, submit to."* Once again, the verb is a present tense, signifying continuous present action. *"Children"* should continue to *"obey their parents in all things."*

Again, if parents tell their *"children"* to kill somebody or something else contrary to the clear teaching of Scripture, they ought *"to obey God rather than men"* (Acts 5:29b). In all the other realms that do not relate to the Bible, *"children"* are to *"obey their parents."*

You *"children"* might not like your parents, but you must *"obey"* them anyway. You might not like what they are telling you to do. You might not want to do all these jobs around the house. Do them anyway. If you are under their roof, if they are feeding you, clothing you, and housing you, it is your obligation, as *"children,"* to be obedient to your mom and dad. That is tough to do sometimes. I was a child once. I was unsaved until I was 17 years of age. Before I was saved, I was rebellious. But after I came to Christ, I had a love for my mom and dad more then I ever had before. I tried to please them as much as possible after I was saved.

Mowing the lawn and taking care of the dog house were my tasks. My dog's name was Gyppy because my dad felt like he paid too much for him. Do you know how much my dad paid for him in the 1940's? Fifty cents! That was too much. I built Gyp a dog house. When I finished the dog house, my mother told me that I did not leave room for his tail. My mom was quite a joker.

"this is well pleasing unto the Lord" It was not a question of whether or not I liked what mom and dad told me to do. It was that I wanted to be *"wellpleasing"* unto the Lord Who had saved me. I was a young boy under my father's roof. I was to *"obey"* my parents *"in all things."* If we don't learn to obey our moms and dads, we may never learn to obey the Lord Jesus Christ.

That is an important lesson to learn. It is the duty of every boy and girl, from the cradle right up until they leave the house, to *"obey"* continuously their parents *"in all things."* Sometimes when children *"obey"* their parents, the parents are astounded that they have obeyed them. That should never be, but sometimes that is the case. It is rare, in some homes, that the children obey the parents. In many homes, sad to say, it is the parents who obey the children. The children dictate what goes on in the house. They just *"pitch a fit"* and the parents bow and scrape to their children. That is contrary to the teachings of the Bible.

Colossians 3:21

"Fathers, provoke not your children *to anger*, lest they be discouraged" Here is another *"stop sign."* We found one in verse 19 where it says: *"Husbands stop being bitter against your wives."* This is a prohibition in the present Greek tense. It means to stop an action already in progress. Apparently, the *"fathers"* were *"provoking their children to anger."* Paul said that the *"fathers"* were to stop that provoking action.

The Greek word for *"provoke"* is ERITHIZO. It means: *"to stir up, excite, stimulate, to provoke."* How do you *"provoke a child to anger"* or cause him to be discouraged? In the first place, parents must start early in discipline. They cannot wait until it is too late to be effective.

Begin Godly Discipline Early

"*Fathers*" you must start early, from birth to age one, two, three and upward. You must bring them up in the proper way. If this is true, you won't "*provoke them to anger*" they will do what they are supposed to do. It is not that we are breaking their spirit. We are controlling their impulses.

I knew of a little girl who had a tremendously powerful spirit when she was a little baby. Right now she is an excellent Christian lady. She has read the Bible ever since she could read English. In fact, she has read the King James Bible through from Genesis through Revelation many times. That is wonderful. When she was a little baby, no one could control that little girl. She had a roll-around, fall-down, pitching-fits type of spirit. Her parents did not break her spirit but tried to control her impulses. Right now that spirit is strong for the Lord Jesus Christ.

We are not interested in breaking the spirit of our children, but we must channel their spirit into proper responses. I had a very strong spirit when I was growing up. I used to bite people. That was a horrible thing. My mother bore in her wrist the scar of one of my bites. Mom has gone Home to Glory now, but I remember going to visit Mom later in life. I saw those scars and I remembered who gave them to her. I was sorry. What a wicked little boy I was. Praise God he saved me and turned me around.

I was not only a biting child, but I did other willful things. When I was bad, my parents would make me stay in a room and put me in a chair. On one occasion, I was so angry that I took my knife and wrote my name on the arm of that chair. I scratched it right in there. I was angry as I could be. My mom was quite a humorist. When she had no more use for that particular chair, she sent it up here to me. We have it up in our bedroom now. I can still see it with my name in the arm. I am so glad that the Lord channeled that willful spirit of mine, after He saved me, and made me strongly motivated to serve the Lord Jesus Christ.

Do Not Discourage Your Children

Fathers we should not *"discourage"* our children. The Greek word for *"discourage"* is ATHUMEO. It means: *"to be disheartened, dispirited, broken in spirit."* It comes from two Greek words, "A" (which means *"no or not"*) and THUMOS which means: *"passion, angry, heat, anger forthwith boiling up and soon subsiding again."* The resultant meaning is a child that is without any passion or feeling or spirit of any kind. Again, I repeat, we must not break the child's spirit, but we must re-direct it and channel it into proper responses.

Horses can be kept in-line. Dogs can be kept in-line. Any kind of animal can be kept in-line. If this is not the case, we can have problems. I had an Arabian mare named Babe. She was a five-gaited horse. She could walk, single-foot, trot, pace, and gallop. She was all horse. She was so frisky that she needed two bits in her mouth in order to control her. She had a straight bit and a curved bit in order to control her. I knew how to control her, but any other rider did not know what to do with her. It is good to have a spirited horse, but that horse must be controlled. So it is with children.

Colossians 3:22

"Servants, obey in all things *your* masters according to the flesh; not with eyeservice, as menpleasers; but in singleness of heart, fearing God:"

"Servants obey in all things *your* masters according to the flesh" In those days there were slaves. We don't have them today in our country. But we do have people who are slaves to drink, and slaves to drugs, but we don't have slavery in this same sense.

What were *"servants"* and slaves to do? They were to obey *"in all things"* the wishes of their masters *"according to the flesh."* Some people wonder why slavery was not addressed in the Bible. Paul was not trying to revolutionize the society of his day. The Roman government had slaves. Even in the Jewish Old Testament, there were slaves. Jews were not supposed to enslave their fellow countrymen, but were allowed to use Gentiles as slaves. They could not have a Jew to be a slave, because that was against the Scriptures. Because in this verse, *"obey"* is in the present tense, it means that the *"servants"* or slaves were to continuously *"obey in all things"* of their *"masters."* Certainly, if there was something contrary to the Word of God, then they should obey God rather than men (Acts 5:29b).

The principles of this teaching about those who are *"servants"* could be applied to present-day employees. We need to obey our employers and do what they say. They pay our salary and we should follow what they say. If we don't follow what they say they might fire us. We should not speak evil of them or disturb the people within the work place.

"not with eyeservice as menpleasers" Notice that this *"obedience"* it is not with *"eyeservice."* The word for *"eyeservice"* in the Greek language is the word from which we get ophthalmology. It is OPHTHALMO-DOULEIA. It means: *"service performed [only] under the master's eyes; for the master's eye usually stimulates to greater diligence; his absence, on the other hand, renders sluggish."* It comes from two Greek words, OPHTHALMOS (the *"eye"*) and DOULEIA (*"service* or *slavery"*). Are you a good worker only when the master is watching? What about when he is not watching? Do you stir up discontent in the work place? What about the Lord Jesus Christ, our Master, if we are saved? He is always watching. As the Negro spiritual says, *"My Lord is watching all the time."*

Not Menpleasing Servants

The *"servants"* are not to be *"as menpleasers."* The Greek word for *"menpleasers"* is ANTHROPARESKOS. It means: *"studying to please man, courting the favour of men."* This is not what the *"servants"* are to be like. A servant is not to work for compliments, but to please God.

"but in singleness of heart, fearing God" The word for *"singleness"* is HAPLOTES. It means: *"singleness, simplicity, sincerity, mental honesty; the virtue of one who is free from pretence and hypocrisy; not self-seeking, openness of heart manifesting itself by generousity."* This is the way we are to serve someone else. Christians should be the most sought-after workers in the world. They should be sought after, but, sad to say, they aren't always sought after. Some people feel if they want something done they don't want to get a Christian. That is a sad commentary on Christians. If you want someone to mow your lawn, some people are reluctant to hire a Christian because they might not do it right. If they don't do it right you can't say anything for fear they will be angry with you. That is not the way it should be. If we are Christians, we ought to be the best *"servants"* in the world.

- **Proverbs 25:19**
  Confidence in an unfaithful man in time of trouble is like a broken tooth, and a foot out of joint.

Obedience From The Heart

We should be the most obedient people of all, following everything we are expected to do. Employers should want to hire Christians who are *"servants"* that do their work diligently and right. Notice we are to do it from the *"heart,"* which is the center and the seat of our spiritual life. We must also do our service *"fearing God."*

Colossians 3:23

"And whatsoever ye do, do *it* heartily, as to the Lord, and not unto men" If it is *"to the Lord"* you are doing something, it must not be done in a haphazard way. If you are pleasing the Lord, He is always looking at you. There is no way we can escape the Lord's gaze upon us, if we are *"servants"* of the Lord. We must do everything *heartily"* as unto the Lord. This verse does not just apply to servants it applies to everyone, *"wives," "husbands,"* and *"children."* Whether it is wives submitting to your husbands, whether it is husbands loving your wives, whether it is children obeying their parents, whether it is fathers not provoking their children, or whether it is servants obeying their masters, we are to do it *"heartily."*

The heart is very important in the Bible. *"Keep thy heart with all diligence; for out of it are the issues of life"* (Proverbs 4:23). The heart is the very source of spiritual growth. Sometimes I wonder if people know they are serving and working for the Lord. Why aren't they doing things for the Lord in a more diligent way? He is the One whom we are to please.

Colossians 3:24

"Knowing that of the Lord ye shall receive the reward of the inheritance: for ye serve the Lord Christ" The service to the Lord Jesus Christ is the most important service that we can offer. There is a gospel song that starts out, *"I serve a risen Saviour He's in the world today. I know that He is living whatever men may say."* This is the theme of this verse. The Lord Jesus Christ does *"reward"* those who follow Him and serve Him. The different crowns are given to the believers who are faithful. This *"inheritance"* is one we have when we are saved. We Christians have an *"inheritance"* when we serve the Lord Jesus Christ faithfully. When we are saved we have eternal life, forgiveness of sins, a Home in Heaven, and we are going to be in Glory one day.

The Five Crowns For Believers

There are five crowns that have been given by the Lord for faithful service after a person becomes a Christian.
1. The crown of rejoicing
2. The crown of glory
3. The incorruptible crown
4. The crown of righteousness
5. The crown of life.

The Greek word for "*Lord*" is KURIOS. It means: "*he to whom a person or thing belongs, about which he has power of deciding; master, lord; the possessor and disposer of a thing; the owner; one who has control of the person, the master.*" That is what the Lord Jesus Christ is to you and to me if we are saved. We belong to him. One gospel song says: "*Now I belong to Jesus, Jesus belongs to me; not for the years of time alone, but for eternity.*" That is the way it is. If I am saved, I belong to Jesus. If He is my "*Lord,*" I belong to Him. The Lord Jesus should control us. He is our Lord. He is our Master. This idea of "*Lordship salvation*" is backwards. It is not Lordship and then salvation. First it is salvation and then it is Lordship. Make Christ Lord of your life after you are saved. You can't make Him truly Lord of your life before you're saved.

Colossians 3:25

"But he that doeth wrong shall receive for the wrong which he hath done: and there is no respect of persons" If you do what is "*wrong,*" God says that "*he that does wrong shall receive for the wrong which he hath done.*" Does that follow through today? No, sometimes it doesn't. You and I would go to jail for perjury, but not President Bill Clinton. He went free. God is not that way. If you do wrong, no matter who you are, small or large, big or little, wealthy or in poverty, God will treat you just the same. For "*there is no respect of persons*" with Him.

- Proverbs 24:23
  These things also belong to the wise. **It is not good to have respect of persons in judgment**.

If a person has done right, he deserves to be rewarded. If he has done wrong he deserves to have his punishment.

- **Proverbs 28:21**
  To have respect of persons is not good: for for a piece of bread that man will transgress.
- **Romans 2:11**
  For there is no respect of persons with God.
- **Ephesians 6:9**
  And, ye masters, do the same things unto them, forbearing threatening: knowing that your Master also is in heaven; **neither is there respect of persons with him.**
- **1 Peter 1:17**
  And if ye call on the Father, **who without respect of persons judgeth according to every man's work**, pass the time of your sojourning here in fear:

The Lord does not *"respect persons."* Those of us who have come to Christ by faith are *"servants"* no matter how long we have been saved. The Lord does not *"respect"* any person. Does He *"respect"* the Apostle Paul more then us? No! The Apostle Paul was a great apostle, but he is just the same as you and I who are saved. God does not *"respect"* one over another. That is a good thing to have is it not? Justice should be that way, but many times it is not. The picture of justice in the Supreme Court is a lady with a balance in her hands and a blindfold over her eyes. That is what it ought to be--blind--no matter who you are, what your color of skin, how tall, how rich, how poor, it should all be the same. Many times that isn't the case in this world, but it is the way the Lord runs His justice. The Lord is no respecter of persons.

Some preachers are *"respecters of persons."* The Greek word for *"respect of persons"* is PROSOPOLEPSIA. It means: *"partiality; the fault of one who when called on to give judgment has respect of the outward circumstances of man and not to their intrinsic merits, and so prefers, as the more worthy, one who is rich, high born, or powerful, to another who does not have these qualities."* That is what it means to *"respect persons."* Some preachers do that, I am sorry to say. Some preachers placate some people in their congregation. They won't say anything about certain things because of their fear of these important people. God wants us to realize that He is a God who does not *"respect persons,"* no matter who he or she is.

Colossians Chapter Four

Colossians 4:1

"Masters, give unto *your* servants that which is just and equal; knowing that ye also have a Master in heaven."

"Masters, give unto *your* servants that which is just and equal" Paul had talked earlier about the *"wives,"* *"husbands,"* *"children,"* *"fathers,"* and *"servants."* In this chapter, Paul talked about *"masters."* In those days, the *"masters"* were the owners of slaves. The Christian *"masters"* were to give unto their *"servants,"* who worked for them, *"that which is just and equal."* The reason for this is that they themselves *"have a Master in Heaven."*

If we apply this today, these *"masters"* would be employers who have hired some people to work for them. They should also be *"just and equal"* with the things they do for their employees. The Greek word for *"master"* is KURIOS. It is the same word from which we get *"Lord."* Though he is not divine, a *"master"* is a person in charge. He is *"one who has the power of deciding."* The Lord Himself is our Master if we are born-again by the Spirit of God. The meaning of the name, *"Lord,"* is *"he to whom a person or thing belongs."* We belong to Jesus, if we are saved. It also means someone who *"has power of deciding."* The Lord should have *"the power to decide"* in our lives what we should or should not do.

Servants and Slaves

The word for *"Servant"* is DOULOS in the Greek language. It is a word used for *"slaves"* and *"bondman."* We are *"servants"* to Christ if we are saved. A *"servant"* is *"one who gives himself up to another's will."* The Lord Jesus Christ was an example of that. He said to His Father in the garden of Gethsemane, *"Not my will but thine be done"* (Luke 22:42b).

The Lord Jesus gave up His own will to do the Father's will and to go to Calvary. *"Servants"* of God are those whose service is used by Christ to extend and advance His cause among men. A *"servant"* is *"one devoted to another to the disregard of his own interest."* If we are *"slaves"* and *"servants"* to the Lord, we should not put our own interests primary, but the Lord's interests first.

In the earthly realm those who are *"masters"* should be *"just"* in dealing with their *"servants"* and *"employees."* Should the employee earn as much as the owner of the shop? No, that is not right, but the employer should give his employees what he can justly afford. We have *The Bible For Today* ministry. It is a ministry that is run by faith. People send us gifts and order some of our materials. We are a faith ministry. We have employees. We try to do what is *"just"* and right by those employees. We can not pay them as much as they deserve, or as much as the world would pay, but we do what we are able. Mike was a temporary employee who worked for nothing. He worked on my computer. He came once for about two hours and then he came back another hour because we had to do a few things, but we did not pay him anything. We thank him for that. Randy is another man who helps us without getting paid. I work for *The Bible For Today* and I don't get paid either. My wife doesn't get paid. We do it because we want to. Joshua came two days last week. We gave him what we could afford. I hope it is helpful to him. We have other employees, too. We have to be *"just"* in our dealings.

"knowing that ye also have a Master in heaven" If we are saved, it is wonderful to know that we have a *"Master in Heaven."* He is One Who knows the whole panoramic view of our lives. In the Greek text, the word, *"have,"* is in the present tense. That means it is a continuous action. There is no one who is saved today and lost tomorrow in this word, *"have."*

Our Constant Master

If you are saved, you *"have"* a *"Master"* continually. He is always your Master. Once you have been saved by genuine faith in the Lord Jesus Christ, you are regenerated by the Holy Spirit of God. You will not lose that salvation. The Lord Jesus Christ is your Master continuously. He is in Heaven. That is the place one day, if we are saved, everyone of us is going to go.

Heaven is where the Lord Jesus has gone before *"to prepare a place"* for us, as He promised (John 14:2). That Master is in Heaven. The Father is in Heaven and the Son is in Heaven. We are going to see the Lord Jesus one day and *"in Him dwelleth all the fulness of the Godhead bodily"* (Colossians 2:9).

Colossians 4:2

"Continue in prayer, and watch in the same with thanksgiving"

"Continue in prayer" Paul is writing to these Colossian Christians from a Roman jail. He wants these believers in Colosse to *"continue in prayer."* *"Prayer"* is talking to the Lord. Only those who are saved can talk to the Lord and have Him hear and respond. Only those who come through Christ can go to the Father. That is what the Lord Jesus Christ told us to do.

- **Matthew 26:40-41**
  And he cometh unto the disciples, and findeth them asleep, and saith unto Peter, What, could ye not watch with me one hour? **Watch and pray**, that ye enter not into temptation: the spirit indeed is willing, but the flesh is weak.

The disciples were to *"watch and pray."* The Lord prayed for an hour, apparently. Then He went back and prayed for another hour (Matthew 26:40-42). This was in the garden of Gethsemane before He went to Calvary. The three disciples, who were with Him, fell asleep. They were tired. Maybe they were bored. Has anyone ever told you that church services are boring? Some people are bored by coming to church. Whatever the reason the Lord Jesus Christ chided them.

- **Matthew 26:41**
  Watch and pray, that ye enter not into temptation: the spirit indeed is willing, but the flesh is weak.
- **1 Peter 4:7**
  But the end of all things is at hand: be ye therefore sober, and **watch unto prayer**.

Peter was one of the ones who fell asleep. I think the Lord spoke to Peter in the hour of Gethsemane when he fell asleep. Peter did not watch and he did not pray. Now, he said to those to whom he writes that they need to *"watch unto prayer."*

Thanksgiving Needed

Along with the *"prayer"* was to be *"thanksgiving."* This *"prayer"* is not just making requests. So many times we have had requests, but the Lord wants us to intercede and pray for others. We are also to include *"thanksgiving."*

- **Psalm 100:4**
  Enter into his gates with thanksgiving, and into his courts with praise: be thankful unto him, and bless his name.

"*Thanksgiving*" is an important part of the Christian faith. That is why I like to sing every Sunday morning in our services, "*Thank you Jesus for all you've done, thank you Lord.*" There is a Latin phrase I remember. It is "REPETITIO MATER ESTUDIORUM EST." This means: "*Repetition is the mother of learning.*" If we sing about thanking the Lord for "*all He has done,*" it is possible that we might learn to be thankful at all times. Let us purpose to be thankful.

- **Philippians 4:6**
  Be careful for nothing; but in every thing **by prayer and supplication with thanksgiving** let your requests be made known unto God.

"*Prayer*" and "*thanksgiving*" go together.

- **Colossians 2:7**
  Rooted and built up in him, and stablished in the faith, as ye have been taught, **abounding therein with thanksgiving**.

We are to be "*abounding*" and overflowing with "*thanksgiving.*" We can't thank the Lord enough for what He has done for us. Then why don't we do it? If He has done so much for us why don't we keep thanking Him for it?

Some people don't "*abound with thanksgiving*" they just say "*thank you*" a little bit. "*Abounding*" means you have a cup that is not only full, but overflowing all over the floor. That is an "*abounding*" cup, and we must have an "*abounding thanksgiving.*"

"and watch in the same with thanksgiving" The Greek word for "*watch*" means: in a metaphorical sense, "*give strict attention to, be cautious, active; to take heed lest through remission and indolence some destructive calamity suddenly overtake one.*" If you don't keep your eyes on the road every second that you are driving, "*calamity*" could come. We must "*watch*" every step of our way. Paul wrote about this. He said: "*let him that thinketh he standeth take heed lest he fall*" (1 Corinthians 10:12). Watch!

Colossians 4:3

"Withal praying also for us, that God would open unto us a door of utterance, to speak the mystery of Christ, for which I am also in bonds." The "*us,*" used here, probably refers to Paul's friends that were with him. He names some of them later. They were Tychicus, Onesimus and other friends. There are many kinds of "*prayers.*" Among other things, "*prayer*" could be intercession, thanksgiving, or praise. For what did Paul want the Colossians to "*pray*"? It was "*that God would open a* *door of utterance."* Isn't that a very descriptive figure of speech--*"a door of utterance"*?

Imprisoned, Yet Still Preaching

The reason Paul was in prison in Rome was that he was preaching the *"mystery of Christ."* He preached that the Lord Jesus Christ could save sinners, that He loved the sinners, and that He came into the world *"to seek and to save that which was lost"* (Luke 19:10). Paul was in *"bonds"* because he spoke about *"the mystery of Christ."* Yet, Paul still wanted more *"doors of utterance"* to speak the *"mystery of Christ."* The officials could not do much more to Paul. He was already in prison. If he wanted to keep preaching, the Romans could not put him in prison again.

If Rome wanted to teach Paul a lesson about preaching Christ, he did not learn it. He kept preaching Christ, even while he was in prison. May we keep preaching Christ by our life and by our lips, regardless what happens to us. Look with me at a number of verses about *"open doors."*

- **1 Corinthians 16:9**
  For **a great door and effectual is opened unto me,** and there are many adversaries.

Though the *"door"* was *"open,"* there were *"many adversaries,"* or opponents. No matter how many *"open doors,"* there are always enemies of the gospel of Christ.

- **2 Corinthians 2:12**
  Furthermore, when I came to Troas to preach Christ's gospel, and **a door was opened unto me** of the Lord

The Lord opens *"doors."* Sometimes He closes doors. He closed the door for Paul in one area of the country, but He opened it to another area.

- **Revelation 3:8**
  I know thy works: behold, I have set before thee **an open door,** and no man can shut it: for thou hast a little strength, and hast kept my word, and hast not denied my name.

Our church, *The Bible For Today Baptist Church*, should always be known as an *"open door that no man can shut."* May the Lord help us in our church to *"keep His Word"* and not *"deny His name."* We have *"open doors"* to the ministry. When the Lord laid on my heart to get back into the harness of preaching the gospel and begin a church in October of 1998, that was a *"door"* that the Lord opened for me in my seventies.

I have never heard of a church that would call a man who is 70 to preach and for him to be their pastor. Many churches turn out their pastors by the dozens when they are in their 60's. Some of my friends aren't even 65 yet and they are resigning from the pastorate. It seems a shame, because many men make better and more mature pastors in their older age.

The Lord gave me an *"open door"* to preach His Word. When you preach, you should prepare. I admit, it seems like many pastors do not prepare very much for their sermons. A preacher must know what he is going to preach. I wanted to prepare. I wanted to study the Words of God in the few years the Lord has given to me while on this earth. I don't know how many more years the Lord will give to me. None of us know this. This *Bible For Today Baptist Church* is one of those *"open doors."* We have had our *Bible For Today* ministry since 1971, with different books and publications. We carry over 3,155, but that wasn't preaching the Word verse by verse. That was a different ministry. That is a necessary ministry, but preaching the Word is also necessary.

Expository Preaching & No CCM

Sorry to say, that pastors who take the Words of God, preaching them in an expository, verse by verse manner, telling what they mean, are few and far between. There are few churches these days that use and defend the King James Bible. There are also few churches that reject "contemporary Christian music" (CCM) and so-called Christian *"rock,"* using only the traditional hymns and gospel songs. So, the Lord opened a *"door."* You people are here this morning, not because somebody twisted your arm, or paid you to come, but because you want to be here.

The ministry of radio is another *"door"* that the Lord has laid on my heart to *"open."* He has given us that outreach. Every single word of the sermons from these church services is heard on a station in Greenville, South Carolina; a station in Elkton, Maryland; Baltimore, Maryland; another one in Pennsylvania. On the Internet, our preaching can be heard all over the world for those who want to tune into it. Our Internet site is **www.BibleForToday.org**. I am glad for Mrs. Waite's program, *"Just For Women"* which is also on the Internet for all to hear. Her program is heard in Greenville, South Carolina, Baltimore, Maryland, Camden, New Jersey, and on the Internet. A recent month's *"downloads"* for all 700 messages on the Internet at that time totaled over 3,700. This included 25 foreign countries and 49 states. I praise the Lord for the vast numbers of people who are downloading our messages in order to listen to them on their own computers.

You might say we are just a tiny band of people meeting in a house, but God in His great grace and mercy has given us many *"doors"* that are wide-open for us to minister to the world. Paul was in prison. He was not in a house. He did not have heat or air conditioning like we do. He was uncomfortable. He did not have much food. Yet, he was still waiting for more *"open doors"* to minister for our Saviour, the Lord Jesus Christ. Paul knew exactly why he was in prison.

Colossians 4:4

"That I may make it manifest, as I ought to speak" Not only did Paul want to have the *"door"* open that he may speak, but also he wanted to make it *"manifest"* as he *"ought to speak."* He wanted to do it right and exactly, as the Lord would have him to *"speak."* That is important. We should not just open up our mouths, let our tongues loose, and say whatever comes out of our mouths. It should be as the Lord would have us speak. Paul wanted to speak and make *"manifest"* the truth of Christ exactly as it should be. We should try very hard, when we talk to people about the Lord Jesus or about the Bible, to use Bible verses. We should show that we are speaking from the Scriptures, rather than about something fanatical.

Colossians 4:5

"Walk in wisdom toward them that are without, redeeming the time." People might ask how are they going to *"walk in wisdom"*? There is only one source of *"wisdom."* That is the Word of God. The Lord Jesus Christ is also made unto the believers *"wisdom."*

- 1 Corinthians 1:30
  But **of him are ye in Christ Jesus, who of God is made unto us wisdom,** and righteousness, and sanctification, and redemption:

Wisdom Found in the Right Bible

The only place we can get real, godly *"wisdom"* is in the Word of God, the Bible. But it should be the right Bible. In the English language, it should be the King James Bible. It should be based on the Hebrew and Greek texts that underlie the King James Bible. We must not only have the right Bible, but we must know what is in that Bible. That is why I urge all Christians to read 85 verses per day to complete the entire Bible from Genesis through Revelation each year.

Once we know the *"wisdom"* found in the Bible, we must walk in the *"wisdom"* that God gives us. That means that we must follow that *"wisdom"* in our daily life, step by step. We have to *"walk in wisdom"* in what we do, what we say, where we go, and what we think. We should *"walk"* this way especially toward *"them that are without."* This refers to those who do not know Christ. They should see in us, nothing contradictory to the gospel. We have to be a walking gospel in shoe leather. That is what they must see if the Lord is to be pleased.

The last part of this verse adds something else. Believers in Christ are to *"redeem the time."* This Greek word is EXAGORAZO. It means: *"to buy up, to buy up for one's self, for one's use; to make wise and sacred use of every opportunity for doing good, so that zeal and well doing are as it were the purchase money by which we make the time our own."*

How many years do you have left on this earth? How do we know if we have so many hours or days, or weeks left on this earth? Job did not know when his trials would end.

- **Job 23:10**
  He knoweth the way that I take and when He hath tried me, I shall come forth as gold.

David left his *"times"* in the hands of the Lord.

- **Psalm 31:15**
  My times *are* in thy hand: deliver me from the hand of mine enemies, and from them that persecute me.

- **Job 7:6**
  My days are swifter than a weaver's shuttle, and are spent without hope.

Life is short. Our days go back and forth like a *"weaver's shuttle."* How are we going to *"redeem"* this time?

- **Job 8:9**
  (For we are but of yesterday, and know nothing, because **our days upon earth are a shadow**:)

How long does a *"shadow"* appear? When the daylight appears it is there. When the night comes, unless you have a street light, there is no shadow.

- **Job 14:1-2**
  Man that is born of a woman is **of few days**, and full of trouble. He cometh forth like a flower, and is cut down: **he fleeth also as a shadow**, and continueth not.

- **Psalm 90:9-11**
  For all our days are passed away in thy wrath: **we spend our years as a tale that is told.** The days of our years are **threescore years and ten**; and if by reason of strength they be **fourscore years,** yet is their strength labour and sorrow; for **it is soon cut off, and we fly away.** Who knoweth the power of thine anger? even according to thy fear, so is thy wrath.

How long is a story? You might be able to tell a story that is a lengthy one to your children, as they are going to bed, but when it is finished, it is finished. That is our life. It is like a *"tale that is told."*

- **Psalm 90:12**
  So **teach us to number our days,** that we may apply our hearts unto wisdom.

That is not just for the 80-year-olds or the 70-year-olds. It is for everyone. We must all *"number our days."*

What is the Number of Your Days?

We don't know when that *"number"* is going to be the last. If we are *"numbering our days,"* we will *"redeem the time."* We will buy up the time for the work of the Lord and not waste it. The opportunities are there. We don't know how much more time we have.

- **James 4:14**
  Whereas ye know not what shall be on the morrow. For what is your life? **It is even a vapour,** that appeareth for a little time, and then vanisheth away.

Our life is like a puff of smoke. That is all life is. We have to *"redeem the time."* How much time do we have left?

You and I have the same number of minutes in one hour. We all have 60 minutes in one hour. Nobody has any more or any less time. We all have 24 hours a day. That is 1,440 minutes. All of us have the same amount. All of us have seven days per week. That is 10,080 minutes a week. All of us have the same amount of time. We have to redeem that time. We have to buy up the opportunities. Everyone of us has 52 weeks in a year. That is 524,160 minutes every year. Nobody has less. Nobody has more. If we are 70 we have 36 million 691 thousand and 200 minutes. What about those who are 80 years? That is 41 million 932 thousand 800 minutes.

Are we" *redeeming the time*"? Are we buying up the opportunities? That is what that word, *"redeem,"* means. As mentioned above, redemption is a purchase by means of a purchase price. It also means *"to buy up, to buy up for one's self, for one's use."* The Lord Jesus provided redemption by His work on the cross.

Colossians 4:6

"Let your speech *be* alway with grace, seasoned with salt, that ye may know how ye ought to answer every man" Paul is lecturing from jail to the Christians at Colosse about their speech--how they should talk and what they should say.

- James 1:19
  Wherefore, my beloved brethren, let every man be swift to hear, **slow to speak**, slow to wrath:
- James 4:11
  Speak not evil one of another, brethren. He that speaketh evil of his brother, and judgeth his brother, speaketh evil of the law, and judgeth the law: but if thou judge the law, thou art not a doer of the law, but a judge.
- James 3:8
  But **the tongue can no man tame**; it is an unruly evil, full of deadly poison.

Our speech is untamable by man. The Lord is able to tame it. The Holy Spirit of God is able to tame that *"speech."*

Somebody called me yesterday and told me that his wife is yelling and screaming all the time and needs to see somebody. This is uncontrolled, or untamed *"speech"* which is full of *"deadly poison."*

- Titus 2:8
  Sound speech, that cannot be condemned; that he that is of the contrary part may be ashamed, having no evil thing to say of you.

Our speaking must please the Lord. It has to be *"sound speech."* It should not be such that it could be in any way *"condemned."*

Gracious Yet Seasoned Speech

The *"speech"* must be *"with grace."* The Greek word for *"grace"* is CHARIS. It means: *"that which affords joy, pleasure, delight, sweetness, charm, loveliness: grace of speech."* The *"speech"* mentioned here must not only be *"with grace,"* but also *"seasoned with salt."*

Why do you think that cows have a salt lick? Because it is good for their bodies. It has minerals that they need. So, they can all come to this one place and they can lick this salt. Recently, we visited a ranch that had 600 cows and 300 calves. The rancher ordered several tons of salt at one time for his cattle. He described for us the various minerals and other ingredients in the salt in order to provide the needed nourishment for his cattle.

Our speech should be gracious and seasoned with salt. Salt is that which makes food seasoned. The Greek word, ARTUO, means *"to season, make savory."* The sacrifices were sprinkled with salt in the Old Testament.

- **Leviticus 2:13**
And every oblation of thy meat offering shalt thou season with salt; neither shalt thou suffer the salt of the covenant of thy God to be lacking from thy meat offering: with all thine offerings thou shalt offer salt.

You don't want to sprinkle too much salt on your food. That would be horrible. It must be just enough salt. We had eggs the other day in a restaurant. At first, they were without salt. I can eat them without salt, but I would rather not. I just went over and put just a little bit of salt on them, not too much salt. Did you know that salt holds liquids in your body?

That is one of the things that my mother had to be warned about when she was in her older age. She was not supposed to eat too much salt because of her health condition. When my sister, Dorothy, turned her back, Mom salted her food as much as she wanted. My dad had just died. My sister and mother bought two coffins, one for Dad and one for Mom. My mom said that Dorothy thought Mom was going to get too fat by using salt. Mom said: *"I know what the width of my coffin is. I just bought it. I will be able to fit in it, no matter how much salt I use."* My Mom was quite a joker. She wasn't afraid to die. She loved the Lord. She was saved. So, our *"speech"* should be speech of *"grace, seasoned with salt."* In this way, it will be meaningful and useful to those who are listening to us.

"that ye may know how ye ought to answer every man" It is difficult sometimes to know how to *"answer"* some people. Often, when a person asks you a question, you may wonder how you should *"answer"* them. Will you hurt their feelings? If it is truth, maybe it will hurt them or maybe it won't. You don't want to lie, but you must have wisdom to *"answer"* every person as you *"ought to answer"* them.

Lord willing, after we finish Philemon, the Lord is leading me into First Corinthians. I might make some enemies, but I will *"preach the Word."* You don't mind if I *"preach the Word"* do you? I will tell it like it is. There are many issues in the Scriptures that may cause some people to squirm a bit. It might also cause the preacher to be tempted to compromise somewhat, but he better not!

Preachers shouldn't be unkind, but they must preach straight and preach faithfully, regardless. You know how this preacher preaches. I try to be kind, but I must be honest, and true to the Lord Jesus Christ, Who has called me into His service.

Colossians 4:7

"All my state shall Tychicus declare unto you, who is a beloved brother, and a faithful minister and fellowservant in the Lord"

"All my state shall Tychicus declare unto you" *"Tychicus"* was the *"beloved brother"* who probably brought this letter to the church at Colosse. Colosse is in what was called Asia Minor. It is now called Turkey. Paul is writing from Rome, where *"Tychicus"* lived. He ministered to Paul. He was going to go across the Adriatic Sea into Macedonia, and then into Asia Minor to deliver the letter.

"who is a beloved brother and a faithful minister and fellowservant in the Lord" *"Tychicus"* was a faithful man. He was going to inform the Colossians how things were going, how the trial was coming along, if Paul were going to be released from prison. Paul was eventually released from his first Roman imprisonment. Notice what Paul said about this man, *"Tychicus."*

Don't Put Down Your Associates

Sometimes people put down their associates. Sometimes they undermine their associates when nobody is looking. This is not what Paul did. Paul respected his fellow workers.

First, *"Tychicus"* was a *"beloved brother."* He was not only a Christian, but he was *"beloved"* and loved by Paul. Christians should love one another with genuine Christian love.

Second, *"Tychicus"* was a *"faithful minister."* He was not a person who started something without finishing it. He was *"faithful."*

- **1 Corinthians 4:2**
  Moreover it is required in stewards, that a man be found **faithful.**

A *"minister"* is a servant. The Greek word for *"minister"* is DIAKONOS. It means: *"one who executes the commands of another, esp. of a master, a servant, attendant, minister.*"

Third, *"Tychicus"* was a *"fellowservant in the Lord."* Paul did not say that *"Tychicus"* was an inferior person compared to Paul, who was an apostle called by the Lord Jesus Christ Himself. He said he was a *"fellowservant."* The Greek word for *"fellowservant"* is SUNDOULOS. It means: *"a fellow servant, one who serves the same master with another."* Though there are different gifts and callings among saved people, there is a fundamental equality among Christian brethren. As some have said, *"the ground is level at the foot of the Cross of Calvary."*

"Tychicus" knew all about Paul's *"state."* He would *"declare"* unto the Colossians all that they needed to know about Paul's situation. He was a real solid Christian gentleman. All of the above three qualities were true of him. May they also be true of us. May people be able to call us, if we are saved, *"beloved"* brothers or sisters. May they be able to call us *"faithful ministers"* as well as *"fellowservants in the Lord."*

Colossians 4:8

"Whom I have sent unto you for the same purpose, that we might know your estate, and comfort your hearts." So, Paul was going to send *"Tychicus,"* not only for them to know Paul's *"state,"* but also, *"Tychicus"* wanted to know the *"estate"* of the Colossians as well. He was what we call a *"people person."* There are some of those kind in our church, as well, who are genuinely concerned and interested in other people and their problems.

Notice also the second purpose for the visit of Tychicus to the Colossians. It was to *"comfort their hearts."* Apparently the Colossian Christians needed some *"comforting."* All of us need *"comforting."*

- Job 16:2
  I have heard many such things: **miserable comforters are ye all**.

The friends of Job had all kinds of answers, but the answers did not go with the real questions. The problem was not solved by the answers these *"friends"* were giving. Job's malady could not be cured by their platitudes. They had the wrong set-up. They were misjudging Job. They were not *"comforting"* him. In fact, they were bringing him discomfort. Job was not all these things that they claimed he was. Here were four friends coming to commiserate with him. Job waited 15 chapters before he finally told these friends that they were *"miserable comforters."*

> ## The Art of Comfort
> I hope, when you go to visit someone in the hospital, you are not a *"miserable comforter"* to them. Sometimes, the best way to bring *"comfort"* to someone who is ill or not feeling good is to remain relatively quiet. Your presence is a *"comfort"* many times.

- **Psalm 23:4**
  Yea, though I walk through the valley of the shadow of death, I will fear no evil: for thou art with me; **thy rod and thy staff they comfort me.**

A *"rod"* is something the shepherd uses to discipline his sheep in order to keep them in line. A *"staff"* had a crook on it and was used by the shepherd to pull his sheep out of a ditch or a pit.

- **Psalm 94:19**
  In the multitude of my thoughts within me **thy comforts delight my soul.**

- **Psalm 119:50**
  This is my comfort in my affliction: for thy word hath quickened me.

The Word of God is indeed a *"comfort."*

- **Romans 15:4**
  For whatsoever things were written aforetime were written for our learning, that we **through patience and comfort of the scriptures might have hope.**

"Tychicus" was sent to *"comfort their hearts."* One of the many purposes of the Word of God is to *"comfort our hearts."* Of course, you must read God's Word in order to receive this *"comfort."*

- **2 Corinthians 1:3-4**
  Blessed be God, even the Father of our Lord Jesus Christ, the Father of mercies, and **the God of all comfort; Who comforteth us** in all our tribulation, **that we may be able to comfort them** which are in any trouble, **by the comfort wherewith we ourselves are comforted of God.**

This is the key section on *"comfort."*

- **2 Corinthians 7:6**
  Nevertheless **God, that comforteth those that are cast down, comforted us by the coming of Titus;**

That means that Titus brought *"comfort"* to Paul. That means that you and I can bring *"comfort"* to other fellow Christians as well. We are to bring *"comfort"* to those who are uncomfortable. It is in our power, if we are saved.

Several weeks ago, remember, I told you I went into our Collingswood post office. There was one postal worker (a woman) who was smiling. I wanted to ask her if she were a Christian, but I did not get her as I went to another postal worker. When I went to the post office the other day, I went right up to this woman and asked her if she were a Christian. She said, *"Yes."* She asked me if her light showed. I told her, *"Yes"*! She said, *"So does yours."* She radiates throughout that whole post office there in Collingswood.

The Need to Comfort

Why is it that some who profess to be Christians have such a sour countenance? You can't see their faith in any way because of the gloom. There is no light. There is not a shine or a glow. How can we bring comfort, if we are troubled ourselves? How are we going to comfort anybody else? If we are in that condition, rather than being able to give *"comfort,"* we are candidates to receive *"comfort."*

Colossians 4:9

"With Onesimus, a faithful and beloved brother, who is *one* of you. They shall make known unto you all things which *are done* here" *"Onesimus"* went along with *"Tychicus,"* to the church at Colosse. Just as Tychicus, Onesimus was a *"faithful and beloved brother."* Being *"faithful"* means that when he said he was going to do something, he did it. When he said he was going to be somewhere, he was there. We all know people who say they will be in church on Sunday and never show up. It is a great thing to be *"faithful."* And he was also *"beloved."* Paul loved Onesimus. He was also a *"brother."* He was *"in Christ"* (2 Corinthians 5:17). That means he was saved. He was born-again. He was regenerated. The Holy Spirit of God has redeemed him by faith in Christ.

Paul said that Onesimus was *"one of you."* That means that he was from Colosse. We see this man, Onesimus, again in the book of Philemon. He was a former unsaved slave of Philemon who ran away. Yes, he was a runaway slave whom Paul led to Christ. Paul sent him back to his former owner. *"Onesimus"* means *"profitable or useful."* If a man has a slave and then the slave runs away, the slave owner is going to be angry. Right? He lost his income. He lost his servant. He lost his slave. He could not do any more work for him. But when Onesimus ran away, he met Paul while he was in prison. Paul led him to Christ, and thus Onesimus became a Christian.

Now the issue for Paul was, should he send Onesimus back to Philemon, or should he keep him to assist him. That is what the book of Philemon is all about. I have combined **Philemon--Preaching Verse By Verse** with this book of Colossians since it is just one chapter in length, and is also a letter written from Paul's first Roman imprisonment. Paul decided to send Onesimus back to his owner, Philemon. Paul reminded Philemon that he had led him to Christ. Philemon owed his eternal life to Paul. The fact was that Onesimus was unprofitable before, but now he was *"profitable."* That is why he is called Onesimus, *"profitable or useful."* Paul sent Onesimus back to Philemon, but it seems like Philemon then returned Onesimus to Paul to help him in his ministry. We don't know what happened for sure, but I think Philemon sent him back to Paul. Paul needed him. Onesimus, who once was a runaway was now a *"faithful and beloved brother."*

Grace For The Chiefest of Sinners

Those of us in the past, who were lost in sin and are now redeemed, have become and can become *"faithful and beloved"* brothers and sisters in Christ. No matter what the past is. The past can be forgiven and forgotten. We have a yard man named Chris. He has been with us over ten years. Chris takes care of our lawn. I invited him to come to church. He said it was a long way from where he lived. He said that he looked at a painting of my wife and me. I told him that it was painted by a prisoner on death row. He killed someone. Chris said, *"Well then, he can't go to Heaven if he killed someone."* I said, *"Yes he can, if he genuinely trusts the Lord Jesus Christ as His Saviour."* Chris did not know that God could forgive a murderer and send him to Heaven, if he is genuinely saved. This man found Christ in prison and is now studying the Word of God. Onesimus was changed and you and I can be changed by our Redeemer as we, *"as new born babes, desire the sincere milk of the Word"* of God (1 Peter 2:2). Let us redeem the time this week, this year, and throughout our lives so we can be *"profitable and useful."*

Colossians 4:10

"Aristarchus my fellowprisoner saluteth you, and Marcus, sister's son to Barnabas, (touching whom ye received commandments: if he come unto you, receive him;)" We see, from this verse, that *"Aristarchus"* was Paul's *"fellowprisoner"* in Rome. He brings greetings to the Colossians as well. He might have been in prison for the same reason as Paul, that is, for preaching the gospel of Christ. However, it could have been that Paul met him in prison, and led him to Christ.

"Marcus" which is *"Mark,"* was also there with Paul. Paul is telling them in Colosse to receive *"Marcus."* *"Marcus"* was the author of the gospel of Mark. Remember also that Mark was the one who departed from Paul on one occasion. He returned to Jerusalem on Paul's first missionary journey. Mark was related to *"Barnabas."* He was *"sister's son"* to him, or his nephew. On the first missionary journey, Paul took Barnabas with him. Mark went with them. Barnabas wanted to bring Mark along on the second missionary journey, but Paul disagreed.

- Acts 15:37-40 .
And **Barnabas determined to take with them John, whose surname was Mark.** But **Paul thought not good to take him with them, who departed from them from Pamphylia**, and went not with them to the work. And the contention was so sharp between them, that **they departed asunder one from the other: and so Barnabas took Mark**, and sailed unto Cyprus; And **Paul chose Silas,** and departed, being recommended by the brethren unto the grace of God.

Mark was not taken on the second missionary journey because on the first missionary journey, he dropped out. I don't know what made him go back, but he was a *"quitter."* Some drop out of church when the going gets tough.

Paul and Barnabas were sent forth in Acts 13 to be the missionaries from the church at Antioch. Mark went with them but left them before the journey was completed. On the second missionary journey Barnabas wanted Paul to bring Mark, also. Paul banned him from this second journey because he did not finish out the first journey.

So, Paul took Silas and Barnabas took Mark. On the second and third missionary journeys, it was Paul and Silas together rather than Paul and Barnabas. Though phased out of the picture for awhile, Mark appears again here. Mark is now profitable to Paul.

When we make mistakes, if we are saved, the Lord can forgive us of those mistakes. He can straighten us out. Paul and Barnabas were split over this problem with John Mark. They broke fellowship when Paul would not take Mark with him. So Paul went one way with Silas, and Barnabas went another way with Mark.

God's Forgiving Grace

Here Mark was visiting Paul in jail in Rome. He is right there as he writes the letter to the people of Colosse. Paul said of Mark, *"if he come unto you, receive him."* Paul is saying, by his own practice, that the Colossians should give the right hand of fellowship to this one who forsook him at one time, but has returned. It is wonderful that the Lord has a saving and forgiving grace. He can make us new creatures in Christ Jesus (2 Corinthians 5:17). Mark even wrote a Gospel. The Lord did not give up on him.

Have you ever wondered if the Lord has given-up on different ones that you know who seem to be washed out? Who knows, later on down in life, the Lord may pick them up and restore them again and use them for His glory.

Think of the apostle Peter, the writer of 1 & 2 Peter. He was nothing to speak of. He denied the Lord three times after the crucifixion. He was asked, while standing around the enemies' fire at the trial, if he knew the Lord Jesus Christ. Peter cursed and swore that he never knew Him. God is able to renew and restore wayward lives. After getting back to the Lord, Peter wrote two of our New Testament books. He was restored as an apostle.

Colossians 4:11

"And Jesus, which is called Justus, who are of the circumcision. These only *are my* fellowworkers unto the kingdom of God, which have been a comfort unto me"

"And Jesus, which is called Justus"

Five Men Named Jesus

Another name for this "*Jesus*" is "*Justus*." There are actually five different people in the New Testament with this name, Jesus:

(1) Joshua

(2) Jesus the son of Eliezer, one of the ancestors of Christ

(3) The Lord Jesus Himself

(4) Jesus Barnabas, the one that was let go instead of Christ at the crucifixion time

(5) Jesus, surname Justus, which is the one right here. He was a Jewish-Christian and a friend of Paul. Both Mark and Justus were saved Jews.

"**These only *are my* fellowworkers unto the kingdom of God, which have been a comfort unto me**" It is unfortunate that Paul could not name scores of people who were "*fellowworkers*" and "*comforters*" with him when in prison. He just named "*Mark*" and "*Justus*." There are a number of verses on "*comfort*."

Job was a man who lost the fellowship of his wife. He lost his seven sons and three daughters. He lost all his servants. He lost his sheep, his oxen, and all his animals. He lost his prestige. He lost his health. So four men came to comfort him.

● Job 16:2
I have heard many such things: **miserable comforters are ye all**.

He called these men "*miserable comforters*." We should not be "*miserable comforters*" when someone is in need. Have you ever felt alone and in need of "*comfort*"?

- **Psalm 23:4**
    Yea, though I walk through the valley of **the shadow of death,** I will fear no evil: for thou art with me; **thy rod and thy staff they comfort me.**

The *"rod and staff"* can comfort the sheep. Something about that phrase, *"the shadow of death"* came to me for the first time.

The "Shadow of Death"

When a saved person meets physical *"death,"* he is walking through a *"shadow."* It is not real. What must be behind a *"shadow"*? It is light. The one behind the "shadow" of "death" for the Christian, is the *"Light of the world,"* the Son of God (John 8:12b)

- **Psalm 94:19**
    In the multitude of my thoughts within me **thy comforts delight my soul.**

The Lord is able to *"comfort"* us.

- **Psalm 119:50**
    This is my comfort in my affliction: for thy word hath quickened me.

- **Romans 15:4**
    For whatsoever things were written aforetime were written for our learning, that **we through patience and comfort of the scriptures might have hope.**

The Scriptures can bring *"comfort"* to our soul.

- **2 Corinthians 1:3-4**
    Blessed be God, even the Father of our Lord Jesus Christ, the Father of mercies, and **the God of all comfort; Who comforteth us** in all our tribulation, **that we may be able to comfort them** which are in any trouble, **by the comfort wherewith we ourselves are comforted of God.**

Our heavenly Father is called the *"God of all comfort."*

- **2 Corinthians 7:6**
    Nevertheless **God, that comforteth those that are cast down, comforted us by the coming of Titus;**

"Titus" was a faithful saint of God. He *"comforted"* Paul on that occasion. Both *"Mark"* and *"Justus"* were *"comforters"* of Paul. These were the only two that he had.

We get that Greek word for "*comfort*" is PAREGORIA. It means: "*comfort, solace, relief, alleviation, consolation.*" We get the word "*paregoric*" from this Greek word. This is a substance that "*soothes or lessens pain.*" "*Paregoric*" comforts the little children when they are in pain. This is what these men were doing for Paul.

Colossians 4:12

"**Epaphras, who is *one* of you, a servant of Christ, saluteth you, always labouring fervently for you in prayers, that ye may stand perfect and complete in all the will of God**" Paul mentioned greetings from "*Epaphras,*" another of his friends. Being "*one of you,*" he was from Colosse. He was a "*servant of Christ.*" The Greek word for "*servant*" is DOULOS. It means: "*one who gives himself up to another's will, those whose service is used by Christ in extending and advancing His cause among men; devoted to another to the disregard of one's own interests; simply doing the will of another.*"

"*Epaphras*" was not only a "*servant,*" but he was also one who was "*always labouring fervently for them in prayers.*" The Greek word for "*labouring fervently*" is AGONIZOMAI. This means: "*to contend, struggle, with difficulties and dangers; to endeavour with strenuous zeal, strive: to obtain something.*" By the word, "*always,*" it means that his "*fervent prayers*" were repeated, constant, and continuous.

What did he want to pray for them? "*Epaphras*" was praying that the Colossian Christians might "*stand perfect and complete in all the will of God.*" "Perfect" has the sense of mature and grown-up.

Full Knowledge of God's Words

Some have said truly that "*A full knowledge of God's will is found in a full knowledge of God's Words.*" It is important that we have the right "*Word*" so that we might know all the "*will of God*" for our lives. In the English language, the right "*Word*s" are found in the King James Bible. In the Hebrew language it is the *Masoretic Hebrew Text* underlying the King James Bible. In the Greek, it is the New Testament *Textus Receptus* that underlies the King James Bible.

There are various references to "*the will of God*" in Scripture.

- Mark 3:35
For **whosoever shall do the will of God**, the same is my brother, and my sister, and mother.

You have a close relationship with the Lord by doing *"the will of God."*
- **Romans 12:2**
  And be not conformed to this world: but be ye transformed by the renewing of your mind, that ye may prove what is that **good, and acceptable, and perfect, will of God.**
- **1 Corinthians 1:1**
  Paul, called to be **an apostle of Jesus Christ through the will of God**, and Sosthenes our brother

Paul's calling by God to be an apostle was *"through the will of God."* The calling of an apostle, a preacher, and leaders in the church should be by *"the will of God."* It should not be by the mother's will, nor the father's will, nor something else. It should be by *"the will of God."* That was the case in the Apostle Paul's call.
- **2 Corinthians 8:5**
  And this they did, not as we hoped, but first gave their own selves to the Lord, **and unto us by the will of God.**

Before he was saved, Paul was against the Christians. He was killing and imprisoning them. The Lord called Paul and changed him around. That was in *"the will of God."* These Corinthian Christians helped Paul. But first, they gave themselves to the Lord and to Paul *"by the will of God."*
- **Ephesians 6:6**
  Not with eyeservice, as menpleasers; but as the servants of Christ, **doing the will of God from the heart**

The Will of God From the Heart

The *"will of God"* must be done *"from the heart,"* and not just from the head, the hands, or from the feet. The *"will of God"* must not be performed in some mechanical fashion. It must be done from our *"heart."*

- **1 Thessalonians 4:3**
  For this is the will of God, even your sanctification, that ye should abstain from fornication

"Sanctification" is the *"will of God."* God prays for everyone of us that we may be holy, sanctified, and set apart unto God from sin.
- **1 Thessalonians 5:18**
  In every thing give thanks: **for this is the will of God in Christ Jesus concerning you.**

That is another part of the *"will of God"* being *"thankful"* Christians.

- **Hebrews 10:36**
  For ye have need of patience, that, **after ye have done the will of God**, ye might receive the promise.
- **1 Peter 2:15**
  For so is the will of God, that with well doing ye may put to silence the ignorance of foolish men

The *"will of God"* is for you to live for Him, and keep on doing what He would have you to do. People will see you doing God's will. That is important to the Lord.

- **1 Peter 3:17**
  For it is better, **if the will of God be so**, that ye suffer for well doing, than for evil doing.

Suffering and the Will of God

It is the *"will of God,"* sometimes, to suffer. You might think that if you are a Christian, all the suffering will go away. No, that is not true. Sometimes the suffering is even greater. There are various kinds of suffering, including physical suffering and pain. There is also spiritual suffering. We are aware of the suffering that comes from being alone, standing on a position which no one else shares. But, despite the kind of suffering that is involved, God says that, if it is the will of God for you to suffer, it is better to *"suffer for well doing than for evil doing."*

- **1 Peter 4:2**
  That he no longer should live the rest of his time in the flesh to the lusts of men, **but to the will of God.**

Our past may have been to the will of men but the future and the present should be living in *"the will of God."*

- **1 Peter 4:19**
  Wherefore **let them that suffer according to the will of God** commit the keeping of their souls to him in well doing, as unto a faithful Creator.

Sometimes suffering is *"according to the will of God."* Beverly, my wife's sister suffered all of her 65 years. She could not talk. She could not eat by herself. Through her suffering, she brought her mother closer to the Lord. She brought her father closer to the Lord. She brought her sister closer to the Lord. She brought others closer to the Lord. Sometimes it is the *"will of God"* to suffer.

- 1 John 2:17
And the world passeth away, and the lust thereof: but **he that doeth the will of God abideth for ever.**

This *"fervent prayer"* of *"Epaphras"* that the Colossians *"stand perfect and complete in all the will of God"* should be the desire of us today.

That Greek word for "stand" is HISTEMI. It means: *"to stop, stand still, to stand immovable, stand firm; of the foundation of a building; to stand; continue safe and sound, stand unharmed, to stand ready or prepared; to be of a steadfast mind; of quality, one who does not hesitate, does not waiver."* If you "stand" for something, you don't slip, you don't slide. You are not *"jelly on the wall"* as Dr. George Dollar wrote in his book, *Fundamentalism in America*. He says those who are New Evangelicals and compromisers are like *"jelly on the wall."* They just slide down. It is very important, in the present battle for our Bible, to stand strong.

A friend from Barbados sent me an e-mail recently. He read my two books called, *Fundamentalist Distortions on Bible Versions*, and *Fundamentalist Misinformation on Bible Versions*. Although this man said he was in favor of me and my ministry, he wondered if I were driving a sharp axe among various Fundamentalists by my taking a firm stand on this Bible issue.

I wrote him back. As I said, he is a friend of mine. I told him that in my opinion this axe should be wielded as far as Fundamentalists are concerned. I am talking about the famous four Fundamentalists Institutions: (1) *Bob Jones University*, (2) *Detroit Baptist Theological Seminary*, (3) *Central Baptist Theological Seminary*, and (4) *Calvary Baptist Theological Seminary*.

These schools, by their written or spoken materials, **DENY THAT GOD EVEN PROMISED to preserve His original Hebrew/Aramaic and Greek Words**.

God Promised to Preserve His Words

God has promised to preserve His Words. That is His Hebrew/Aramaic and Greek Words. God always keeps His promises. Therefore, I believe that because He has promised to preserve His Words that He has preserved His Words. I believe He has preserved these Words in the *Masoretic Hebrew Text* which underlies the Old Testament in our King James Old Testament and the *Textus Receptus* Greek Text which underlies our King James New Testament.

Those of the four Fundamentalist schools mentioned earlier teach that God has not promised to preserve His **Words** and that He has, therefore, not preserved

His **Words**. They teach only that God promised and has preserved His "**Word**," which does not mean "**Words**." It means either: (1) message, (2) ideas, (3) concepts, (4) thoughts, or (5) voice (MICTV for short). But, to these people, "**Word**" of God does not mean "**Words**" of God. They say we don't have God's **Words**. They believe that these **Words** have been lost. You must understand that when these kinds of Fundamentalists say they believe in Bible Preservation, that Preservation is only of the **Word** (meaning no more than message, ideas, concepts, thoughts, or voice--MICTV for short), but not the **Words** of Hebrew/Aramaic and Greek.

My friends, this position on bibliology (the doctrine of the Bible) is false teaching. It is a modernistic position. It is an apostate position. It is a heretical position. I intend to continue to drive that home. If this splits Fundamentalists, it should be split. It is a serious and fundamental issue.

Fundamentalists and Bible Preservation

Fundamentalists who do not have a proper conviction on the Bible and the preservation of its Hebrew/Aramaic and Greek Words are not Fundamentalists in that area. If history teaches any lessons for us, if this false view of the Bible prevails, it won't be too many decades before these famous four Fundamentalist schools will not be Fundamentalist in other areas, if indeed Fundamentalist in any. That indicates a pathetic slide and drift in the Fundamentalist theological position.

I was very kind as I wrote back our friend from Barbados, but I said the figure of speech picturing an axe may be needful. The sooner people know it the better. If only the message, ideas, concepts, thoughts, or voice (MICTV) is preserved, then why should you care about what Bible you have. Take the *New American Standard*. Take the *New International Version*. They have the message, ideas, concepts, thoughts or voice of God, but they are based on the false Westcott and Hort Greek text. It has 356 erroneous doctrinal passages in it. Yet these brethren, if they were honest about it--and I do call them and treat them as brethren, don't care about these 356 doctrinal errors in the *NASV* and the *NIV*. Nor do they care about the false translation techniques used by these modern versions whereby they add to, subtract from, or in other ways, change God's **Words**.

Doctrinal error is serious. The battle is with us now, and the lines are drawn. Who is on this side and who is on that side, who knows? Part of the *"will of God"* is to *"stand perfect"* (that is mature and full grown) and *"complete in all the will of God."* That is why we as preachers of the gospel and expositors of Scriptures should want to *"preach the Word"* (2 Timothy 4:2) in all areas, and not just a few areas. *"All the counsel of God"* (Acts 20:27) must be proclaimed.

Colossians 4:13

"For I bear him record, that he hath a great zeal for you, and them that are in Laodicea and them in Hierapolis." Paul is giving a testimony of the *"great zeal"* that *"Epaphras"* had for those in Colosse, as well as those in the two neighboring towns of *"Laodicea"* and *"Hierapolis."* Paul wanted those believers in all three towns to *"stand perfect and complete in all the will of God."* *"Epaphras"* also had *"great zeal."* This is an important quality for Christians to have.

- **Romans 10:2**
  For **I bear them record that they have a zeal of God**, but not according to knowledge.

The Greek word for *"zeal"* is ZELOS. It means: *"excitement of mind, ardour, fervour of spirit; zeal, ardour in embracing, pursuing, defending anything; zeal in behalf of, for a person or thing."* If you are saved, you should be fervent, but you should also have knowledge to go along with it. Misspent fire will burn a house down. A lady in the Philadelphia area had her house burnt down recently because of fire. *"Zeal"* is like fire.

It is good to have fire and warmth, but without knowledge it is not good either. Someone asked me the other day why I sometimes stop preaching and fill up with tears in my eyes. I told them I don't plan that. I am not one of these preachers who has it in his notes to cry here. Sometimes, when the Lord gets hold of my heart, I just have to stop. Would you rather have a preacher who is stone-cold, with no heart and never being able to show any emotion or feeling? Or, would you rather have a warm-hearted preacher who loves the Lord, loves his people, and sometimes, when the Lord touches his heart, he is a little bit emotional and feels it? You will have to answer these questions yourself.

Faithful to the Fight
(2 Timothy 4:7)

Faithful to the fight, Faithful to the Faith,
Faithful to the finish for God
Faithful to the right, Faithful in His might,
Faithful to the Word of God.
Faithful in the fray, Faithful every day,
Faithful in the fight for the Faith.
Faithful to the fight, Faithful to the Faith,
Faithful to the finish for God.

"Faithful to the Fight"

When we were singing that song, *"Faithful to the Fight"* written by my mother-in-law, it brought tears to my eyes, because I remember her writing that song and dedicating it to me, a preacher of the gospel. It was taken from 2 Timothy 4:7: *"I have fought a good fight, I have finished my course, I have kept the faith."* She knew I was a warrior. She knew there was a *"fight"* for the truth of God. She knew there was a *"faith"* to be kept and guarded. She knew that I wanted to *"finish my course"* for His glory, so she wrote that song. Zeal is great, but make sure there is knowledge to go along with it.

- **Philippians 3:6**
  Concerning zeal, persecuting the church; touching the righteousness which is in the law, blameless.

Make sure your *"zeal"* is in the right direction. I am sure that Epaphras's *"zeal"* was in the proper direction. He wanted the other people there in *"Laodicea"* and *"Hierapolis"* (not only Colosse) to *"stand perfect and complete in all the will of God."*

Colossians 4:14

"Luke, the beloved physician, and Demas, greet you."

"Luke, the beloved physician," was the one who wrote the Gospel according to Luke. He was also the writer of the book of Acts. He joined Paul on one of his missionary journeys.

Paul evidently was comforted by *"Luke, the beloved physician."* Apparently, Luke was there with Paul at Rome. Maybe Paul needed some medical care also.

- **Colossians 4:14**
  Luke, the beloved physician, and Demas, greet you.
- **2 Timothy 4:11**
  Only Luke is with me. Take Mark, and bring him with thee: for he is profitable to me for the ministry.

This was not Paul's first Roman imprisonment. It was his second Roman imprisonment where he died. He was beheaded as a martyr for his faith in the Lord Jesus Christ. He brings Luke into the picture in this second Roman imprisonment also. Luke was a faithful friend to Paul in prison. I hope if any of us go to prison that those who are left will be faithful in visiting these people. That is important.

At this time, *"Demas"* was with Paul and sent his greetings to the Colossian Christians. He was called a *"fellowlabourer"* in Philemon 24. In 2 Timothy, however, it says that *"Demas hath forsaken me, having loved this present world"* (2 Timothy 4:10). He is no longer with Paul. We have seen flip-flops with people many times. One day people are for you, and the next day they are against you. Luke was a steady friend of Paul both in his first and second Roman imprisonment. Demas was only with Paul in his first Roman imprisonment, not during his second.

- **2 Timothy 4:10**
  For **Demas hath forsaken me, having loved this present world, and is departed** unto Thessalonica; Crescens to Galatia, Titus unto Dalmatia.

Stay On Track For the Lord

"*Demas*" was not steady. "*Mark*" was unstable, but got back on track later. "*Demas*," on the other hand, started out all right, but ended up in the wastebasket, as far as service for Christ was concerned. Mark recovered himself and continued service for Christ. Peter started out all right, went bad, and finally came out and was restored as a faithful servant for Christ. We have flip-flops of people in the New Testament. Is it any wonder that we who are living today find many who are flip-flop people? Let us keep strong for the Lord. Let us stay on track for Christ.

Colossians 4:15

"Salute the brethren which are in Laodicea, and Nymphas, and the church which is in his house"

House Churches in the Bible

Paul greeted the *"brethren"* in *"Laodicea"* and especially Nymphas who had a *"church in his house."* We have a *"church in our house."* Is this a Biblical practice, or is it not? If it is in the Bible, it is *"Biblical"* is it not? This is not an outlandish or foolish idea. There may come a day when many of the churches which are now in buildings and structures will have to close down because of persecution. Maybe many believers will have to worship in their houses. This is practiced often in Communist nations and in other places. There are at least four places that talk about *"churches in houses."*

- Romans 16:5
  Likewise greet **the church that is in their house**. Salute my wellbeloved Epaenetus, who is the firstfruits of Achaia unto Christ.
- 1 Corinthians 16:19
  The churches of Asia salute you. Aquila and Priscilla salute you much in the Lord, **with the church that is in their house**.
- Colossians 4:15
  Salute the brethren which are in Laodicea, and Nymphas, **and the church which is in his house**.

- **Philemon 1:2**
  And to our beloved Apphia, and Archippus our fellowsoldier, **and to the church in thy house:**

These were gatherings of believers that were in a *"house."* A *"house"* is simply a place where people live. We live here in our *"house."* There is space in our large living room, so we just invited you to come worship with us, and here you are.

Not only do we have the church and the ministry in the house, but also we have it on the radio. It is a wonderful thing to be able to project these services here by way of radio. Through the Greenville station the services are projected all over the world via the Internet. My wife also has this broadcast *"Just For Women."* She is not a woman-preacher. She is talking just for women and things that women need to know. We also broadcast our messages by way of the Internet on **www.BibleForToday.org** under our **"Audio Sermons."** During a current month, as of this writing, we had 700 messages available on our site and over 3,700 people from almost all states and many foreign countries have downloaded these onto their own computers for future listening. That is a record monthly download number for us as of this date. All our messages are put on both audio and video cassettes. At present, many families receive our services for their own families to see and hear. We have also been able to put five of our messages preached verse by verse into five books for future reading and impact. The *"church in thy house"* should have and does have good effects all over the world.

Colossians 4:16

"And when this epistle is read among you, cause that it be read also in the church of the Laodiceans; and that ye likewise read the *epistle* from Laodicea" Paul urges the Colossian Christians to read this letter. Reading of the Word of God is urged throughout the Scriptures.

- **Deuteronomy 17:18-19**
  And it shall be, when he sitteth upon the throne of his kingdom, that **he shall write him a copy of this law in a book** out of that which is before the priests the Levites: And it shall be with him, and **he shall read therein all the days of his life: that he may learn to fear the LORD his God, to keep all the words of this law and these statutes, to do them:**

That is one of the major problems with the kings of Israel and the kings of Judea. They did not write their own copy of God's Word as commanded, nor did they read those words *"all the days"* of their lives.

- **Joshua 8:34**
  And afterward **he read all the words of the law**, the blessings and cursings, according to all that is written in the book of the law.
- **Nehemiah 8:8**
  So **they read in the book in the law of God distinctly, and gave the sense, and caused them to understand the reading**.
- **Nehemiah 8:18**
  Also **day by day, from the first day unto the last day, he read in the book of the law of God**. And they kept the feast seven days; and on the eighth day was a solemn assembly, according unto the manner.

This was the revival during Ezra and Nehemiah's time after they came back from captivity.

- **Nehemiah 9:3**
  And they stood up in their place, and **read in the book of the law of the LORD their God one fourth part of the day**; and another fourth part they confessed, and worshipped the LORD their God.

If the day is 12 hours of light a fourth would be three hours wouldn't it? That is quite a long service. He "*read*" the Word of God.

- **Isaiah 34:16**
  Seek ye out of the book of the LORD, and read: no one of these shall fail, none shall want her mate: for my mouth it hath commanded, and his spirit it hath gathered them.
- **Matthew 19:4**
  And he answered and said unto them, **Have ye not read**, that he which made them at the beginning made them male and female,

The Lord Jesus criticized the Pharisees and Sadducees of his day who had not "*read*" the Old Testament.

- **Matthew 21:16**
  And said unto him, Hearest thou what these say? And Jesus saith unto them, **Yea; have ye never read**, Out of the mouth of babes and sucklings thou hast perfected praise?
- **Matthew 21:42**
  Jesus saith unto them, **Did ye never read in the scriptures**, The stone which the builders rejected, the same is become the head of the corner: this is the Lord's doing, and it is marvellous in our eyes?

- **Acts 8:30**
  And Philip ran thither to him, and heard him read the prophet Esaias, and said, Understandest thou what thou readest?

  Paul urged the Colossian Christians to *"read"* this book to those in *"Laodicea."* He also wanted the letter to Laodicea to be read by the Colossians. This is the way the letters in the New Testament originated. They were copied, recopied, and then passed around. Some believe that *"the epistle from Laodicea"* could be a reference to the book of Ephesians.

- **1 Thessalonians 5:27**
  I charge you by the Lord that this epistle be read unto all the holy brethren.

God's Book--Read It and Heed It

God has not given us this Book, not just to defend, but to *"read,"* and not only to *"read"* but to heed. Reading alone without heeding is wasteful and useless. We must heed what we *"read."* We can't heed it if we don't *"read"* it from Genesis to Revelation wherein is found *"the whole counsel of God."* Remember what was said earlier, *"Full knowledge of God's will is found in full knowledge of God's Word."*

- **2 Corinthians 3:2**
  Ye are our epistle written in our hearts, **known and read of all men**

  Paul says that Christians are *"epistles"* that can be something that people can and do *"read."*

  You remember when the first President Bush said, *"Read my lips."* People are reading, not only our lips and our faces, but also our actions, words, and lives. People don't look only at the preacher, but they look at all of us who are born-again. They are ready to laugh at us, if we make a mistake. They are ready to slap us down, if we disagree with them. We have to keep marching on. *"Read"* the Word and then *"heed"* the Word. Then people will *"read"* you and maybe they will *"heed"* you. Who knows? Maybe people will follow the Lord Jesus Christ because you are following Him.

  Remember that old saying, *"Good, better, best. Never let it rest. 'Till your good is better and your better is best."*

> ## Good, Better, Best, Never Let It Rest
> Remember another saying that I like to use often:
> > "*The Bible in the hand is <u>good.</u>*
> > *The Bible in the head is <u>better.</u>*
> > *The Bible in the heart is <u>best</u>.*"
>
> My mother always used to say: "<u>*Good, better, best, never let it rest*</u>, *'till your good is better and your better's best!*"

The Bible will never pass away. They can take away your Bible during persecution, but if it is in your heart, you will always have it.

Colossians 4:17

"And say to Archippus, Take heed to the ministry which thou hast received in the Lord, that thou fulfil it."

Paul wanted the believers to give a message to *"Archippus."* He might have been the pastor of the church at Colosse. Paul was concerned about the *"ministry"* which Archippus *"received in the Lord."* He was to *"take heed'* to this ministry and *"fulfil it."*

- **1 Corinthians 3:10**
  According to the grace of God which is given unto me, as a wise masterbuilder, I have laid the foundation, and another buildeth thereon. But **let every man take heed** how he buildeth thereupon.
- **1 Corinthians 10:12**
  Wherefore **let him that thinketh he standeth take heed** lest he fall.

It is important to *"take heed."*

- **1 Timothy 4:16**
  Take heed unto thyself, and unto the doctrine; continue in them: for in doing this thou shalt both save thyself, and them that hear thee.

Pastors must have their own life in order and then, after that, they should be concerned about their *"doctrine."*

We had a lady call this week and ask about a pastor. She was formally one of the members of his church. This pastor is a graduate of *Dallas Theological Seminary*, the same as I am. He is positive about *"doctrine,"* but does not seem to be concerned about his life, and the life of his church. She talked about all the child molestation that goes on in that church. I asked permission to interview her about this situation. We have a lot of information about this pastor. He is a false teacher in many areas. This child molestation is another dimension that I did not know about. God told pastor Timothy to take heed to himself first and then to *"doctrine."* It is not enough to have sound *"doctrine."* Our lives must be in line first and foremost.

Paul wanted *"Archippus"* to *"fulfil"* the *"ministry"* that he *"received in the Lord."* Paul himself wanted to *"finish his course."*

- **Acts 20:24**
  But none of these things move me, neither count I my life dear unto myself, so that I might finish my course with joy, and the ministry, which I have received of the Lord Jesus, to testify the gospel of the grace of God.

Paul was interested in *"finishing"* his ministry even if it meant death in Jerusalem.

- **2 Corinthians 5:18**
  And all things are of God, who hath reconciled us to himself by Jesus Christ, and hath given to us the ministry of reconciliation

- **1 Timothy 1:12**
  And I thank Christ Jesus our Lord, who hath enabled me, for that he counted me faithful, putting me into the ministry

Paul was *"put into the ministry"* and *"counted faithful"* by the Lord.

- **2 Timothy 4:5**
  But watch thou in all things, endure afflictions, do the work of an evangelist, make full proof of thy ministry.

Fulfil Your Ministry

What is your service? What is your ministry? All of us who are Christians should have a service or a ministry for the Lord. It is important that we *"fulfil it"* and finish that ministry the Lord has given us.

- **Luke 9:62**
  And Jesus said unto him, No man, having put his hand to the plough, and looking back, is fit for the kingdom of God.

I have never plowed, except when I helped a friend of mine plow his field. It is like mowing lawns. I certainly have mowed lawns. You can imagine mowing a lawn while you are looking back. It would be a very poor job of mowing if we *"looked back"* instead of looking forward while mowing. We must continue our ministry faithfully and *"fulfil it."*

- **Matthew 5:17**
  Think not that I am come to destroy the law, or the prophets: I am not come to destroy, **but to fulfil**.
- **Colossians 1:25**
  Whereof I am made a minister, according to the dispensation of God which is given to me for you, **to fulfil the word of God**;
- **2 Thessalonians 1:11**
  Wherefore also we pray always for you, that our God would count you worthy of this calling, **and fulfil all the good pleasure of his goodness**, and the work of faith with power:

I don't know how many years the Lord will let me have in this ministry here in our Bible For Today Baptist Church. Who knows? As long as I am the pastor, I will try to *"fulfil"* the ministry that the Lord has given to me. As a minister of the gospel, called unto the gospel ministry, I try to be faithful to the Lord and His ministry and His Word everywhere I go.

As I have said before, the Lord laid on my heart to begin our church here in our house in October of 1998. He has put on my heart to *"preach the Word"* (2 Timothy 4:2) as faithfully as I am able. I preach verse by verse, by way of expository preaching, using the King James Bible and the Hebrew and Greek texts that underlie it. In order to fulfill the ministry that the Lord Jesus has given to me, we have our *Bible For Today* ministry all over the world in different areas. We have over 3,155 titles that we carry defending the Scriptures and many other topics.

In the ministry of our Bible For Today Baptist Church, I trust that God will enable me to fulfill it. As you see, I am going through Bible books, verse by verse, taking half a chapter each Sunday. As of this date, I have preached through Romans, 1 Peter, Galatians, Ephesians, Philippians and am now finishing Colossians. Lord willing, I will begin Philemon next week. How many books will the Lord enable me to go through and to preach and teach in an expository manner? And how many of those books will the Lord enable us to put into print so that, after I go Home to be with the Lord, people can read if they want. How many books? Who knows?

What I am interested in, as far as the Lord is concerned in my life, as a preacher, is to *"fulfil"* what God has given me the desire to do. I want to do this honestly, honorably, and faithfully. That is what Paul urged *"Archippus"* to do.

Take Your Ministry Seriously

When the Lord gives you a ministry, don't take it lightly. It is never to be taken lightly. It is serious business and fervent business.

Colossians 4:18

"The salutation by the hand of me Paul. Remember my bonds. Grace *be* with you. Amen"

From the words, *"the salutation by the hand of me Paul"* we conclude that Paul himself wrote this letter to the Colossian church and signed it. Sometimes he used a secretary to write the letters for him. When he wrote, *"Remember my bonds,"* he was telling the church at Colosse to keep praying for him. He wanted to be released from Roman imprisonment if it were the Lord's will. Paul was finally released. They did *"remember his bonds."* During his time in prison, Paul was Christ's freeman, but Rome's prisoner.

As we think of this last part of Colossians, may we *"stand perfect and complete in all the will of God."* That is what the Lord would have all of us to do, in order that the Lord Jesus Christ might be honored and glorified in our ministry that He has given to us. Paul wished that God's *"grace"* might be with the Colossians. All believers need that *"grace"* daily.

GRACE

Hard is the pathway of training,
Stern is the way He may use
To take our dim eyes from the earth things,
To make us His own will to choose.

How often our hands seem to cling to
The baubles and toys of this sphere,
But a wonderful wise overseer
Will give us of things far more dear.

He seats us in Heavenly places,
Enfolds us around with His care,
Bestows on us gifts for His glory
That we may be used everywhere.

He lets us see failure in others,
Permits us to weep over loss
For all of this, while He is turning
Our eyes from this world to His cross.

Philemon

Introductory Remarks

The book of Philemon is one of the four prison epistles. The other three are the books of Ephesians, Philippians, and Colossians. This book is a story about a slave owner, Philemon, and one of his slaves, Onesimus. Philemon lived in Colosse. This city was located in the province of Asia Minor, which is now known as the country of Turkey. Colosse (found on the map below) is about 50 miles east and a little south of the city of Ephesus. Paul wrote this letter from Rome, Italy, which was clear across the Mediterranean Sea.

This is a personal letter. Though it is not a doctrinal book as such, it does

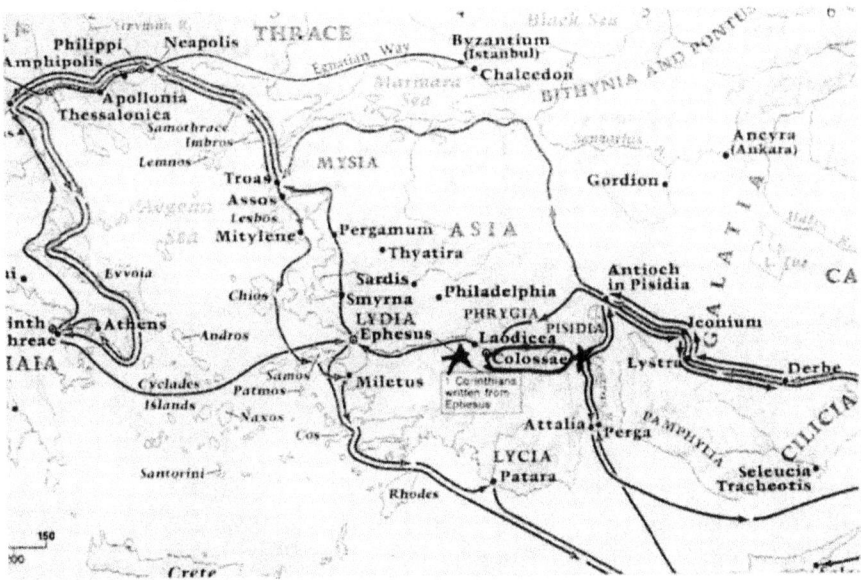

have some doctrine by implication. Though many of Paul's epistles were written by secretaries, this brief letter was written with his own hand.

While Paul was a prisoner in Rome, he met a former slave, Onesimus. Onesimus had run away from Philemon, had stolen some of his money, and ended up in Rome. Paul led Onesimus to a genuine saving faith in the Lord Jesus Christ. Though he was a Christian now, he was still a slave who was owned by Philemon.

Paul could do one of two things. (1) Paul could keep Onesimus there in Rome with him because he needed him for the ministry, or (2) Paul could send him back and hope that Philemon would return him to Rome to help Paul. The second alternative is the way Paul wanted things to happen. He wanted Philemon to send Onesimus back to him voluntarily, without any force on Paul's part.

Philemon 1

"Paul, a prisoner of Jesus Christ, and Timothy *our* brother, unto Philemon our dearly beloved, and fellowlabourer" Evidently, *"Timothy"* was with Paul when he wrote this letter. Paul mentioned that he was a *"prisoner"* because of his faith in, and service for, the Lord Jesus Christ. Philemon was a wealthy man who lived in the city of Colosse. He was not only *"dearly beloved,"* but also a *"fellowlabourer"* with Paul. We will see later in this letter that Paul was the one who led him to Christ. So Paul wrote this letter and reminded Philemon that he was a prisoner in Rome. There are at least seven passages that mention that Paul was a *"prisoner."*

- Acts 23:18
  So he took him, and brought him to the chief captain, and said, **Paul the prisoner** called me unto him, and prayed me to bring this young man unto thee, who hath something to say unto thee.

He was in prison in the book of Acts. He was taken from prison in Jerusalem all the way to Rome.

- Acts 28:17
  And it came to pass, that after three days Paul called the chief of the Jews together: and when they were come together, he said unto them, Men and brethren, though I have committed nothing against the people, or customs of our fathers, **yet was I delivered prisoner from Jerusalem into the hands of the Romans.**

He was *"delivered"* as a *"prisoner."*

- Ephesians 3:1
  For this cause I Paul, **the prisoner of Jesus Christ for you Gentiles,**

The reason that Paul was a prisoner, just like in Philemon 1:1, was because he was a faithful preacher and minister of *"Jesus Christ."* That is a good reason to be put in prison.

- **Ephesians 4:1**
  I therefore, the prisoner of the Lord, beseech you that ye walk worthy of the vocation wherewith ye are called,
- **2 Timothy 1:8**
  Be not thou therefore ashamed of the testimony of our Lord, **nor of me his prisoner**: but be thou partaker of the afflictions of the gospel according to the power of God;

He was writing to Timothy from the jail in Rome. As mentioned earlier, the four letters that Paul wrote from his first Roman imprisonment were: Ephesians, Philippians, Colossians, and Philemon. Many feel that Paul was in prison in Rome a second time when he wrote 1 Timothy, 2 Timothy, and Titus. I believe it is certain that he was in jail when he wrote 2 Timothy. The question is, *"Did Paul learn his lesson?"* What is the lesson? I think the lesson Rome was trying to teach Paul was for him to stop preaching the Lord Jesus Christ. I hope none of us will stop preaching or witnessing for the Lord, no matter what may happen to us. Paul ended up in prison again because he did not learn Rome's lesson.

This was his second Roman imprisonment. He said to preacher Timothy, the pastor of the church of Ephesus *"not to be ashamed of the testimony of our Lord nor of me His prisoner."*

- **Philemon 1**
  Paul, **a prisoner of Jesus Christ**, and Timothy our brother, unto Philemon our dearly beloved, and fellowlabourer,
- **Philemon 9**
  Yet for love's sake I rather beseech thee, being such an one as Paul the aged, **and now also a prisoner of Jesus Christ**.

"Iron bars do not a prison make" as the saying goes. Though imprisoned, Paul was free in Christ. We praise the Lord for that. He was a prisoner writing to Philemon who was *"dearly beloved."* Paul loved Philemon.

When you lead someone to Christ, you usually have a special affection for them. You want to help them, encourage them, and draw them close to Christ that their lives may be in conformity to the life of the Lord Jesus Christ.

Philemon 2

"And to *our* beloved Apphia, and Archippus our fellowsoldier, and to the church in thy house:"

"Apphia" means *"fruitful."* Paul is writing not only to Philemon, but also *"Apphia"* and *"Archippus."* This name comes from two Greek words, ARCHE *"leader, ruler, or master"* and HIPPOS *"horse."* It means *"the master of the horse."*

"Archippus" is called Paul's *"fellowsoldier."* Did you know there is a battle for the things of Christ today? Among many other battles, there is a battle

about various Bible doctrines such as the Blood of Christ. There is a battle about evolution versus creation. There is a battle about Biblical separation. There is a vital battle about Bible preservation of the Hebrew and Greek Words of God. There is a battle about Bible versions. Are you in these battles? If you are saved you are already in the battle because you are wearing the uniform of the King of Kings and Lord of Lords against whom all the worldly forces of the Devil are arrayed in opposition. Some battles find other born-again Christians arrayed against you as well. As soon as you take on the uniform of Christ you become a *"fellowsoldier"* of the Lord.

Here was a *"fellowsoldier."* Paul was glad, I am sure, that Archippus was one of his *"fellowsoldiers."* Notice that Paul wrote to the *"church in thy house."* Does that make you feel more comfortable? Not only is the church at 900 Park Avenue, Collingswood, New Jersey in a *"house,"* but also the church that Apphia and Archippus attended was in a *"house."* There are a number of *"house"* churches spoken about in the New Testament.

- **Romans 16:5**
   Likewise greet **the church that is in their house.** Salute my wellbeloved Epaenetus, who is the firstfruits of Achaia unto Christ.
- **1 Corinthians 16:19**
   The churches of Asia salute you. Aquila and Priscilla salute you much in the Lord, **with the church that is in their house.**
- **Colossians 4:15**
   Salute the brethren which are in Laodicea, and Nymphas, **and the church which is in his house.**
- **Philemon 2**
   And to our beloved Apphia, and Archippus our fellowsoldier, **and to the church in thy house:**

Here we see the various New Testament churches that met together to worship and serve the Lord Jesus Christ in *"houses."* What is wrong or unscriptural with this practice? I do not think anything is wrong with it. Some people wonder how it is possible for a *"church"* to meet in a house. These folks are of the firm belief that a church must meet in a larger building. Though meeting in such buildings has been the practice of Christians for many centuries, what is really wrong with going back to this unquestioned Biblical custom of meeting in *"houses"*? The *"church"* is not a building. It is a called-out group of saved people meeting to glorify their Saviour. In other words, a church is a gathering of Christian people. The Greek word for *"church"* is EKKLESIA. It comes from EK (*"out from"*) and KALEO (*"to call"*). It refers to people who have been *"called out"* from the world by personal faith in Christ and who gather together in one place to worship and to serve the Lord. The word, "church," in the New Testament, refers to *"people"* and not to a *"building."*

Can the church, a called-out assembly of believers who are saved by faith in Christ, meet in a *"house"*? Certainly they can. We in our Bible For Today Baptist Church are doing it. We have been doing it since October of 1998. Of course, we have some limitations by meeting in the" *house,"* but we also have some blessings. It is much closer fellowship. In many churches, with a huge meeting place, when the pastor leaves, most of the people leave, too, and the large building is left empty.

Many churches have been built which are now almost empty. Dr. Carl McIntire's Bible Presbyterian Church is a good example of that. When we came to Collingswood we attended that church for a short while. I was an associate for the ministry of his broadcast for about three years. Our family attended there until we could find a Fundamental Baptist Church where we would agree in doctrine and practice. There must have been about 1,000 people in that big building in 1965 when we entered Collingswood. As of this writing, I have been told that, for some reason, there are only about 35 to 60 attending there today. That many people could meet in our *"house."*

The *"house"* is a place of blessing. It is a place of closeness. It is a place of beautiful instrumental music by Mr. Dick Carroll. We have beautiful acoustics. There may be a day when we will have to move out of the house, but for me and my house we would like to have you here. Not that we are trying to be small on purpose, but we are not trying to be big on purpose either.

Philemon 3

"Grace to you, and peace, from God our Father and the Lord Jesus Christ."

"Grace to you" The Greek word for *"Grace"* is CHARIS. It speaks *"of the merciful kindness by which God, exerting his holy influence upon souls, turns them to Christ, keeps, strengthens, increases them in Christian faith, knowledge, affection, and kindles them to the exercise of the Christian virtues."*

God's Grace Is Undeserved

"Grace" is *"getting something we do not deserve."*

That's God's grace. It is *"something that affords joy and pleasure."* Paul gave His greeting by using the term, *"grace,"* which was the Greek greeting of that day. It is CHARIS. The modern Greeks use this even today when they say, EUCHARISTO. This is both a greeting like *"hello"* and also *"thank you."*

"and peace" Then, Paul gave the Hebrew greeting which is *"peace."*

This word is SHALOM in the Hebrew language. In the Greek, it is EIRENE. As I have said many times before, *"peace,"* in the Christian sense, is:
> *"the tranquil state of a soul assured of its salvation through Christ, and so fearing nothing from God and content with its earthly lot, of whatsoever sort that is."*

God's Peace Brings Joy
"Peace" causes us to rejoice in the Lord.

"from God our Father and the Lord Jesus Christ" The modernists and liberals of our day seem to divide God the Father and God the Son. They say that God the Son is inferior to God the Father. The Unitarians do not even believe that the Lord Jesus is God. The Scripture, however, always declares both Persons of the Godhead to be co-equal, co-powerful, co-extensive, and co-eternal. Each Person, including God the Holy Spirit, shares equally with the other Persons in the Godhead so far as attributes are concerned. Paul says *"grace"* and *"peace"* not only *"from God our Father,"* but also from *"the Lord Jesus Christ."*

Philemon 4

"I thank my God, making mention of thee always in my prayers" Paul here expresses his thanksgiving to his God. Paul, at this point, has not asked for a thing. He hasn't required a thing. He hasn't suggested a thing. Paul will ask of Philemon something of great importance later on in the letter. You do not have to come out with a big issue right at first. You can start slowly. Philemon is the subject of Paul's constant *"prayers."*

We must remember in prayer those that we led to Christ. Though we may be led to pray for others, we must not neglect those the Lord has used us to lead to Him, out of darkness and into the Light. So, Paul continuously thanks God for Philemon and constantly makes mention in prayers unto the Lord for him. That's important.

Paul and Prayer
Paul was a man of prayer.

We should be men and women of prayer as well.

Philemon 5

"Hearing of thy love and faith, which thou hast toward the Lord Jesus, and toward all saints," Paul heard from his prison in Rome the news from Colosse, which was over 1,000 miles away. He heard of Philemon's *"love and faith."* *"Love"* is an emotion. *"Faith"* is also an emotion, but not exactly the same kind.

Philemon and Love
Philemon was a man of *"love."*

He had *"love and faith"* not only for the Lord, but also for the *"saints."* We must have a *"love"* that is not narrow, but all-encompassing, extending to all the believers in Christ.

Saved people are often called *"saints"* in the Bible.

"Saints" Not Limited to Rome
Don't let the Roman Catholic Church take the word, *"saints,"* away from us.

Some people (probably of Roman Catholic origin) use the expression, *"Saints preserve us."* That is calling on the *"saints"* that Rome has canonized to help. Those *"saints"* are not going to preserve a soul. Even genuinely saved *"saints"* in heaven can do nothing for us here on earth. Let us be clear about that. They are dead. If they have not trusted Christ as their Saviour they are lost and in conscious suffering, awaiting their final destiny in the Lake of Fire. Those lost *"saints"* of Rome are in judgment and pain even now.

There may be some Roman *"saints"* whom they have *"sainted"* that are saved. I am not saying there are not some. But, if they are trusting in their works, as Rome teaches; if they are trusting in their baptism, as Rome teaches; if they are trusting in extreme unction, as Rome teaches; if they are trusting in the Mass for their salvation, as Rome teaches, they are not born-again. They are not with the Lord. They are outside the Lord. There may be some exceptions, as I said, but don't let Rome take away our Biblical title of *"saints."*

If you are trusting Christ as the Lord and Saviour of your life, you are a *"saint,"* according to the Scriptures.

Modern Versions and "Saints"

Do not let the new versions take away our understanding of the word, *"saint."* These modern versions often remove *"saint."*

Look with me at nine passages where the Lord does call the saved ones *"saints."*
- Acts 9:13
  Then Ananias answered, Lord, I have heard by many of this man, how much evil he hath done **to thy saints at Jerusalem**:

Jerusalem Saints Were Alive

The *"saints"* in Jerusalem where not dead. They were living believers.

- Acts 26:10
  Which thing I also did in Jerusalem: and **many of the saints did I shut up in prison**, having received authority from the chief priests; and when they were put to death, I gave my voice against them.

Paul said that before he was saved he shut up the *"saints"* or believers in prison.
- Romans 1:7
  To all that be in Rome, beloved of God, **called to be saints**: Grace to you and peace from God our Father, and the Lord Jesus Christ.

The Greek word for *"saint"* is HAGIOS. It comes from HAGIAZO and means *"set apart ones or holy ones."* From this Greek word, HAGIOS, you get the English word *"hag."* We are *"hags,"* or *"holy and separated ones."* When you see a *"hag"* they usually look ugly. They are so ugly that they are *"set apart"* completely from other people. That is what that means to be *"separated or set apart"* in a good sense of that term. We are *"set apart"* for the Lord and His Words.

- Romans 8:27
  And he that searcheth the hearts knoweth what is the mind of the Spirit, **because he maketh intercession for the saints** according to the will of God.

That does not mean the Roman Catholic *"saints,"* but God the Holy Spirit makes intercession for every believer.

- **Romans 12:13**
  Distributing to the necessity of saints; given to hospitality.
- **1 Corinthians 6:2**
  Do ye not know that the saints shall judge the world? and if the world shall be judged by you, are ye unworthy to judge the smallest matters?

The believers will be with the Lord Jesus Christ during the judgment of the lost at the Great White Throne judgment (Revelation 20:11).

- **1 Corinthians 16:1**
  Now concerning the collection for the saints, as I have given order to the churches of Galatia, even so do ye.
- **2 Corinthians 13:13**
  All the saints salute you.

"*Love*" is so needful in this wicked world. Remember, the fruit of the Spirit in Galatians 5:22-23? That very first part of His fruit is "*love.*" If you do not have human "*love*" for the "*saints,*" the Holy Spirit of God can put that "*love*" in your heart for them. You may not agree with all the "*saints.*" They may have different doctrines from you in some areas, but if they are "*saints*" you still should "*love*" them because they are one of Christ's children. It does not mean you have to go to their church if their doctrine or practice is different from yours. We can still have "*love*" and respect for them.

Our *Dean Burgon Society*, for example, is not a Baptist organization. It is a Bible-believing organization. It is a separated organization. It stands for the Hebrew and Greek texts which underlie our *King James Bible*. It stands for six literal days of creation. It stands for the Blood of Christ as cleansing us from sins. There are many doctrinal distinctives, but it is not Baptist as such. Most of us in the *Dean Burgon Society* are Baptists. We have some who are not. We still "*love*" them as brethren. Though for fellowship in our local churches we must stand on doctrines, but it is a wonderful thing to have "*love*" for all the true "*saints*" of God.

Philemon 6

"That the communication of thy faith may become effectual by the acknowledging of every good thing which is in you in Christ Jesus." Paul wanted the "*communication of the faith*" in Christ to be "*effectual.*" He wanted it to work. That is what he is trying to say. "*Effectual*" "*faith*" is "*faith*" that works. The "*communication of faith*" means that it is spread abroad. It results in our telling others about this "*faith*" in our Saviour. This is what Paul wanted.

If we are saved, we should count up "*every good thing*" that is ours because we have salvation by faith in our Lord Jesus Christ. He has given to us forgiveness of our sins, redemption by His blood, a home in heaven and all of the many other promises for us in God's Word. They form a part of *"every good thing."*

Philemon was a Christian. He trusted Christ. Paul prayed that the *"communication"* of his *"faith"* in the Lord Jesus Christ might be *"effectual."* Here are several passages that mention that word, *"effectual,"* in our King James Bible.

- **1 Corinthians 16:9**
  For a great door and effectual is opened unto me, and there are many adversaries.

"Effectual" means it is workable. It must be energized by the Holy Spirit of God.

- **Ephesians 3:7**
  Whereof I was made a minister, according to the gift of the grace of God given unto me by **the effectual working of his power.**

That is the *"working"* that is genuine and the *"working"* that really works.

- **James 5:16**
  Confess your faults one to another, and pray one for another, that ye may be healed. **The effectual fervent prayer of a righteous man availeth much.**

The Wrong Greek Text

The ASV (1901), NASV, NIV, RSV, NRSV, New Century, and many other modern versions have the wrong Greek text here. The Westcott and Hort (UBS or Nestle-Aland) all read: *"sins."* They don't have PARAPTOMATA which is *"faults."* They have HAMARTIAS which is sins.

These modern versions translate this as if we must confess our *"sins"* like Roman Catholics do to their priests in the confessional box. That's Romanism. The *King James Bible* and the Received Greek text which underlies it says, *"confess your faults one to another."* There is nothing wrong with that. If we get in trouble one with another we must talk directly to the person or persons involved (and no one else). Agree that we were wrong about something, and try to make things right with those we have wronged.

Philemon 7

"For we have great joy and consolation in thy love, because the bowels of the saints are refreshed by thee, brother." Paul was glad for the *"love"* that Philemon had for the *"saints."*

He had *"great joy and consolation in that love."* The Greek word for *"bowels"* is SPLAGCHNON. It means the following:

> *"The bowels were regarded . . . by the Hebrews as the seat of the tenderer affections, esp. kindness, benevolence, compassion; hence our heart (tender mercies, affections, etc.)"*

It meant to the Hebrews something like the "heart" might mean to us today. We might say *"the heart of the saints is refreshed."*

The Greek word for *"refreshed"* means: *"to cause or permit one to cease from any movement or labour in order to recover and collect his strength; to give rest, refresh, to give one's self rest, take rest; to keep quiet, of calm and patient expectation."*

Apparently Philemon was a man who had people stay for a while at his house. He *"refreshed"* them. That is, he gave them food and lodging. That enabled them to be relaxed before they had to resume their long journeys. He was hospitable. Paul thanked him for this. He was very grateful and wanted him to continue to do this. They did not have motels or hotels in those days. They had Christian homes. When believers came into a city they stayed in the homes of fellow Christians. That was Philemon's joy to give assistance the to the *"saints"* who traveled through his city.

Philemon 8

"Wherefore, though I might be much bold in Christ to enjoin thee that which is convenient," Paul said that he could be very bold and forthright with Philemon. He could *"enjoin"* or command him to do something. He was not going to do it. He could command him to send Onesimus back to him at Rome. Paul could have said that. He could have been bold to do that. He didn't do that, but he could have done it. You know the old saying, *"Rank has its privilege."*

Paul, the apostle, had rank on Philemon. He led him to Christ. He was his father in the faith. Fathers have what is known as *"command presence"* with their children. Am I right? They should anyway. Unfortunately, many children don't believe that. In fact, some children command their parents.

Philemon 9

"Yet for love's sake I rather beseech *thee*, being such an one as Paul the aged, and now also a prisoner of Jesus Christ." As I mentioned before, Paul could have enjoined, ordered, dictated, or commanded Philemon. This could happen just as, in the military, the higher ranking officer can issue commands to the lower ranking men or women. Paul could have done that, too.

Because he loved Onesimus and because he loved the Lord, Paul *"besought"* him. The Greek word translated *"beseech"* is PARAKALEO. It means, among other things, *"to beg or entreat."* It has the sense of asking someone to do something with the hope that they will do it. It is not commanding, but simply urging. *"Beseeching"* means to ask and to hope that you'll do it. It is not commanding, but simply urging someone to do something. This is what Paul was asking of Philemon.

Paul mentioned two reasons for this request of Philemon. The first reason was that Paul was *"aged."* He was saying that he was older than Philemon. As such, he out-ranked him and had privilege over him. Usually, but not always, older people have the determining vote over the younger ones. It is not that way in the age in which we live, but I will tell you, in the Oriental world, the ancient ones always command the respect of the younger ones. They almost worship their elders. We in the western world do not agree with this, but they have deference for the aged.

The second reason was that Paul was a *"a prisoner of Jesus Christ."* He was in chains. Paul didn't have freedom like Philemon had. Because of this, he is *"beseeching"* Philemon.

There are a number of places where the word, "beseech," is found in the New Testament.

- **Mark 7:32**

    And they bring unto him one that was deaf, and had an impediment in his speech; **and they beseech him to put his hand upon him.**

Who were they to bring this poor soul and command that the Lord Jesus put His hand upon him. They did not command, but they *"besought"* him. This means that they *"asked, begged, entreated, requested, or urged"* Him.

- **Romans 12:1**

    I beseech you therefore, brethren, by the mercies of God, that ye present your bodies a living sacrifice, holy, acceptable unto God, which is your reasonable service.

In this verse, Paul addressed the Christians at Rome. He did not command them to *"present their bodies,"* but he *"besought"* them. Again, this means he *"asked, begged, entreated, requested, or urged"* them. By application, Paul would urge those who are saved people also to *"present our bodies"* in the same manner.

- **2 Corinthians 5:20**

    Now then we are ambassadors for Christ, **as though God did beseech you by us**: we pray you in Christ's stead, be ye reconciled to God.

The believers in Corinth were called *"ambassadors for Christ."* "God did beseech" them by Paul to be *"reconciled to God."* Again, this is the idea of his having *"asked, begged, entreated, requested, or urged"* them to do this.

- **Ephesians 4:1**
  I therefore, the prisoner of the Lord, **beseech you** that ye walk worthy of the vocation wherewith ye are called,

Paul *"besought"* the Ephesian believers to *"walk worthy."* He was a *"prisoner of the Lord."*

- **1 Peter 2:11**
  Dearly beloved, **I beseech you as strangers and pilgrims**, abstain from fleshly lusts, which war against the soul;

Peter wrote to his *"dearly beloved"* Christians and *"besought"* them as well.

There are times in Scripture and times in life that we could command, but that is often ineffectual. You might issue commands to certain people until you are, as they say, *"blue in the face,"* but they will not follow them. If you *"beseech"* these same people in a polite manner, they might respond favorably. There is no guarantee either way, however. When you have authority over people who are working for you, you can command them to do this or that. When you are a preacher, an apostle, or one who is trying to lead people toward Christ and to love Christ all you can do is *"beseech."* That's not so bad. You can catch more flies with honey than you do with vinegar. Sometimes you must *"beseech"* a little bit and people often react in a positive manner.

That was all Paul was doing. *"For love's sake"* he beseeches him, being *"Paul the aged."* Remember, in verse eight, Paul had said he could have been bold enough to "enjoin" or command Philemon, but he did not choose to do this.

Philemon 10

"I beseech thee for my son Onesimus, whom I have begotten in my bonds" Paul used *"beseech"* in this verse also. He is finally getting down to the subject of this letter. It concerns his *"son Onesimus."* Onesimus was not one of Paul's natural *"sons,"* but a *"son"* whom he had *"begotten in his bonds"* while in the Roman prison. This was Paul's spiritual *"son."* Now, he has two special *"sons"*--Philemon and Onesimus--in addition to the other men he led to the Lord. In addition to being one of Paul's spiritual *"sons,"* Onesimus is also a runaway slave who stole money from Philemon. It is important to realize that, once we come to Christ, whether we are slaves or whether we are free, we are sons of God by faith in Christ Jesus. We are all on the same plane, as far as the way God sees us.

Paul took a special interest in Onesimus. Paul knew Onesimus was a runaway slave who had stolen money. Though Philemon owed Paul some favors, he *"beseeches"* him on behalf of Onesimus. He really intercedes for this slave. Have you ever interceded for anybody? When someone has gotten into trouble have you ever helped by saying a few encouraging words to help them? That's what this is. Paul, with his pastoral heart, *"besought"* Philemon on behalf of Onesimus, his "*son*" in the faith.

Prison Did Not Stop Paul's Witness

The fact that Paul led Onesimus to Christ while in prison indicates that Paul did not stop his witnessing for Christ while in prison. Here was a soul that he had led to Christ. There are others also that Paul led to Christ. These are mentioned in his other prison letters. The word, "*Onesimus,*" means "*profitable or useful.*" Though he was unprofitable before his conversion, he is very profitable to Paul now that he has been saved.

Remember, the reason Paul was put into this Roman prison was because he was proclaiming Christ as his Saviour. That is why, in Acts 23:18, he was called a "*prisoner.*" In Acts 25:27 and in Acts 28:17 he was called a "*prisoner.*" His imprisonment came as a result of his proclamation that the Lord Jesus Christ was the Messiah Who would one day come back and redeem Israel. Paul also preached the bodily resurrection of the Lord Jesus Christ. Resurrection was denied by the Sadducees.

The Jews would have killed Paul had he not appealed unto Caesar.

Appealing Your Rights
There is a time and a place to appeal your rights.

The Lord Jesus did not appeal His rights. He could have appealed to His Father and avoided the cruel cross with its suffering and pain. But it was His Father's will to have His Son suffer, bleed, and die for the sins of the whole world. His Father's will was His will, as He said, "*Not my will, but thine, be done*" (Luke 22:42).

The Jews wanted to take Paul from Caesarea back to Jerusalem. There was a group of forty men who had bound themselves by an oath to kill Paul before he ever got back to Jerusalem (Acts 23:21). They were waiting for him. Paul got word of that and immediately refused to go back to Jerusalem for trial. Instead, he appealed unto Caesar at Rome.

Philemon 11

"Which in time past was to thee unprofitable, but now profitable to thee and to me" In the past, Onesimus was *"unprofitable"* to Philemon, and Paul admitted it.

"Unprofitable" to the Lord?

Have you ever been *"unprofitable"* to the Lord at some point in your life?

If you are saved through faith in Christ, you are *"profitable"* to the Lord. God wants you, He wants me, to be His servant. He wants us to serve Him with everything that we are and everything that we have. Yes, though we all have different gifts and abilities. God still wants us to be *"profitable."*

Before we were saved we were all *"unprofitable."* We had nothing good in ourselves. We were all bound for Hell. We were all sinners by nature and sinners by practice. When Christ came into our life and saved us, if we are saved, He made us *"profitable."* This is the difference that the cross of Calvary can make in a life. If the life does not become *"profitable"* to the Lord after trusting Christ as Saviour, then woe is that life. That's not why God saves us just *"to have a fire escape from Hell"* as they say. It is true that we are escaping Hell, if we trust in Christ and are saved. He wants us to be profitable.

Not only was Onesimus *"profitable"* to *"thee"* (Philemon) but also *"to me"* (Paul). There were two profitabilities. The practical problem was, how could Onesimus be in two places at the same time, both in Colosse and in Rome?

Paul was a very clever writer. He knew that Philemon would send that slave immediately back to Rome as soon as he reads this letter. That's why he could write that. Paul implied that Onesimus would be a better slave then ever. He would also be *"profitable"* to Paul because he knew that Philemon would send him back to him soon. He would be Paul's servant and helper. He would even help Paul preach the gospel in Rome. Paul already had confidence as to what was going to happen in the future. There are many *"profitable"* things in Scripture.

- 1 Timothy 4:8
  For bodily exercise profiteth little: but **godliness is profitable unto all things**, having promise of the life that now is, and of that which is to come.

"Godliness" is *"profitable."*

- **2 Timothy 3:16**
  All scripture is given by inspiration of God, **and is profitable for doctrine**, for reproof, for correction, for instruction in righteousness:

The "*Scripture*" is "*profitable.*"

- **2 Timothy 4:11**
  Only Luke is with me. Take Mark, and bring him with thee: for **he is profitable to me for the ministry.**

"*Mark*" is the one who fled from Paul on the first missionary journey, but now even he had become "*profitable*" to Paul.

- **Titus 3:8**
  This is a faithful saying, and these things I will that thou affirm constantly, that they which have believed in God might be careful to maintain good works. **These things are good and profitable unto men.**

"*Good works*" certainly are "*profitable.*" You are not saved by "*good works,*" but they are "*profitable*" unto others as a testimony to the saving grace of the Lord Jesus Christ.

Philemon 12

"Whom I have sent again: thou therefore receive him, that is, mine own bowels" Paul told Philemon that he was returning his slave, Onesimus, once again. Philemon was to "*receive*" Onesimus. This particular word for "*receive*" is an interesting word. The usual Greek word for "*receive*" is LAMBANO. The form of the word used here has the prefix, PROS, before it. The Greek word is PROS- LAMBANO. The effect of it is as follows:

> "*to take or receive into one's home, with the collateral idea of kindness ; to receive, i.e. grant one access to one's heart.*"

Remember King David and Absalom his son? Absalom was a wicked and rebellious son. Finally, after partially forgiving him, David brought him back to Jerusalem, but never saw him. King David received Absalom into his city, the Jerusalem area, but he never received him into his heart. That was not the kind of reception that Paul wanted Philemon to have for his slave, Philemon.

What would you do to a person who had robbed you and then run away from you? In your natural flesh, what would you do? Paul didn't want Philemon to beat him up, or kill him, but "*receive him into his heart.*" Paul wanted Philemon to "*take him to yourself*" (PROSLAMBANO) and "*receive him.*"

"him that is, mine own bowels:" When Paul identified Onesimus as "mine own bowels," he was using a Hebrew expression. The

Greek word for "bowels" is SPLAGCHNON. Here is what it meant to the Hebrews:

> "*the bowels were regarded as the seat of the more violent passions, such as anger and love; but by the Hebrews as the seat of the tenderer affections, esp. kindness, benevolence, compassion; hence our heart (tender mercies, affections, etc.)*"

Paul was showing Philemon that he had tender affections toward this man, Onesimus. Paul still loved Onesimus, though he was a slave who stole money and then ran away. Since he was now saved, the Lord Jesus Christ had forgiven him all of these things.

When you lead someone to Christ do you just let him or her go and forget about them? I hope not. I hope you would be concerned for them, follow up with them and show them how they can "*grow in grace, and in the knowledge of our Lord and Saviour Jesus Christ*" (2 Peter 3:18). Paul was that same way. He didn't want to let Onesimus go. He wanted to take care of him. I don't know how he got back to Colosse. I am sure it was by ship.

Christianity Is Forgiveness

We must forgive people once they have repented of their sin of harming us and come back to us after they have hurt us or harmed us. Do not hate them or be mean to them even though they may hate you. That is the nature of the Christian faith. We have love even for those who may be unlovely. God loved us when we were unlovely. Christianity is centered on forgiveness. Harry Rimmer once wrote: "The only permanent pain and harm that can come to me from the offenses committed against me is the irreparable injury I do myself by hatred of those who wrong me!"

Paul urged Philemon to forgive Onesimus when he returned home. We should have the same forgiving spirit.

The profitability of Onesimus had now resurfaced. Since he has been converted, he was going to be "*profitable*" both to Philemon as well as to Paul. May you and I be "*profitable*" to the Lord Jesus Christ.

Philemon 13

"**Whom I would have retained with me, that in thy stead he might have ministered unto me in the bonds of the gospel:**" Paul says, talking about Onesimus, the runaway slave. He said, "*I would have retained with me.*" Paul really didn't want to send Onesimus back to Philemon, he wanted to keep him.

Paul had a purpose for wanting to keep Onesimus. He told Philemon that, in his place, Onesimus *"might have ministered unto him in the bonds of the gospel."* Philemon wasn't in Rome, but Onesimus was. Paul really wanted to keep him in Rome so he could minister to Paul and help him in the prison conditions.

Sharing in the Gospel

When Paul said, *"in thy stead,"* he was saying that Onesimus could take Philemon's place in helping him. This is the way the gospel is. The gospel message is not always given by those on the firing line, the preachers, missionaries, or evangelists. It is also shared by those at home praying, giving money so that missionaries can be sent out, and doing other business for the Lord.

Is this not what we have here? Onesimus could stay and minister to Paul in the place of Philemon, the rich land owner and the one who owned this slave. He could minister in his place *"in the bonds of the gospel."* Our church does not go to Australia with the Bennetts, or to Papua New Guinea with the Guerrants, or to London with the Moormans, or the Kenderdines in Cambodia. This is our missionary outreach. The ones who are back home holding the ropes are also ministering *"in the bonds of the gospel"* as we send forth others. This is a missionary verse here in Verse 13. There are *"bonds"* in the gospel that holds us. There is a *"bond"* of service, a *"bond"* of preaching, and so on. This is a very important *"bond"* indeed.

Paul was a minister of the *"gospel"* even while he was in prison. That *"gospel"* was the good news about the bad news. The bad news is we are sinners, we are lost, we are undone, and we are headed for Hell. The good news is that the Lord Jesus Christ came to redeem us from sin, redeem us from hell, and give us everlasting life and forgiveness. The good news is by genuine faith in Him, we can trust Him and be saved. The bonds of the *"gospel"* are important.

Philemon 14

"But without thy mind would I do nothing; that thy benefit should not be as it were of necessity, but willingly"
Paul did not want to do something against the wishes of Philemon. He did not want to retain him without Philemon's permission. That is an important point. Paul was writing this letter in order to see what Philemon would do. Paul indicated this caution by his words, *"without thy mind."* He wanted Philemon's

input and counsel. Paul wanted to have Philemon's actions voluntary. He wrote: *"that thy benefit should not be as it were of necessity, but willingly."* There would be a *"benefit"* to Philemon before this matter was resolved. God would bless him.

Willing Service Needed

The Lord wants us to do everything *"willingly."* The Lord Jesus Himself was a willing missionary. The only missionary that God the Father ever sent from Heaven was His Son. He *"willingly"* came to earth, leaving His place in a sinless and perfect heaven to come into a sinful world. Then, *"willingly"* he went to the cross of Calvary to die for the sins of the world. Nobody forced Him. He said to His Father in prayer, *"not my will, but thine be done"* (Luke 22:42). He came to do His Father's will. It was a willing offering.

That is the way that Abraham's son, Isaac, reacted. Isaac was a willing subject. As Abraham took his son into the land of Moriah to sacrifice, Isaac did not question. It is like the Lord Jesus Christ who went to Mount Calvary. He did not question. He went willingly all the way along.

When the Lord Jesus saves us by His grace through genuine faith, He wants us to be willing servants of His. He does not crack the whip on us. He does not make us do things against our will. He does not force us. He does not push us around. That is not the way He created us. He did not make us machines. If we were machines, He could simply push the buttons on the machinery and He could make us do what He wanted us to do. That is not the way He created us. He created us free to love Him, free to serve Him, and free to give Him our lives. That *"willingness"* is the way we are made. That's the only thing God really expects of us.

Nobody made you come to church at our *Bible For Today Baptist Church*. Nobody took a whip to you and said, *"If you don't come I will whip you."* Nobody said, *"If you do not come. I will kill you."* You were not threatened. You came by your own free will. We come to worship our Saviour *"willingly."* We read our Bibles *"willingly."* We witness and give tracts out *"willingly."* In the Old Testament we read in the book of Exodus.

- **Exodus 25:2**
Speak unto the children of Israel, that they bring me an offering: of every man **that giveth it willingly with his heart** ye shall take my offering.

This pertained to the Tabernacle.

- **1 Chronicles 29:9**
  Then the people rejoiced, for that **they offered willingly**, because with perfect heart **they offered willingly** to the LORD: and David the king also rejoiced with great joy.

This was in the building of the Temple.

- **Proverbs 31:13**
  She seeketh wool, and flax, and **worketh willingly with her hands.**

As they say, "*a woman's work is never done,*" but is it willing work? The virtuous woman of Proverbs 31 works willingly around the house to help her husband and her children.

- **1 Corinthians 9:17**
  For if I do this thing willingly, I have a reward: but if against my will, a dispensation of the gospel is committed unto me.

- **1 Peter 5:2**
  Feed the flock of God which is among you, taking the oversight thereof, not by constraint, but **willingly**; not for filthy lucre, but of a ready mind;

Peter is talking to the preachers, teachers, elders, and bishops. Preachers and pastors also should minister to the people of the Lord Jesus Christ willingly.

This is what he says. Paul wanted Philemon "*willingly*" to say, "*All right, Paul, you can keep Onesimus. I will send him back to you so he can be a helper to you.*" Paul didn't want to force Philemon to do that. He could have. He could have pulled rank. "*Rank has its privilege*" as they say. This certainly is true. The apostle has rank over his spiritual "*son*" in the faith whom he led to Christ. He was a convert of Paul. He could have said, "All right, Philemon, I led you to Christ and you know that. I order you to release Onesimus to me." Paul did not do that. He wanted Philemon to act "*willingly*" without any pressure from him.

Philemon 15

"For perhaps he therefore departed for a season, that thou shouldest receive him for ever" What Paul was saying here was that Onesimus "*departed for a season*" from Philemon in order that Philemon would "*receive him*" back in his home, and "*for ever*" in heaven because he was now saved. Onesimus, as well as Philemon and Paul, are in Heaven today. They are rejoicing together around the Lord Jesus Christ their Saviour. The departure was part of the plan of God.

Sometimes we do things without knowing really why we are doing them. They are silly things. Here was a slave who stole some money, took it away from his slave master, and then ran away. That was not nice. I suppose, after he was saved, he realized he should not have stolen that money and run away.

We do some foolish things, but sometimes the Lord is able to use our folly for His glory. We must try to understand these things. The departure of Onesimus was only "for a season." This return of Onesimus was going to be permanent. He was not going to run away again because he had been saved and redeemed. Redeemed ones stay with their masters unless released by these masters.

Paul did not write a lesson on abolitionist slavery. That wasn't his mission. We had slavery in this country for many years. We don't have it now except for white slavery, narcotic slavery, drug addiction slavery, and other slavery to sin. We have plenty of that, I am afraid.

Now, this new drug that the young people are taking, ecstasy, is very dangerous. Our governor of New Jersey said there are some strict laws of prohibition of sales and use of ecstasy. Our Declaration of Independence and our U. S. Constitution have given us political freedom in our country. These young people who take this ecstasy hurt and damage their minds immediately, perhaps forever. As the governor said in the broadcast we heard this morning, that is just one drug. There will be some new drugs that will take the minds of our young people away, just for a momentary pleasure.

We used to have physical slaves, but now we have all of this other kind of slavery. Paul wanted to redeem the souls of sinners whether they were slaves who needed to be redeemed by the blood of Christ, or whether they were free people that were enslaved to sin. He wanted to set those in slavery spiritually free in Christ. He also wanted to set people free spiritually who were free but enslaved by sin.

Philemon 16

"Not now as a servant, but above a servant, a brother beloved, specially to me, but how much more unto thee, both in the flesh, and in the Lord?" Onesimus was a *"servant."* The Greek word for this is DOULOS. This means:
> *"one who gives himself up to another's will, those whose service is used by Christ in extending and advancing His cause among men; devoted to another to the disregard of one's own interests."*

Onesimus was *"doing another's will."* But now that he was a Christian, he was *"above a servant."* He had another title, a *"brother beloved."* He was saved and had the same Heavenly Father as Paul had. Onesimus had the same Heavenly Father that Philemon, the slave owner, had. He is not now just your servant, Philemon, he is your brother.

Those who are the meanest, the lowest, and the ugliest kind of people, when they are saved, sometimes become the most *"beloved."* This was the case of Onesimus. He was a shining example for whom Paul could praise and thank the Lord. He was not a "flash in the pan" as some converts are. They say they believe in Christ, but they are back into the world the next day. Onesimus was a glorious convert through Paul's ministry. He was a convert of the Lord Jesus Christ. He was a *"brother beloved"* especially to Paul. Paul loved Onesimus, but how much more was Onesimus unto Philemon. He was now a *"beloved brother"* both in the flesh and now unto the Lord since has been redeemed by faith in Christ. There can be fellowship one with another in the Lord.

- **Galatians 3:28**
  There is neither Jew nor Greek, there is neither bond nor free, there is neither male nor female: for **ye are all one in Christ Jesus**.

In Christ, bondage goes. Freedom goes. All spiritual distinctions are wiped out in the Lord. Now, this slave can be not only a servant, but also a *"brother beloved"* both *"in the flesh, and in the Lord."*

Philemon 17

"If thou count me therefore a partner, receive him as myself." Paul was using an *"if"* here. He could have said, *"I am your partner, you know. I led you to the Lord in Colosse. We have been friends for many years."* Instead, he put an *"if"* in his sentence. He left it to Philemon to decide whether or not he was Paul's *"partner."* The Greek word for partner is KOINONOS. It means,

  "a partner, associate, comrade, companion; . . . sharer, in anything"

A Partner With Paul

Paul wanted Philemon to realize that he was truly his *"partner."* After Paul established his *"partnership,"* he gave Philemon a command to *"receive him as myself."* It was just as if Paul were coming to Philemon's house. He meant that Onesimus was a part of him, and should be *"received"* in the same manner if it were Paul himself.

I am coming ; to you receive him as me. That word for receive is not simply the regular LAMBANO which is the normal Greek word for receive. It's got a prefix, PROS. The whole word is PROSLAMBANO. It means:

  "to take by the hand in order to lead aside; to take or receive into one's home, with the collateral idea of kindness; to receive, i.e. grant one access to one's heart."

This word denotes reception into a close fellowship. Paul did not want Philemon to receive Onesimus and put him in the woodpile, or in a shack. He wanted Philemon to *"receive"* him into his home and into his heart.

In the Gospels it says to those who have visited the sick or have visited the prisoner, the Lord Jesus said, *"Inasmuch as ye have done it unto one of the least of these my brethren, ye have done it unto me."* (Matthew 25:40). The *"brethren"* of the Lord are a part of the Body of the Lord Jesus Christ, as are all saved believers.   When Paul, the persecutor, was saved on the road to Damascus, on the way to kill Christians, he put them into prison, and harmed them, the Lord Jesus met Paul and blinded him with a light far brighter than the sun light. The sun was shining. It was midday, but the Lord Jesus, the Light of the world, was the One that blinded Paul. Christ asked Paul, *"Why persecutest thou me?"* Paul said, *"Who art thou, Lord?"* And the Lord said, *"I am Jesus of Nazareth, whom thou persecutest"* (Acts 22:7-8) The Lord Jesus Christ was in heaven. He was in Glory. He was not here on earth any more. He was not crucified again. But, because Paul was persecuting Christ's people, His Christians, His saved ones, Paul was persecuting the Lord Jesus Christ Himself. This is very important.

Taking Things Personally

Do you take things personally when people go after you and attack you? I think most people do. So does our Saviour. When people are attacking us, His saints, the saved ones, He takes it personally. We must stand together, unit

---

Paul said,
> *"Please receive him. Take him into your heart. Take him into your home. Take him into your friendship, just like you would do to me if I were out of this prison and back there with you. He is just the same as I am."*

You can't say that about too many people. You may have some friends about whom you can say that. Maybe you have a friend that you could send to somebody who lives in another part of the country and ask them to take them in just as they would take you in. How many people do you know that you could say to that host, *"Receive that one (boy or girl, man or woman) just as you would receive me."* How many? There are very few that are so close that you could say that. This was how close Paul and Onesimus were.

Philemon 18

"If he hath wronged thee, or oweth *thee* ought, put that on mine account" Paul began the sentence again with "if" as he had done in verse 17. Certainly Onesimus had wronged his master. He had *"wronged"* him by leaving him. He had *"wronged"* him by stealing from him. He had *"wronged"* him perhaps in some other ways. Maybe he took some things that were very precious possessions of Philemon. Paul said that, regardless of what had happened, if he *"owed"* Philemon, he was to put it on Paul's *"account."* The Greek verb translated *"to put on an account"* is ELLOGEO. It means,

"to reckon in, set to one's account, lay to one's charge, impute."

Onesimus had stolen money or merchandise, perhaps. Maybe he stole rings or necklaces of gold or silver.

Have we *"owed"* anything to God? Have we hurt our Lord? Have we stolen from our God in heaven? The Lord Jesus Christ says to any of us who come to Him by faith to put all those things on the Lord Jesus' *"account."*

- **Isaiah 53:6**
  All we like sheep have gone astray; we have turned every one to his own way; **and the LORD hath laid on him the iniquity of us all**.

Our Sins Put on Christ's Account

God the Father laid the *"iniquity"* of the entire world on His Son, the Lord Jesus Christ on Calvary's cross. That includes your sins and mine. It was as though the Lord Jesus said to His Father, concerning our sins, *"Put that on My account."* Your sin, my sin, all the sins of the world. Yes, all these sins were put on Christ's *"account."* He died *"the just for the unjust"* (1 Peter 3:18). He bled and died for our misery, our sins, our mistakes, our wickedness, our corruptness. What about the sins of the saved ones after we have come to Christ?

We sin day by day in word, thought, and deed. That is why 1 John 1:9 is in our Bible.

- **1 John 1:9**
  If we confess our sins, **he is faithful and just to forgive us our sins**, and to cleanse us from all unrighteousness.

What about the sins we do afterwards? We must confess them. The Greek word for *"confess"* is HOMOLOGEO. It means, *"to say the same thing."* We must *"say the same thing"* about our sin as God says about it. We must agree with God that these thoughts, words, or deeds are sins. We must take them to God immediately. When this is done, God is *"faithful and just to forgive us our sins and to cleanse us from all unrighteousness."* Only then can our fellowship with God be restored. God can accomplish this because our sins have been put on the *"account"* of the Lord Jesus Christ. He has paid for every one of them.

What about the sins we are going to commit in the future? If we are under the blood of Christ and are saved , the Lord Jesus says *"put them on my account"* also. That's a pretty big bill. That is why John the Baptist said of the Lord Jesus Christ:

- **John 1:29**
  The next day John seeth Jesus coming unto him, and saith, Behold the Lamb of God, which taketh away the sin of the world.

God the Father put the sin of the whole world on the Lord Jesus Christ's *"account."* That's the gospel message. It's not simply the account of those who are of the elect. It is the sin of the whole world that was reckoned to Christ's *"account."* Every man, woman, boy, or girl can be born again by repenting of their sins and trusting Christ in sincerity and truth. *"The Lord laid on Him the iniquity of us all"* (Isaiah 53:6).

- **2 Corinthians 5:21**
  For he hath made him to be sin for us, who knew no sin; that we might be made the righteousness of God in him.

"Put that on my account." Paul said if Onesimus had wronged Philemon, if he were a criminal in some way, if he hurt you, if he damaged you, if he harmed you, if he owes you money, *"put that on my account."* This is what the Lord Jesus has done for us who are saved. We praise God for that.

This is just like a bookkeeping transaction. Most of us have bank accounts. Some old-timers don't trust the banks. They remember 1929, when the banks crashed, and they could not get their money. Because of this, some of them have secretly hidden their money under their mattress or in some other hiding place. Most of us have a savings account or a checking account.

Can you imagine running up a bill on your Visa, or your Master Card, or whatever credit card you may have? Then, can you imagine that somebody came forward and said concerning all those bills, *"put that on my account, I will pay for all of it."* You might say to this person, *"You cannot afford to do that."* You may have bought a car. You may have bought a house. You may have bought a boat.

> ## Jesus Paid It All
>
> Can you imagine anyone foolish enough to come forward and say to you and to me, *"Put that on my account, I will pay for it?"* That is exactly what the Lord Jesus Christ has done for us with our sins. He has put on His own personal omnipotent account all the sins of all the world. He has paid for them in full. That's why the hymn writer could write, *"Jesus paid it all, All to Him I owe. Sin had left a crimson stain. He washed it white as snow."* Praise God for that.

Remember the good Samaritan that was kind to the man who was beaten by thieves and left for dead on the road to Jericho? The Priest looked at him and passed by on the other side without giving him any help. The Levite also came by, saw him and went on the other side of the road without giving him assistance. But this despised Samaritan came right over where that man was lying. He picked him up, dressed his wounds, put oil upon his head, and put the sick man on his own beast. The Samaritan walked back to the city and the man, that was beaten by thieves, rode on the Samaritan's own animal. When he came into the city, the Samaritan went to the inn keeper and put up the infirmed man for the night. The Samaritan told the innkeeper to take care of him. This is told in the Gospel of Luke,

- **Luke 10:35**
  And on the morrow when he departed, he took out two pence, and gave them to the host, and said unto him, Take care of him; and whatsoever thou spendest more, when I come again, **I will repay thee**.

Then the good Samaritan said, "whatsoever thou spendest more," he would pay it. Whatever the bill is, whatever food he eats, however long he stays, *"I will repay thee"* when I come back. *"Put that on my account."* It is a similar kind of situation.

Philemon 19

"I Paul have written *it* with mine own hand, I will repay *it*: albeit I do not say to thee how thou owest unto me even thine own self besides" Paul wanted to make clear to Philemon that this letter was not a forgery. He had *"written it with his own hand."* He said *"I will repay"* anything Onesimus has stolen.

Then, Paul was careful how he words the next part of this verse. He said, he *"did not say"* something, and yet, by his very mention of what he did not say, that very thing is mentioned. Notice how he phrased this: *"I do not say to thee how thou owest unto me even thine own self besides."* He reminded him that he had led him to Christ, and that Philemon owed his own salvation and eternal life to Paul's ministry. Oh that people today would treasure the pastors who have led them to Christ and/or those who have given of themselves to teach them the Word of God!

Philemon 20

"Yea, brother, let me have joy of thee in the Lord: refresh my bowels in the Lord" Paul did not give any specific suggestions. In effect, he was saying *"Do as you will."* Paul did make a request, however. He said: *"Let me have joy of thee in the Lord."* In other words, Paul was implying that he hoped that Philemon would do the right thing and release Onesimus back to him.

The Greek word translated *"refresh"* is ANAPAUO. It means,
"to give rest, refresh, to give one's self rest, take rest; to keep quiet, of calm and patient expectation"
Paul was saying, "give me a patient expectation" of what you are going to do. That's what refresh means.

The Greek word for "bowels" is
"the bowels were regarded as the seat of the more violent passions, such as anger and love; but by the Hebrews as the seat of the tenderer affections, esp. kindness, benevolence, compassion; hence our heart (tender mercies, affections, etc.)"
This word is used in the Scripture just like we say *"my heart belongs to this one or that one."* It is the inner feelings of kindness and compassion. Paul was saying he wanted to be *"refreshed before the Lord that I may have a joy that you are doing the right thing."* That's what Paul meant.

Philemon 21

"Having confidence in thy obedience I wrote unto thee, knowing that thou wilt also do more than I say." In this verse, Paul showed that he had *"confidence"* in Philemon's *"obedience."* Paul is quite a strategist. He has *"confidence."* He *"knew"* that not only would Philemon do what he suggested and let Onesimus come back to help Paul in prison, but also that he would do more than Paul *"said."* That's being positive. Paul had *"confidence"* in Philemon because he knew him well enough to know that he would do as his *"father"* in the Lord had requested that he do. This is how Paul knew Philemon would do what he asked and even more than he asked.

Philemon 22

"But withal prepare me also a lodging: for I trust that through your prayers I shall be given unto you." Paul asked Philemon to *"prepare"* him a *"lodging."* Not only did Paul want Philemon to prepare a place for Onesimus, but also for him. Paul expected to be released from this Roman imprisonment as a result of Philemon's *"prayers."* He was later released. The books of Ephesians, Philippians, Colossians, and Philemon were all written during Paul's first Roman imprisonment. After his release, I believe he was arrested again and returned to a prison in Rome. During the second Roman imprisonment some feel Paul wrote what we call the pastoral letters of 1 Timothy, 2 Timothy, and Titus. Though there may be some question about 1 Timothy and Titus, I feel certain that Paul wrote 2 Timothy from that second Roman imprisonment.

I am sure that, when Philemon read this, he thought twice about any action that would be adverse to Onesimus. Would you not think twice if the Apostle Paul, the man who led you to the Lord, would write unto you and tell you that he was coming with Onesimus and for you to prepare him a place? Philemon might think something like this: *"If Paul is coming and I put Onesimus in chains and if I don't treat him right, Paul is going to know about that. I can't escape it. I can't hide it."* So, Paul made doubly sure. He reminded Philemon that he led him to Christ. Then he reminded him that he thought he would do more than he said.

Let us review what Paul had said. Paul told Philemon that he was coming with Onesimus. He asked Philemon to pray for him. Paul told Philemon that because of his prayers, he was going to be released from prison. He told him he was coming to see Philemon so as to be able to observe what he would do with his slave, Onesimus. Paul did not come out plainly and say these things, but they were clearly implied.

Paul had confidence that he would be released and he was released. Prayer changes things. Prayer released Peter. Remember in of Acts chapter 12? The whole church was praying for Peter's release (verse 12). Peter was knocking on the door. Rhoda went to the door (verse 13). She heard *"Peter's voice"* (verse 14). Rhoda believed him and told the others that Peter was at the door (verse 14). The church doubted Rhoda's testimony (verse 15) until he came into the room. Peter was released by prayer. I am sure that Paul and Silas were released by prayer. They praised God in the prison in the Philippian jail (Acts 16:25). The jail doors were opened and their chaines fell off (verse 26). The Lord answered prayer. *"Prayer changes things,"* as we say.

Paul said that he had confidence that the Lord was going to answer Philemon's prayer and that he was going to be released from prison. He was sure that the Lord was going to use him for some more ministry and service. In the second Roman imprisonment, it was not that way. Paul wrote 2 Timothy from his second Roman imprisonment.

- **2 Timothy 4:7**
  I have fought a good fight, **I have finished my course,** I have kept the faith:

Paul was ready to be offered because he knew that, in this second Roman imprisonment, the Lord's work for him had been *"finished"* upon this earth.

- **2 Timothy 4:6-7**
  For **I am now ready to be offered**, and the time of my departure is at hand. I have fought a good fight, I have finished my course, I have kept the faith:

Paul was a warrior for Christ. Some warriors for Christ never finish the fight. They drop out because of sin, wickedness, or corruption. It is sad to say, but there are some that do that. Paul said he had *"fought a good fight."* He had *"finished his course."* He had *"kept the faith."* He did not swerve. He was just the same when he was in prison as he was out of the prison. He was ready to die. He was just as ready to go Home to be with the Lord as when he was first saved. May we be the same. May we fight the *"good fight"* of faith, lay hold on eternal life, and *"finish our course"* with joy.

Don't Depart From The Faith!

There are many people who, in their old age, depart from the faith. Did you know that? Some, even old preachers, start one way and end up another. That is not the way Paul was. He was an old man at this time-- older than when he started, obviously. He was just as strong. He had the same faith as he had at the start. Paul could say that he was faithful to the finish. He wanted to be released through prayers. God was not finished with him yet.

God could have cut off my life in 1985 and 1986 when I had Hodgkins Disease which is cancer of the lymph glands. It was a serious and deadly malady. My sister-in-law, Audrey June Sanborn, died from that disease in the 1950's when she was 20-years old. My neck was swelling up from the disease. Some of you people who knew me at that time, knew that situation. You remember what I looked like. The Lord intervened and raised me up to health again.

The question is why did the Lord spare my life and restore my health? I believe that the Lord had other work for me to do and other ministries to perform. I take my pledge from that to be faithful. I have stared death in the face. I have been to death and back. Maybe you who have been healthy all your life do not realize what this is like. I have faced the Grim Reaper. Some, perhaps you, have also faced the Grim Reaper and the Lord has also restored your soul and your body.

I have a different attitude toward life that perhaps you who have not faced death do not have. Think about that. Years earlier, I had faced death (or so it seemed). This occurred when a young Marine Lieutenant took me up for a ride in his dive bomber. I was a young Naval Chaplain at the time. The pilot did many of his dive bombing maneuvers, purposely trying to get me sick. He succeeded. I felt like I was going to die anyway. I was so sick that I did not care if I died.

When you face death in a real way, such as when you have cancer, and come back from death, you are a different person. I believe that is why Paul was the good apostle that he was. He was stoned and left for dead at Lystra. I believe he died (Acts 14:19; cf. 2 Corinthians 12:2-4). The Lord raised him up from the dead. He was a missionary for the rest of his life. He was faithful to the end. Paul said prayer was going to be answered for him, and it was true.

Philemon 23

"There salute thee Epaphras, my fellowprisoner in Christ Jesus" Here were some greetings that Paul was giving to Philemon. Perhaps Paul led *"Epaphras,"* his *"fellowprisoner,"* to the Lord Jesus Christ also. He saluted Philemon believer to believer. The name, *"Epaphras,"* means "lovely." He was a *"fellowprisoner"* who was in the Roman prison with Paul.

Philemon 24

"Marcus, Aristarchus, Demas, Lucas, my fellowlabourers" These other four men also greeted Philemon. They were Paul's *"fellowlabourers."* Mark was the one who wrote the gospel of Mark. He was apparently with Paul in Rome, laboring with him. That was good. As you might remember, Mark left Paul on the first Missionary journey (Acts 15:37-38). He was then a disappointment, but now, apparently, he was restored. He got back with the Lord and with Paul.

"Aristarchus" means *"the best ruler."* He was there helping. *"Demas"* was also there. He was now a companion of Paul. 2 Timothy 4:10 mentions that Demas did not stand with Paul. He forsook him. It says that *"Demas hath forsaken me, having loved this present world."* He went back into the world and stopped being Paul's helper. Now *"Demas"* was back with Paul. *"Luke"* is the physician, the author of the gospel of Luke and the author of the book of Acts. He also was greeting Philemon.

Paul had some *"fellowlabourers."* Can you imagine a prisoner having *"fellowlabourers"* working for him? A prisoner usually is working for someone else. He is in chains. Yet Paul had some workers and *"fellowlabourers."* I wonder what their labor was all about. Do you think they were making bread? Do you think they were tidying up the prison? Do you think they were making shoes? What do you think they were doing laboring? Do you think they were out in the fields? Do you think they were picking cotton or something? No! They were laboring for the Lord Jesus Christ. They were soul-winning for Christ. I think that is a labor. The hymn writer has put it this way, *"Let us labor for the Master from the dawn till setting sun. Let us talk of all His wondrous love and care. Then when all of life is over and our work on earth is done, And the roll is called up yonder, I will be there."* That's the labor I believe they were doing. The *"labour of love"* for Christ (1 Thessalonians 1:3).

Philemon 25

"The grace of our Lord Jesus Christ *be* with your spirit. Amen." Paul left this letter to Philemon with the grace of our Lord Jesus Christ. Grace is a wonderful word. It means *"loving kindness, getting something we do not deserve."* God is gracious.

- 2 Corinthians 8:9
   For ye know the grace of our Lord Jesus Christ, that, though he was rich, yet for your sakes he became poor, that ye through his poverty might be rich.

The Lord Jesus Christ can give us something we do not deserve. He is giving us riches in glory. The Greek word for "grace" is CHARIS. It means *"The merciful kindness by which God, exerting his holy influence upon souls, turns them to Christ, keeps, strengthens, increases them in Christian faith, knowledge, affection, and kindles them to the exercise of the Christian virtues."*

Paul wanted God's *"grace"* to be with Philemon's *"spirit."* Perhaps Philemon had a hard spirit. Perhaps he had a mean spirit. Paul prayed that he would have a *"gracious"* spirit. How is our spirit? Is it gracious? Is it mean? Is it ugly? Is it ferocious? I trust that it is *"gracious"* as well.

The Runaway Returned Home

I feel sure this runaway slave, Onesimus, made it back to Philemon safely. Paul could trust him. Could you trust a runaway slave when you released him from Rome to go a thousand miles with hard travel (without an airplane ticket or anything of the kind} and go back to where he was sent?

Very few people could you trust. He was a runaway to start with, and Paul trusted Onesimus. I am sure he got back to Philemon. Paul also trusted Philemon, the slave owner. He trusted him to do what was right. He trusted him to forgive Onesimus of his sin and to welcome him back home with open arms. Paul also trusted that Philemon would put whatever Onesimus owed him on Paul's *"account."* Paul trusted that Philemon would remember that he owed his eternal life to him and that he would receive Onesimus back home just as he would receive Paul himself.

This has been a wonderful book. It has been a small book, a tiny book. This is a book that does not abound too much with doctrine, although doctrine is here. It is a personal letter. It is a letter written by Paul himself. He sent it back to Philemon to Rome by Onesimus the runaway slave. Onesimus could have dropped it. He could have thrown it away. He could have burned it up. He could have forgotten the whole thing, but I am sure that Onesimus delivered it; that Philemon forgave him; and that he sent him back to Paul to help him in Rome.

Index of Words and Phrases

$10,000	103
$100,000	76
1 & 2 Peter	142
1 Chronicles 5:1	26
1 Corinthians	6, 10, 11, 31, 38, 42, 46, 52, 56, 67, 90, 95, 97, 108, 128, 129, 131, 136, 146, 153, 157, 164, 169, 170, 180
1 Corinthians 1:1	146
1 Corinthians 1:30	131
1 Corinthians 10:12	128, 157
1 Corinthians 12:13	67
1 Corinthians 13	108
1 Corinthians 15:19	6
1 Corinthians 15:20	90
1 Corinthians 15:53-54	95
1 Corinthians 15:58	56
1 Corinthians 16:1	169
1 Corinthians 16:19	153, 164
1 Corinthians 16:9	129, 170
1 Corinthians 2:14	42
1 Corinthians 2:8	52
1 Corinthians 3:10	157
1 Corinthians 3:11	38
1 Corinthians 4:14	46
1 Corinthians 4:17	11
1 Corinthians 4:2	10, 136
1 Corinthians 6:19-20	31
1 Corinthians 6:2	169
1 Corinthians 9:17	180
1 John 1:9	69, 70, 108, 184
1 John 2:17	14, 148
1 Peter 1:17	124
1 Peter 1:4	6
1 Peter 2:11	173
1 Peter 2:15	147
1 Peter 3:17	14, 147
1 Peter 3:22	91
1 Peter 4:19	147
1 Peter 4:2	14, 147
1 Peter 4:7	127

1 Peter 4:8 108
1 Peter 5:2 180
1 Peter 5:9 57
1 Thessalonians 1:10 .... 21, 98
1 Thessalonians 2:12 16
1 Thessalonians 3:2 51
1 Thessalonians 4:3 .... 14, 146
1 Thessalonians 5:14 46
1 Thessalonians 5:18 .... 14, 146
1 Thessalonians 5:27 156
1 Timothy 2, 25, 28, 39, 62, 63, 157, 158, 163, 175, 187
1 Timothy 1:12 158
1 Timothy 3:16 .... 25, 28, 62, 63
1 Timothy 4:16 .... 39, 157
1 Timothy 4:8 175
1,000 people 165
1,440 minutes 133
10,080 minutes a week 133
120 disciples assembled 2
17 years of age 17, 118
1929 stock crash 185
1940's, prices cheaper 118
1948, our marriage 116
1965, entered Collingswood 165
1971, Bible For Today began 130
1985, cancer began 189
1986, cancer ended 189
2 Corinthians 7, 13, 21, 22, 27, 34, 44, 49-51, 53, 55, 58, 103, 104, 129,
         138, 139, 142, 144, 146, 156, 158, 169, 172, 185, 190, 191
2 Corinthians 1:1 13
2 Corinthians 1:10 21
2 Corinthians 1:3-4 .... 50, 138, 144
2 Corinthians 11:3 55
2 Corinthians 12:2-4 190
2 Corinthians 13:11 51
2 Corinthians 13:13 169
2 Corinthians 2:12 129
2 Corinthians 3:2 156
2 Corinthians 4:7 53
2 Corinthians 5:17 .... 27, 103, 104, 139, 142
2 Corinthians 5:18 .... 34, 158
2 Corinthians 5:20 172

Index of Words and Phrases

2 Corinthians 5:21 .... 22, 185
2 Corinthians 5:7 58
2 Corinthians 7:6 .... 51, 138, 144
2 Corinthians 8:5 146
2 Corinthians 8:9 .... 44, 191
2 Peter 3:18 .... 5, 40, 177
2 Thessalonians 1:11 159
2 Thessalonians 2:11 103
2 Thessalonians 3:6 61
2 Timothy 2, 11, 18, 21, 39, 150-152, 158, 159, 163, 176, 187, 188, 190
2 Timothy 1:8 163
2 Timothy 2:2 11
2 Timothy 3:11 21
2 Timothy 3:14 39
2 Timothy 3:16 176
2 Timothy 4:10 .... 152, 190
2 Timothy 4:11 .... 152, 176
2 Timothy 4:17 .... 18, 21
2 Timothy 4:17-18 21
2 Timothy 4:5 158
2 Timothy 4:6-7 188
2 Timothy 4:7 .... 151, 188
2,886 Greek words shorter (Westcott-Hort Text) 43
3 John 9 31
3,155 titles, plus, in Bible For Today 159
3,700 people downloaded messages in one month 154
35 to 60 people in a church today 165
356 doctrinal passages in error in false Greek text 43, 149
356 doctrinal passages 44
356 erroneous doctrinal passages 149
36 million 691 thousand and 200 minutes=70 years 133
41 million 932 thousand 800 minutes=80 years 133
5,604 places where Westcott-Hort text departs from T.R. 43
50 miles, Colosse is east of Ephesus 1, 161
524,160 minutes every year 133
600 cows a man had 135
600,000 men, plus women and children came out of Egypt 19
70 years old, most don't want preachers that old 130, 133
700 messages on the Internet as of now 130, 154
85 verses per day, takes you through the Bible in a year 131
856-854-2464, our FAX number i
856-854-4452, our phone number i

900 Park Avenue, our address .... i, 164
A Scarce Commodity 19
About the Author iv
Absalom 176
account, put that on my (Paul to Philemon) 184-186
Acknowledgments .... ii, iv
Acts 1:15-26 2
Acts 13 .... 39, 141
Acts 13:43 39
Acts 14:19 190
Acts 14:22 39
Acts 15:37-38 190
Acts 15:37-40 141
Acts 16:1 2
Acts 16:40 50
Acts 18:11 46
Acts 2 .... 67, 90
Acts 2:32-33 90
Acts 20:24 158
Acts 20:29-30 46
Acts 22:7-8 183
Acts 23:18 .... 162, 174
Acts 23:21 174
Acts 23:6 6
Acts 24:15 7
Acts 25:27 174
Acts 26:10 168
Acts 28:17 .... 162, 174
Acts 28:31 47
Acts 5:29b 114, 117, 120
Acts 5:3 102
Acts 5:31 90
Acts 5:42 46
Acts 7:55-56 90
Acts 7:58 41
Acts 8:30 156
Acts 9:13 168
Acts 9:31 50
adultery 80, 92
afflictions 21, 40, 57, 158, 163
Age of Grace, this present dispensation 73, 74
AGON 49

Index of Words and Phrases

AGONIZOMAI	47, 145
AISCHROLOGIA	101
Aland, Kurt, from Munster, Germany	23, 170
ANAPAUO	187
ANECHOMAI	106
angel	77
angels	25, 26, 61, 72, 76, 78, 91
anger	100, 105, 106, 116, 118, 120, 133, 176, 187
Anna Waite, our granddaughter	41
ANTHROPARESKOS	121
aorist tense, in Greek	73, 102, 115
APALLOTRIOO	35
APEKDUOMAI	72
APHESIS	23, 24
APO	23
APOIKODOMEO	59
APOLUTROSIS	22
apostate	57, 63, 149
apostates	43, 57
apostle	2, 13, 45, 70, 89, 124, 137, 142, 146, 171, 173, 180, 188, 190
Apostle Paul	45, 89, 124, 188
Arabian mare, Babe, the author's horse	120
ARCHE	163
Are You "Faithful"?	11
argue	92
ark	74, 98
Ark of Refuge	98
ARTUO	135
Asia Minor	1, 99, 136, 161
ASV, American Standard Version, 1901	170
ATHUMEO	120
atoms	27
attribute of Deity of Christ	63
attributes of Christ	4, 33, 52, 63, 79, 166
audience	iii
audio	iii, 154
Audrey June Sanborn, author's sister-in-law	189
Australia	178
Author	iv, 2, 91, 141, 190
AXIOS	16
Babe, author's horse	120
Baltimore, Maryland	130

baptism 8, 65-69, 90, 167
Baptist .. ii, iii, 5, 29, 31, 32, 46, 57, 60, 71, 79, 82, 101, 129, 130, 148, 159, 165, 169, 179, 184
Baptized by the Spirit When Saved 67
Barbados 148, 149
Barbara Egan, Bible For Today secretary ii
BARBAROS 105
Barnabas 39, 141-143
Begin Godly Discipline Early 119
believers . 3, 4, 7, 9, 11, 13, 15, 19, 20, 36, 41, 42, 44-46, 53-56, 59-61, 64, 66-70, 73, 76, 79-82, 92, 93, 95, 96, 100, 101, 103, 106, 107, 110, 122, 123, 127, 131, 132, 150, 153, 154, 157, 160, 165, 167-169, 171-173, 183
Bennetts, Dr. David and Pam 178
Beverly Grace Sanborn 147
Beware of These Five Sins! 97
Beware! 60
BFT #2977VC1-2 iii
BFT@BibleForToday.org, our e-mail address i
Bible .. i, 5, 7, 9, 10, 16, 17, 23, 26, 28, 30-32, 42, 43, 46, 53, 55, 57, 59-63, 74, 77, 79-82, 89, 111, 112, 114, 115, 117-120, 122, 126, 129-132, 145, 148, 149, 153, 157, 159, 164, 165, 167, 169, 170, 179, 184
Bible Baptist Institute, where the author teaches each week 60
Bible exposition iii
Bible For Today .... i-iii, 5, 9, 10, 46, 79, 126, 129, 130, 159, 165, 179
Bible For Today Baptist Church ... ii, iii, 5, 46, 79, 129, 130, 159, 165, 179
Bible For Today Press i
Bible Presbyterian Church 165
Bible preservation 30, 149, 164
Bible Version issue 111
BibleForToday.org, our website .... i, iii, 154
bibliology 149
bickering 5, 7
Bill Clinton 123
birthright 26
Bishop B. F. Westcott 29
bishops 180
bite 119
BLASPHEMIA 101
blasphemy 63, 100
BLEPO 60
blessings 25, 32, 66, 155, 165

Index of Words and Phrases

blood ... 14, 21-24, 27, 33, 35-37, 42, 58, 70, 72, 75, 98, 164, 169, 181, 184
Blood of Christ 24, 42, 70, 72, 75, 164, 169, 181, 184
Bob Jones University 148
boil over 19, 106
bondage 21, 24, 73, 182
born-again ... 3, 5, 6, 18, 21, 31, 42, 45, 62, 89, 95, 96, 101, 125, 139, 156, 164, 167
bowels, the inner feelings of compassion 105, 170, 171, 176, 186, 187
BRABEUO 110
broadcast, our radio .... iii, 154, 165, 181
building 30, 32, 59, 65, 148, 164, 165, 179
Calvary 14, 34, 37, 44, 71-73, 78, 81, 126, 127, 137, 148, 175, 179
Calvary Baptist Theological Seminary 148
Cambodia 178
Camping, Harold 8
cancer 189, 190
Catholic 3, 42, 61, 167, 168
CCM, Contemporary Christian Music 113, 130
Cedarville University 85
Cedarville, Ohio 85
Chapter Four .... iv, 125
Chapter One .... iv, 1
Chapter Three .... iv, 89
Chapter Two .... iv, 49
CHARIS 4, 113, 134, 165, 191
Charismatics 67
checking account 185
CHEIROGRAPHON 71
Christ . 2-34, 36-48, 50-56, 58, 60-81, 83-87, 89-99, 101, 103-107, 109-113, 115, 118, 119, 121-129, 131, 132, 136-146, 152, 153, 156, 158, 160, 162-186, 188-191
Christ Could Not Have Sinned 64
Christian Scientists 63
Christians 2, 5-7, 10, 12, 14-17, 19, 20, 24, 35, 39-41, 49, 51, 60, 69, 73, 76, 82-84, 92, 96, 97, 100-103, 105, 107-109, 112, 114, 116, 121, 122, 127, 131, 134, 136, 137, 139, 145, 146, 150, 152, 154, 156, 158, 164, 171-173, 183
Christians Are Not "Make-Overs" 103
church . i-iii, 2, 3, 5, 6, 8-15, 19, 30-32, 38, 41, 42, 46, 49, 50, 54, 56-58, 61, 64, 79, 80, 82, 85, 105, 107, 108, 110, 112, 113, 127, 129, 130, 136, 137, 139-141, 146, 151, 153, 154, 157, 159, 160, 163-165, 167, 169, 178, 179, 188

circumcision 65, 104, 143
Clinton, President Bill 123
coeternal 4
coexistent 4
coffin 22, 135
Collingswood .... i, iii, 5, 139, 164, 165
Collingswood, New Jersey .... i, iii, 164
Colosse ... 1, 3-5, 10, 16, 19, 36, 40, 49, 51, 54, 56, 66, 73, 76, 83, 99, 102, 109, 112, 127, 134, 136, 139, 141, 142, 145, 150, 151, 157, 160-162, 167, 175, 177, 182
Colossians . i, iii, iv, 1-3, 5, 6, 9-13, 15, 17, 20, 22, 24-27, 29, 30, 32, 33, 35, 36, 38-42, 44, 45, 47, 49, 52, 54, 56, 58, 60, 62, 64-66, 69, 70, 72-74, 76, 78, 81, 83, 84, 89, 90, 92, 93, 96, 97, 99, 100, 102-106, 108, 109, 111, 113-115, 117, 118, 120, 122, 123, 125-128, 131, 134, 136, 137, 139-143, 145, 148, 150, 152-154, 156, 157, 159-161, 163, 164, 187
Colossians 1:25 .... 41, 159
Colossians 2:12 .... 66, 89, 90
Colossians 2:19 .... 32, 78
Colossians 2:7 .... 58, 128
Colossians 2:9 .... 33, 62, 126
Colossians 3:1 .... 69, 89, 90
Colossians 3:10 .... 27, 103
Colossians 3:16 .... 47, 111
Colossians 4:12 .... 13, 145
Colossians 4:14 152
Colossians 4:15 .... 153, 164
Colossians 4:2 .... 39, 127
Colossians 4:7 .... 11, 136
comfort 46, 50, 51, 74, 137-139, 143, 144
comforted 49-51, 138, 144, 152
comforters 137, 143
Communist 84, 153
concepts 149
concupiscence 96, 97, 99
confess 24, 44, 69, 70, 108, 170, 184
confidence 47, 52, 121, 175, 187, 188
conflict 49, 115
congregation .... ii, 39, 124
Consider Him 17
copowerful 4
copyright i

Index of Words and Phrases

corrupt versions	61
Cosby, Audrey Dianne	ii
covetousness	96, 97, 99
cows	135
created	16, 25-30, 103, 104, 179 |//

corrupt versions 61
Cosby, Audrey Dianne ii
covetousness 96, 97, 99
cows 135
created 16, 25-30, 103, 104, 179
Created for the Lord Jesus Christ 27
Creator 26-30, 147
Crosby, Fanny Jane, hymn writer 80
cross . . 23, 24, 33-36, 42, 44, 70-73, 78, 81, 87, 91, 134, 137, 160, 174, 175, 179, 184
crown 123
crucifixion 36, 38, 85, 142, 143
Dallas Theological Seminary 157
Damascus 2, 183
Dan Waite 41
Daniel ii
Daniel S. Waite ii
David 132, 176, 179
Dean Burgon Society 169
Declaration of Independence 181
Dedicated Christians Must Grow 40
Defend the True Words of God 111
Deity 4, 28, 33, 52, 62-64
Delilah 55
deliverance 13, 20
Deliverance From the Evil World 13
Demas 152, 190
deny that God even promised to preserve His Hebrew & Greek Words . 148
Detroit Baptist Theological Seminary 148
Deuteronomy 17:18-19 154
devil 21, 55, 72, 73, 102, 164
DIAKONOS 11, 40, 41, 136
Dianne W. Cosby ii
Diotrephes and His Relatives 32
dispensational 74
dispensations 74
dive bomber 189
Divine love 12
Do Not Discourage Your Children 120
Do You Have All of God's Words? 43
doctrinal passages, 356 of them falsified in the Westcott-Hort text . . 44, 149
doctrine . . . 23, 29, 33, 39, 43, 55, 57, 59, 60, 63, 77, 85, 149, 157, 161, 165,

	169, 176, 191
doctrine of the Bible	149
dogs	120
Dollar, Dr. George	60, 148
Don't Put Down Your Associates	136
Dorothy Waite Benedict, the author's sister	135
DOULEIA	121
DOULOS	125, 145, 181
doxology	57
Dr. George Dollar	60, 148
Dr. H. A. Ironside	iii
drug addiction	181
drugs	86, 105, 120, 181
Durham, Dr. Richard	85
Egan, Barbara	ii
Egypt	19
EIRENE	166
EK	30, 164
EKKLESIA	164
elders	81, 172, 180
elect	8, 24, 105, 185
Elijah	19
Elkton, Maryland	130
ELLOGEO	183
EMBATEUO	77
English Bibles	43
entice	55
Epaphras	10-13, 190
Ephesians	1, 11, 13, 16, 18, 27, 28, 32, 47, 51, 66, 68-70, 78, 89, 91, 100, 104, 107, 109, 114, 124, 146, 156, 159, 161-163, 170, 173, 187
Ephesians 1:20	91
Ephesians 1:22	32
Ephesians 1:7	70
Ephesians 2:1	69, 78
Ephesians 2:10	27, 104
Ephesians 2:14	109
Ephesians 2:5	69
Ephesians 2:6	66, 68, 89
Ephesians 3:1	162
Ephesians 3:16	18
Ephesians 3:9	28
Ephesians 4:1	16, 163, 173

Index of Words and Phrases

Ephesians 4:11 47
Ephesians 4:15 32
Ephesians 4:26 100
Ephesians 4:32 107
Ephesians 5:22 114
Ephesians 5:23 32
Ephesians 6:12 27
Ephesians 6:21 11
Ephesians 6:22 51
Ephesians 6:6 .... 13, 146
Ephesians 6:9 124
Ephesus 1, 2, 161, 163
Episcopal Churches 57
EPITHUMIA 96
ERITHIZO 118
eternal Son of God 30
ETHELOTHRESKEIA 84
EUAGGELION 9
EUCHARISTO 165
evangelists 47, 178
Every Attribute of Deity 63
EXAGORAZO 132
EXALEIPHO 70
Exodus 25:2 179
exposition .... ii, iii
expository preaching .... iii, 46, 130, 159
Expository Preaching & No CCM 130
false   7, 8, 23, 25, 26, 28, 34, 43, 54, 55, 60, 61, 63, 67, 77-79, 84, 100, 102-104, 111, 149, 157
false cults 61, 63, 84
false doctrine 55, 60
false gospel 7, 8
false Greek texts 23
false theories 60
Family Radio 8
Fanny Crosby 80
faults 170
fellowship ... 28, 35, 59, 69, 82, 97, 108, 110, 142, 143, 165, 169, 182, 184
females 104
fifty cents, the cost of the author's dog in the 1940's 118
fighting 5, 7, 49
filthy communication 100

finished work	37
firm	59, 60, 66, 148, 164
Five Men Named Jesus	143
football	101
foreign languages	67
Foreword	**iii, iv**
Forgiven All Trespasses	87
forgiving	98, 106, 107, 142, 176, 177
fornication	14, 92, 96, 97, 99, 146
forty men wanted to kill Paul	174
foul language	101
foul mouth	101
fowls	26
fruit-bearers	10
Fulfil Your Ministry	158
Full Knowledge of God's Words	14, 145
Fundamental Baptist Church	165
Fundamentalist	33, 63, 64, 148, 149
Fundamentalist Distortions on Bible Versions	148
Fundamentalist Misinformation on Bible Versions	148
Fundamentalists	33, 43, 52, 63, 64, 148, 149
Fundamentalists and Bible Preservation	149
Galatians	13, 19-21, 42, 66, 99, 109, 159, 169, 182
Galatians 1:4	13, 21
Galatians 2:20	66, 99
Galatians 3:28	182
Galatians 5:22	19, 20, 109, 169
Galatians 5:22-23	20, 169
GARBC, General Association of Regular Baptist Churches	82
Garden of Gethsemane	72, 125, 127
Garden State Fellowship	82
Genesis	14, 15, 17, 42, 55, 65, 112, 119, 131, 156
Genesis 17:11	65
Genesis 22	42
Genesis 3:13	55
Genesis 32:10	15
Genesis through Revelation	14, 17, 112, 119, 131
Gertrude Grace Sanborn	17, 117
Gethsemane	72, 125, 127
Gnostics	23, 26

God . iii, 2-18, 20-22, 24-30, 32-39, 41-55, 57-63, 65, 66, 68-75, 77-83, 85-87, 89-95, 97-101, 103-105, 107-115, 117, 119-126, 128, 130-132,

Index of Words and Phrases

    134, 135, 138-151, 154-160, 163-166, 168-170, 172, 173, 175-180, 184-186, 188, 189, 191
God Equips the Saved Ones 20
God Is Both Wrathful and Loving 99
God Lets No Sin Slide 37
God Promised to Preserve His Words 148
God the Father   4, 24, 25, 29, 33, 34, 44, 52, 62, 63, 69, 72, 91, 92, 166, 179, 184, 185
God the Holy Spirit 4, 12, 21, 24, 25, 29, 52, 53, 62, 166, 168
God the Son 24, 30, 52, 62, 91, 166
God Wants Us Holy 37
Godhead 4, 33, 62-65, 126, 166
God's Book--Read It and Heed It 156
God's Forgiving Grace 142
God's Peace 4, 109, 110, 166
God's Will and God's Words 14
good Samaritan 186
Good, Better, Best, Never Let It Rest 157
gospel ... 7-9, 26, 28, 29, 38, 41, 42, 45, 51, 60, 67, 95, 105, 122, 123, 129, 130, 132, 141, 142, 149, 151, 152, 158, 159, 163, 175, 177, 178, 180, 185, 186, 190
gospel ministry 159
Gospel of John 26, 29
grace . 3, 5, 9, 10, 17, 22, 38-40, 42, 44, 47, 58, 69, 70, 73-75, 80, 83, 95, 98, 100, 111, 113, 117, 131, 134, 140-142, 157, 158, 160, 165, 168, 170, 176, 177, 179, 191
Grace For the Chiefest of Sinners 140
Gracious Yet Seasoned Speech 134
Great White Throne 169
Greek ... iii, 2-4, 11, 12, 16, 18, 19, 22-26, 28, 30, 31, 34, 35, 38, 40-43, 47, 49, 51, 52, 54, 56, 57, 59, 60, 62, 65, 70-73, 75, 77-79, 81, 84, 89, 92, 100-102, 104-106, 108, 110-115, 117, 118, 120, 121, 123-126, 128, 131, 132, 134-137, 145, 148-150, 159, 163-166, 168-172, 176, 181-184, 187, 191
Greek word . 2-4, 11, 16, 18, 19, 22-24, 30, 31, 34, 35, 38, 40-42, 47, 49, 51, 52, 54, 56, 57, 59, 60, 65, 70-72, 75, 77-79, 81, 84, 92, 100-102, 105, 106, 108, 110, 112-115, 117, 118, 120, 121, 123-125, 128, 132, 134-137, 145, 148, 150, 164, 165, 168, 171, 172, 176, 181, 182, 184, 187, 191
Greek Words   iii, 19, 23, 25, 30, 43, 104, 106, 112, 120, 121, 148, 149, 163, 164
Greenville 130, 154

Greenville, South Carolina	130
grounded	38, 57, 58
Guerrants, Pastor and Mrs. Edward	178
Gyppy, the author's dog	118
HAGIOS	42, 168
HAGIOUS	3
HAMARTIAS	170
HAPLOTES	121
Harold Camping	8
Harry Potter	77
Hearts Need Comfort	51
Heaven	6, 7, 21, 26, 29, 30, 32, 36-40, 44, 45, 53, 54, 59, 62, 64, 65, 74, 75, 77, 78, 90-92, 94, 95, 98, 103, 111, 122, 124-126, 140, 167, 169, 179, 180, 183, 184
Heaven and Hell	78
Hebrew Words	43
Hebrew/Aramaic and Greek Words	148, 149
Hebrews 1:3	91
Hebrews 10:12	40, 91
Hebrews 10:36	14, 147
Hebrews 12:2	91
Hebrews 2:14	21, 72
Hebrews 2:14-15	21
Hebrews 2:15	73
Hebrews 5:12	47
Hebrews 8:1	91
Hebrews 9:12	75
Hebrews 9:22b	23, 35
Hell	9, 21, 37, 71, 78, 98, 99, 175, 178
heresy	8, 33, 52, 62-64, 84
Heresy Among Fundamentalists	63
Heresy by Some "Fundamentalists"	33
Heresy on Christ's Omniscience	52
heretical	23, 33, 149
HIEMI	23
High School senior	101
HIPPOS	163
HISTEMI	148
History of Fundamentalism in America	60
Hodgkins disease, cancer of the lymph glands	189
Holding Fast	78, 79
holiness	64

Index of Words and Phrases

holy .. 2, 4, 12, 17, 18, 20, 21, 24-26, 28, 29, 31, 36, 37, 44, 46, 50, 52, 53, 62, 66-68, 72-75, 77, 79, 89, 90, 92, 102, 103, 105, 109, 110, 117, 126, 134, 139, 146, 156, 165, 166, 168-170, 172, 191
Holy of Holies 28
Holy Place 28, 75
Holy Spirit 2, 4, 12, 18, 20, 21, 24, 25, 29, 31, 44, 50, 52, 53, 62, 66-68, 79, 89, 92, 103, 109, 110, 126, 134, 139, 166, 168-170
Home . 32, 41, 44, 45, 63, 65, 77, 91, 95, 111, 119, 122, 149, 159, 169, 176-178, 180, 182, 183, 189, 191
home schoolers 41
HOMOLOGEO 184
homosexuality 92
Hope Beyond the Grave 6
horse, author's horse, Babe 120, 163
Hort, Fenton John Anthony, an apostate 23, 26, 29, 149, 170
house . 19, 32, 41, 45, 46, 50, 55, 56, 59, 116-118, 131, 150, 153, 154, 159, 163-165, 171, 180, 182, 185
House Churches in the Bible 153
husbands 52, 90, 114-116, 122
HYMNOS 112
hymns 28, 47, 111-113, 130
HYPAKOUO 117
HYPOTASSO 114
I.O.U. 71
ideas 149
idolatry 97
impeccability of Christ 63
Importance of Qualitative "Increase" 80
Imprisoned, Yet Still Preaching 129
imprisonment 2, 24, 136, 140, 152, 160, 163, 174, 187, 188
Index of Words and Phrases .... iv, 193
indicative mood in Greek 89
Internet 9, 38, 39, 130, 154
Iraq 53
Ironside, Dr. H. A. iii
Isaiah 34:16 155
Isaiah 43:25 71
Isaiah 44:22 71
Isaiah 53:6 .... 184, 185
Italy 1, 161
jail 123, 127, 134, 142, 163, 188
James 1:19 134

James 3:8 134
James 4:11 134
James 4:14 133
James 5:16 170
Jerusalem 2, 3, 53, 81, 141, 158, 162, 168, 174, 176
Jesus Christ . 2-9, 11-13, 15, 16, 19-34, 36-41, 43, 44, 46, 47, 50, 52-54, 58, 60-65, 68, 70-75, 77-81, 83, 85-87, 89-95, 98, 99, 103-105, 107, 109, 110, 113, 115, 118, 119, 121-123, 125-127, 129, 131, 136-138, 140, 142, 144, 146, 152, 156, 158, 160, 162-166, 168-172, 174, 176-185, 190, 191
Jesus Holds the World Together 30
Jewess 2
Jews 30, 39, 44, 63, 67, 82, 110, 112, 120, 143, 162, 174
Job 7, 18, 34, 71, 92, 108, 116, 132, 137, 143, 158
Job 14:1-2 132
Job 16:2 .... 137, 143
Job 19:25 7
Job 19:26 7
Job 23:10 132
Job 7:6 132
Job 8:9 132
John 1:1 .... 26, 29
John 1:10 28
John 1:12-13 58
John 1:15 29
John 1:17 75
John 1:1-2 29
John 1:29 185
John 1:3 28
John 1:4 94
John 1:48 52
John 10:10 94
John 10:27-30 .... 66, 83
John 10:28 94
John 11:25 94
John 14:2 .... 45, 65, 126
John 14:23 44
John 14:6 95
John 15:5 10
John 15:9 39
John 2:24-25 52
John 21:3b 38

Index of Words and Phrases

John 3:16	8, 22, 94
John 3:30	31
John 3:36	94, 97
John 4:18	52
John 5:26	94
John 5:40	94
John 6:33	94
John 6:35	94
John 6:47-48	94
John 8:31	39
John 8:44	102
john 8:56-58	30
jokes	45
Joshua 8:34	155
Judas Iscariot	2
Judges 14:15	55
judgment	10, 65, 98, 99, 123, 124, 167, 169
justification	37, 109, 111
KAKIA	100
KALEO	30, 164
Kenderdines, John and his family, our missionaries	178
King David	176
King James Bible	i, 3, 42, 43, 62, 77, 80, 111, 114, 119, 130, 131, 145, 159, 169, 170
Kingdom	16, 20-22, 39, 47, 74, 143, 154, 158
Kingdom Age	74
KJB, King James Bible	28
Knit Together	32, 49, 51, 78, 79
KOINONOS	182
KOPIAO	47
KRATEO	79
KURIOS	123, 125
Lamb	16, 37, 71, 87, 98, 185
LAMBANO	176, 182
languages	8, 67
Laodicea	49, 150, 153, 156, 164
Law of Moses	73-75, 81
lesbian	104
Leviticus	23, 24, 135
Leviticus 16:10	23
Leviticus 16:21-22	24
Leviticus 2:13	135

liberal	6, 28
lie	92, 102, 103, 135
London	178
longsuffering	17-19, 109
Lord Jesus Christ	2-9, 11-13, 15, 16, 19-34, 36-41, 43, 44, 47, 50, 52-54, 58, 60-65, 70-75, 77-79, 81, 83, 85-87, 89-95, 98, 99, 103-105, 107, 109, 110, 113, 115, 118, 119, 121-123, 125-127, 129, 131, 136-138, 140, 142, 144, 152, 156, 160, 162-166, 168-170, 174, 176-185, 190, 191
lordship	9, 123
lordship salvation	9
Lord's Day	110
love	5, 6, 8, 12, 14, 32, 39, 45, 49, 51, 61, 63, 79, 83, 84, 87, 97, 98, 105, 108-110, 115, 116, 118, 136, 167, 170, 171, 173, 176, 177, 179, 187, 190
Loving Even Though Unlovely	116
Luke	2, 10, 22, 46, 72, 107, 125, 129, 152, 158, 174, 176, 179, 186, 190
Luke 10:35	186
Luke 11:1	46
Luke 11:24-26	22
Luke 16:10	10
Luke 17:3-4	107
Luke 22:42	72, 174, 179
Luke 24:49	2
Luke 9:62	158
lymph glands, cancer of	189
Lystra	2, 21, 190
magnet	93, 96
mainline	57
MAKROS	19, 106
MAKROTHUMIA	18, 19, 106
males	65, 104
malice	100
mare	120
Marine Lieutenant, pilot	189
Mark	13, 52, 81, 98, 141-143, 145, 152, 153, 172, 176, 190
Mark 3:35	13, 145
Mark 7:13	81
Mark 7:32	172
Mark 7:9	81
Mark 9:33-34	52
marriage	80, 96, 115, 116

Index of Words and Phrases

Masoretic Hebrew text 111, 145, 148
Master . 11, 20, 40, 41, 79, 105, 121, 123-126, 136, 137, 163, 180, 183, 185, 190
Master Card 185
Matthew 11:28 98
Matthew 15:1-3 81
Matthew 18:21 107
Matthew 19:4 155
Matthew 21:16 155
Matthew 21:42 155
Matthew 25:21 10
Matthew 26:40-41 127
Matthew 28:19 .... 46, 67
Matthew 5:17 159
Matthew 6:19-21 53
Mediterranean Sea 1, 161
message .... iii, 8, 10, 42, 149, 157, 178, 185
Messiah 174
Methodist 57
MICTV 149
military term 114
ministry 9, 34, 39, 50, 79, 126, 129, 130, 140, 148, 152, 154, 157-160, 162, 165, 176, 181, 186, 188
MISHNA 82
missionaries 2, 9, 31, 85, 141, 178
Modernist and Liberal Denials 28
modernistic 6, 57, 149
Modernists 28, 63, 97, 166
Molenkott, Virginia Ramey, a loud lesbian 104
Mom, author's mother 118, 119, 135
monks 85
Moormans, Dr. and Mrs. Jack, missionaries in London, England 178
Mosaic Law 61, 73-75
Moses 19, 73-75, 81
Mount Calvary 179
Mount of Transfiguration 19
music 80, 113, 165
Muslims 63, 69
mystery 25, 28, 42, 44, 49, 52, 128, 129
narcotics 92
NASV, New American Standard Version 25, 149, 170
negative commands 73, 115

Negative Commands in Greek 73
Nehemiah 8:18 155
Nehemiah 8:8 155
Nehemiah 9:3 155
Nestle=Aland Greek Text 23, 170
New American Standard (NASV) 23, 25, 28, 43, 149
New Century Version 170
New International Version (NIV) 23, 25, 28, 43, 55, 149
New Revised Standard Version (NRSV) 23, 25, 43
New Testament ... 10, 15, 19, 20, 26, 31, 43, 44, 46, 65, 67, 108, 111, 142, 143, 145, 148, 153, 156, 164, 172
NIV, New International Version 25, 149, 170
No Choice in the Rapture 95
Noah Amatucci 17
Northern Baptist Convention 57
Not Menpleasing Servants 121
NOUS 112
NOUTHETEO 112
NRSV, New Revised Standard Version 25, 170
Numbers 20:12 19
Numbers Mania 80
Obedience by Children 117
Obedience From the Heart 122
obedient 42, 117, 118, 122
obscene 101
October of 1998 .... 129, 159, 165
OIKONOMIA 41
Old Testament . 7, 15, 25, 35, 42-44, 51, 55, 65, 74, 111, 112, 120, 135, 148, 155, 179
omnipotence 33, 63
omnipresence 33, 63
omniscience 33, 52, 63
Onesimus 128, 139, 140, 161, 162, 171-178, 180-188, 191, 192
Only Two Positive Commandments 82
ONOMA 104
order ... iv, 32, 41, 44, 56, 58, 63, 71, 85, 93, 112, 120, 126, 130, 135, 138, 157, 159, 160, 169, 171, 178, 180, 182
Order Blank Pages iv
orderly 56
ordinances 31, 70, 81
ORGE 100
other verses .... iii, 108

Index of Words and Phrases

Our Constant Master	126
Our Worthy Saviour	16
pain	17, 85, 100, 105, 145, 147, 167, 174, 177
Papua New Guinea, where the Guerrant's minister	178
PARAKALEO	172
PAREGORIA	145
partner	182
Pastor D. A. Waite	i, iii
pastoral letters	187
pastors	47, 130, 157, 180, 186
PATHOS	96

Paul . iii, 1-3, 5-7, 10, 12-21, 25, 31, 35, 38-42, 44-47, 49, 51, 54-56, 58-61, 65, 66, 73, 74, 76, 78, 82, 84, 89, 92, 95, 97, 100-102, 109, 115, 118, 120, 124, 125, 127-129, 131, 134, 136-146, 150, 152-154, 156-178, 180-183, 185-192

Paul Wanted to Obey Completely	42
peace	3, 4, 33, 34, 51, 86, 109, 110, 165, 166, 168
peace with God	4, 33, 109
Pennsylvania	41, 130
Pensacola	101
Pentecost	2, 67
Pentecostals	67
perfect Deity	62-64
perfect human body	36, 44, 62, 63
perfect human nature	44
persecution	69, 153, 157

Peter . 2, 5, 6, 14, 27, 38, 40, 57, 91, 102, 107, 108, 124, 127, 140, 142, 147, 153, 159, 173, 177, 180, 184, 188

Pharisees	6, 7, 30, 81, 94, 155
Philadelphia	60, 150

Philemon . i, iii, iv, 1, 135, 139, 140, 152, 153, 159, 161-167, 169-173, 175-178, 180-183, 185-188, 190-192

Philemon 1	153, 162, 163
Philemon 1:2	153
Philemon 2	163, 164
Philemon 9	163, 171
Philippians	1, 4, 7, 18, 42, 44, 45, 65, 72, 110, 128, 151, 159, 161, 163, 187
Philippians 1:21	65
Philippians 1:23	7, 45
Philippians 2:8	72
Philippians 3:6	151
Philippians 4:13	18

Philippians 4:6 .... 4, 128
Philippians 4:7 110
Philippines 85
Philistines 55
philosophy 60, 61
PHUSIOO 78
physician 152, 190
piano 112
PISTIS 38
pitching-fits 119
planets 26
PLEONEXIA 97
PLEROO 65
plough 158
plow 158
POIEO 104
Pope 61
PORNEIA 96
power ... 2, 16-22, 24, 28, 29, 48, 53, 54, 58, 63, 65, 70, 72, 73, 90, 91, 93,
            109, 110, 123, 125, 133, 139, 159, 163, 170
prayer 4, 5, 14-16, 39, 49, 51, 127, 128, 166, 170, 179, 188, 190
praying 5, 6, 12, 15, 31, 46, 56, 128, 145, 160, 178, 188
preachers 6, 41, 46, 64, 124, 136, 149, 150, 178, 180, 189
preaching .... i, iii, 18, 21, 31, 40, 45-47, 129, 130, 140, 141, 150, 159, 163,
                178
preaching verse by verse 140
Presbyterians 65
present .. 12, 13, 21, 36, 38, 45, 52, 69, 73, 76, 92, 102, 110, 111, 114, 115,
            117, 118, 120, 121, 126, 147, 148, 152, 154, 172, 190
present tense in Greek 12, 73, 76, 102, 110, 114, 115, 117, 120, 126
preservation 30, 149, 164
preserved 43, 111, 148, 149
President Bill Clinton 123
President Bush 156
prison ... iii, 1, 5, 10, 40-42, 50, 56, 95, 109, 129, 131, 136, 140, 141, 143,
            152, 160-163, 167, 168, 173, 174, 177, 178, 183, 187-190
prison epistles 1, 161
prisoner 16, 41, 49, 140, 160-163, 171-173, 182, 190
prohibition 73, 76, 102, 118, 181
promised 19, 44, 83, 126, 148, 149
promises 14, 148, 170
PROS 176, 182

Index of Words and Phrases

PROSLAMBANO	176, 182
PROSOPOLEPSIA	124
PROTEUO	31
PROTO	25
PROTOTOKOS	25
Proverbs 10:12	108
Proverbs 24:23	123
Proverbs 25:19	121
Proverbs 28:21	124
Proverbs 31:13	180
Proverbs 4:23	122
Psalm 100:4	128
Psalm 103:12	72
Psalm 119:105	77
Psalm 119:50	138, 144
Psalm 22	42
Psalm 23:4	138, 144
Psalm 31:15	45, 132
Psalm 51:1	71
Psalm 51:9	71
Psalm 90:12	133
Psalm 94:19	138, 144
PSALMOS	112
Psalms	47, 96, 111-113
PSEUDOMAI	102
PSEUDOS	102
publisher's data	iv
pulpit committee	57
radio	iii, 8, 9, 38, 39, 130, 154
rank	56, 171, 180
ransom	22-24
Reckoning Ourselves Dead	68, 93
redeemed	5, 15, 22, 23, 37, 70, 71, 86, 100, 113, 139, 140, 180, 181
redemption	22-24, 70, 75, 131, 134, 169
Redemption and Forgiveness	23
refresh	171, 186, 187
Release from Bondage	24
resurrection	6, 7, 38, 40, 44, 68, 73, 91, 94, 109, 174
Reuben	26
Revelation	14, 16, 17, 29, 43, 74, 75, 78, 98, 99, 112, 119, 129, 131, 156, 169
Revelation 10:6	29

Revelation 11:1 74
Revelation 19:15 99
Revelation 20:11 169
Revelation 3:4 16
Revelation 3:8 129
Revelation 4:11 .... 16, 29
Revelation 5:12 16
Revelation 6:16-17 98
Revised Standard Version (RSV) 23, 25, 28, 43
Rhoda 188
right . 12, 28, 33, 40, 49, 56, 57, 69, 74, 81, 84, 86, 89-91, 97, 102, 107, 109, 112, 113, 115, 118, 119, 121-123, 126, 131, 139, 142, 143, 145, 151, 153, 166, 170, 171, 180, 186-188, 191
righteous 30, 37, 100, 170
righteousness 16, 22, 63, 123, 131, 151, 176, 185
rock music 80, 113
Roman Catholic 3, 42, 61, 167, 168
Roman Catholic Church 3, 42, 61, 167
Roman Catholics 43, 170
Roman imprisonment 2, 136, 140, 152, 160, 163, 187, 188
Roman prison 42, 56, 173, 174, 190
Romanism 170
Romans .. 3, 4, 13, 33-35, 50, 68, 70, 72, 74, 85, 86, 89-91, 93, 95, 98, 109, 124, 129, 138, 144, 146, 150, 153, 159, 162, 164, 168, 169, 172
Romans 1:12 50
Romans 1:7 168
Romans 10:2 150
Romans 12:1 172
Romans 12:13 169
Romans 12:2 .... 13, 146
Romans 15:13 109
Romans 15:31 3
Romans 15:32 13
Romans 15:4 .... 50, 74, 138, 144
Romans 16:15 3
Romans 16:2 3
Romans 16:5 .... 153, 164
Romans 4:7 70
Romans 5:1 .... 4, 33, 109
Romans 5:10 34
Romans 5:9 98
Romans 6:11 93

Index of Words and Phrases

Romans 6:2 93
Romans 6:23 95
Romans 6:3-4 68
Romans 6:6 68
Romans 6:8 .... 89, 93
Romans 8:27 .... 13, 168
Romans 8:34 .... 90, 91
Romans 8:8-9 86
Rome . 1, 10, 49, 85, 129, 136, 141, 142, 152, 161-163, 167, 168, 171, 172,
174, 175, 177, 187, 190-192
Rome, Italy 1, 161
Rome's False Authorities 61
rooted 59, 66, 128
roots 58
Rose Durham 85, 116
RSV, Revised Standard Version 25, 170
runaway 139, 140, 173, 177, 191
Sadducees 6, 7, 155, 174
Saint Christopher 3
Saint Nicholas 3
saints 3, 5, 6, 12, 13, 20, 42-44, 80, 167-171, 183
salt lick 135
Samaritan 111, 186
Samson 55
Sanborn, various family members .... ii, 17, 117, 189
Satan 27, 41, 70, 72, 73, 77, 98, 102
Satan's power 20, 73
Saul 41
saved   iii, 2, 3, 5-11, 15, 20-22, 24, 31, 34, 36, 38, 44, 45, 53, 57, 58, 62, 64-
67, 69, 72, 73, 75, 79, 81, 83, 85, 86, 89, 92, 93, 95, 98, 99, 101,
103-106, 108-113, 118, 119, 121-127, 135, 137, 139-141, 143, 144,
146, 150, 164, 165, 167-169, 172, 174-178, 180, 181, 183-185,
189
Saviour .. 5, 7, 8, 16, 23, 26, 29, 31-33, 36-38, 40, 44, 45, 50, 58, 60, 62, 65,
70, 74, 78, 80, 85, 90, 95, 97, 98, 100, 105, 110, 122, 131, 140,
164, 167, 169, 174, 175, 177, 179, 180, 183
Scripture iii, 11, 15, 26, 28, 29, 38, 74, 77, 82, 112, 114, 117, 145, 166, 173,
175, 176, 187
Scriptures ... 11, 15, 33, 50, 68, 74, 111, 112, 115, 120, 131, 135, 138, 144,
150, 154, 155, 159, 167
sea 1, 26, 29, 136, 161
second Roman imprisonment 152, 163, 187, 188

senior 90, 101
separatist 43
sermons .... ii, iii, 130, 154
servant 10, 13, 15, 40, 121, 136, 137, 140, 145, 153, 175, 181, 182
servants 2, 11, 13, 18, 40, 121, 122, 125, 143, 146, 179
Servants and Slaves 125
service . 3, 8, 10, 80, 122, 123, 126, 136, 145, 153, 155, 158, 162, 172, 178, 179, 181, 188
Set Your Affections Above 92
sexual 14, 96
sexual relations 14, 96
shadow 45, 74, 75, 132, 138, 144
SHALOM 4, 166
Shekinah 75
Silas 141, 142, 188
sin ... 8, 9, 14, 22, 26, 34, 37, 45, 55, 64, 68, 70, 71, 78, 93, 95-97, 99-101, 103, 107, 140, 146, 177, 178, 181, 184, 185, 189, 191
Sinai 23
sinlessness 63, 64
SKIA 75
slave   60, 61, 68, 105, 120, 139, 140, 161, 162, 173, 175-178, 180-182, 188, 191
slave owner 139, 161, 181, 191
slavery 61, 105, 120, 181
slaves 35, 72, 105, 120, 125, 161, 173, 181
Smith, Dr. Edward ii
smoke 133
Son of God 28, 30, 99, 144
Southern Baptist Churches 57
Spirit .. 2, 4, 12, 13, 18, 20-22, 24, 25, 29, 31, 42, 44, 45, 50, 52, 53, 56, 62, 63, 66-68, 79, 86, 89, 92, 103, 107, 109, 110, 119, 120, 125-127, 134, 139, 150, 155, 166, 168-170, 177, 191
Spirit of God .. 12, 18, 20, 21, 42, 50, 66, 86, 103, 107, 109, 125, 126, 134, 139, 169, 170
spiritualists 77
stars 7, 26, 93
Stay on Track for the Lord 153
steal 53, 92, 94, 97, 114
steel 53, 96
Stephen 41, 91
stewards 10, 136
stewardship 10

Index of Words and Phrases

STOICHEION	81
stoned	41, 190
stop	22, 39, 73, 76, 77, 99, 102, 108, 115, 116, 118, 148, 150, 163, 174
Stop Letting People "Beguile" You	77
Stop Walking in These Sins!	99
Submission	114
submit	114, 115, 117
suffering	40, 42, 85, 147, 167, 174
Suffering and the Will of God	147
SUMBIBAZO	51, 79
sun	2, 12, 100, 183, 190
SUNDESMOS	108
SUNDOULOS	137
SUNISTAO	30
Supreme Court	124
swear	101
tabernacle	10, 74, 75, 179
Table of Contents	iv
Take Your Ministry Seriously	159
Tamie Waite, the author's daughter-in-law	41
TAPEINOPHROSUNE	84
Tarot Cards	76
TAXIS	56
tea leaf readers	77
technique	43
TELEIOTES	108
Ten Commandments	82
tenderness	14
Textus Receptus	28, 43, 111, 145, 148
thanks	5, 14, 20, 113, 146, 166
thanksgiving	4, 5, 39, 60, 110, 127, 128, 166
Thanksgiving Needed	127
The Art of Comfort	138
The Believers' Position in Christ	69, 89
The Believer's Treasure	53
The Dangers of Philosophy	61
The Error of "Oneness" Teaching	62
The Essence of a Local Church	30, 31
The Five Crowns For Believers	123
The Gospel Is Good News	9
The Greek Meaning of "Lie"	102
The History of the "Cross"	35, 72

The House of Bitterness 116
The Lord Jesus Was not Created 25
The Lord Jesus' Treasures 53
The Love that Bonds 109
The Meaning of Longsuffering 18
The Meaning of Patience 18
The Meaning of "Beguile" 54
The Meaning of "Build Up" 59
The Meaning of "Stedfast" 57
The Ministry of Comfort 50
The Need for Strong Standards 41
The Need to Comfort 139
The Only Antidote for Sins 36
The Suffering Saviour 85
The Three Major Bible Dispensations 74
The Trinity 24, 52, 62, 92
The Warmth of Love 12
The Will of God From the Heart 13, 146
The "Fruit" of Paul's Labor 10
The "Handwriting of Ordinances" 71
The "Hyper-Calvinist" Heresy 8
The "Shadow of Death" 144
Theological Heresies of Westcott and Hort 29
theology 43, 61
thieves 53, 186
thoughts 9, 54, 60, 61, 70, 138, 144, 149, 184
Thought-Life Dangers 35
Three Bible "Heavens" 7
THUMOS 19, 100, 106, 120
TIKTO 25
Timotheus 2, 11, 51
Timothy .. 2, 11, 13, 18, 21, 25, 28, 39, 62, 63, 150-152, 157-159, 162, 163, 175, 176, 187, 188, 190
TITHEMI 112
Titus 7, 51, 134, 138, 144, 152, 163, 176, 187
Titus 2:13 7
Titus 2:8 134
Titus 3:8 176
TOKOS 25
tongues 67, 103, 131
transcription iii
translated 19, 20, 22, 24, 25, 30, 47, 54, 79, 172, 183, 187

Index of Words and Phrases

translators	43
Trinity	24, 52, 62, 92
Turkey	1, 99, 136, 161
TV	76, 77, 101, 103
two ordinances	31
Two Primary Baptisms	67
U. S. Constitution	181
UBS, United Bible Societies	170
uncleanness	96, 97, 99
under-shepherd	31, 79
Unforgiving Members Frost a Church	107
Unitarians	63, 166
United Bible Society	23
United Methodist Church	57
United States	45, 46, 85
unsaved	17, 35, 42, 66, 97, 104, 118, 139
unworthily	15
vapour	133
Vatican	23
verses	ii, iii, 15, 20, 27, 49, 81, 90, 93, 108, 112, 129, 131, 143
versions	25, 26, 43, 55, 61, 80, 114, 148, 149, 164, 168, 170
video	iii, 17, 154
video cassettes	154
Virginia	104
Virginia Molenkott, a loud lesbian	104
Visa	185
voice	16, 66, 83, 113, 149, 168
Waite, various family members	i-iii
warnings	46, 60
warrior	151, 189
WD-40	108
We Must Be "Stablished"	66
We Must Continue in the Faith	38
We Need God's Working Power	48
weak	17, 19, 46, 55, 59, 117, 127
Weak as Water, or Strong?	59
website	i, iii
Westcott and Hort, two apostates	23, 26, 29, 149, 170
What Baptism Pictures	68
What Is Confession?	70
What Is the Number of Your Days?	133
What Is "Completeness"	65

willingly 178-180
wind 12
wisdom 12, 15, 16, 45, 47, 52-54, 61, 84, 111, 112, 131, 133, 135
Wisdom Found in the Right Bible 131
wishy-washy 60, 66
witch 76
wives 90, 114-116, 118, 122
wizards 77
woman-preacher 154
Word of God ... 15-17, 41, 42, 46, 57, 61, 75, 77, 79, 81, 82, 110, 112-114, 120, 131, 138, 140, 151, 154, 155, 159, 186
Words . iii, iv, 2, 7, 14, 15, 19, 23, 25, 27, 30, 32, 37, 43, 44, 46, 54, 55, 58, 59, 62, 70, 73, 76-78, 82, 83, 101, 102, 104, 106, 107, 111-115, 120, 121, 130, 145, 148, 149, 154-156, 160, 163, 164, 168, 173, 178, 184, 186, 193
Words of God .... iii, 58, 59, 78, 111, 112, 130, 164
works .. 7-9, 20, 27, 35, 48, 50, 58, 64, 85, 92, 103, 129, 167, 169, 170, 176, 180
worthy 15-17, 29, 124, 159, 163, 173
wrath 21, 94, 97-100, 116, 133, 134
www.BibleForToday.org, our Bible For Today website .... i, iii, 154

Yvonne Sanborn Waite, the author's wife ii
zeal 47, 61, 132, 145, 150, 151
ZELOS 150
"ENTICING WORDS" 54, 55
"Faithful to the Fight" 151
"jelly on the wall" 148
"Just For Women" 130
"no posse pecare" 64
"Puffed Up" 78
"Voluntary Humility" 76
"Will Worship" 84

About the Author

The author of this book, Dr. D. A. Waite, received a B.A. (Bachelor of Arts) in classical Greek and Latin from the University of Michigan in 1948, a Th.M. (Master of Theology), with high honors, in New Testament Greek Literature and Exegesis from Dallas Theological Seminary in 1952, an M.A. (Master of Arts) in Speech from Southern Methodist University in 1953, a Th.D. (Doctor of Theology), with honors, in Bible Exposition from Dallas Theological Seminary in 1955, and a Ph.D. in Speech from Purdue University in 1961. He holds both New Jersey and Pennsylvania teacher certificates in Greek and Language Arts.

He has been a teacher in the areas of Greek, Hebrew, Bible, Speech, and English for over fifty-two years in ten schools, including one junior high, one senior high, three Bible institutes, two colleges, two universities, and one seminary. He served his country as a Navy Chaplain for five years on active duty; pastored three churches; was Chairman and Director of the Radio and Audio-Film Commission of the American Council of Christian Churches; since 1971, has been Founder, President, and Director of THE BIBLE FOR TODAY; since 1978, has been President of the DEAN BURGON SOCIETY; has produced over 700 other studies, books, cassettes, or VCR's on various topics; and is heard on both a five-minute daily and thirty-minute weekly radio program IN DEFENSE OF TRADITIONAL BIBLE TEXTS, presently on 25 stations. Dr. and Mrs. Waite have been married since 1948; they have four sons, one daughter, and, at present, eight grandchildren. Since October 4, 1998, he founded and has been the Pastor of the 𝕭𝖎𝖇𝖑𝖊 𝕱𝖔𝖗 𝕿𝖔𝖉𝖆𝖞 𝕭𝖆𝖕𝖙𝖎𝖘𝖙 𝕮𝖍𝖚𝖗𝖈𝖍 in Collingswood, New Jersey. His sermons are heard both on radio and the Internet over "www.BibleForToday.org/audio_sermons.htm"

Order Blank (p. 1)

Name:_____

Address:_____

City & State:_____Zip:_____

Credit Card #:_____Expires:_____

[ ] Send *Colossians & Philemon--Preaching Verse by Verse* by Pastor D. A. Waite ($12+$5 S&H) hardback, 240 pages.
[ ] Send *Philippians--Preaching Verse by Verse* by Pastor D. A. Waite ($10+$5 S&H) hardback, 176 pages.
[ ] Send *Making Marriage Melodious* by Pastor D. A. Waite ($7+$3 S&H), perfect bound, 112 pages.
[ ] Send *Ephesians--Preaching Verse by Verse* by Pastor D. A. Waite ($12+$5 S&H) hardback, 224 pages.
[ ] Send *Galatians--Preaching Verse By Verse* by Pastor D. A. Waite ($12+$5 S&H) hardback, 216 pages.
[ ] Send *First Peter--Preaching Verse By Verse* by Pastor D. A. Waite ($10+$5 S&H) hardback, 176 pages.
[ ] Send *Fundamentalist MIS-INFORMATION on Bible Versions* by Dr. Waite ($7+$3 S&H) perfect bound, 136 pages
[ ] Send *Holes in the Holman Christian Standard Bible* by Dr. Waite ($3+$2 S&H) A printed booklet, 40 pages
[ ] Send *Central Seminary Refuted on Bible Versions* by Dr. Waite ($10+$3 S&H) A perfect bound book, 184 pages
[ ] Send *Fundamentalist Distortions on Bible Versions* by Dr. Waite ($6+$3 S&H) A perfect bound book, 80 pages
[ ] Send *Burgon's Warnings on Revision* by DAW ($7+$3 S&H) A perfect bound book, 120 pages in length.
[ ] Send *The Case for the King James Bible* by DAW ($7+$3 S&H) A perfect bound book, 112 pages in length.
[ ] Send *Foes of the King James Bible Refuted* by DAW ($10+$4 S&H) A perfect bound book, 164 pages in length.
[ ] Send *The Revision Revised* by Dean Burgon ($25 + $4 S&H) A hardback book, 640 pages in length.

Send or Call Orders to:
THE BIBLE FOR TODAY
900 Park Ave., Collingswood, NJ 08108
Phone: 856-854-4452; FAX:--2464; Orders: 1-800 JOHN 10:9

Order Blank (p. 2)

Name:_____

Address:_____

City & State:_____Zip:_____

Credit Card #:_____Expires:_____

Other Materials on the KJB & T.R.

[ ] Send *The Last 12 Verses of Mark* by Dean Burgon ($15+$4 S&H) A hardback book 400 pages.
[ ] Send *The Traditional Text* hardback by Burgon ($16 + $4 S&H) A hardback book, 384 pages in length.
[ ] Send *Summary of Traditional Text* by Dr. Waite ($3 +$2)
[ ] Send *Summary of Causes of Corruption*, DAW ($3+$2)
[ ] Send *Causes of Corruption* by Burgon ($15 + $4 S&H) A hardback book, 360 pages in length.
[ ] Send *Inspiration and Interpretation*, Dean Burgon ($25+$4 S&H) A hardback book, 610 pages in length.
[ ] Send *Summary of Inspiration* by Dr. Waite ($3 + $2 S&H)
[ ] Send *Contemporary Eng. Version Exposed*, DAW ($3+$2)
[ ] Send *Westcott & Hort's Greek Text & Theory Refuted by Burgon's Revision Revised--Summarized* by Dr. D. A. Waite ($7.00 + $3 S&H), 120 pages, perfect bound.
[ ] Send *Defending the King James Bible* by Dr.Waite $13+$4 S&H) A hardback book, indexed with study questions.
[ ] Send *Guide to Textual Criticism* by Edward Miller ($7 +$4)
[ ] Send *Westcott's Denial of Resurrection*, Dr. Waite ($4+$3)
[ ] Send *Four Reasons for Defending KJB* by DAW ($3+$3)
[ ] Send *Vindicating Mark 16:9-20* by Dr. Waite ($3+$3 S&H)
[ ] Send *Dean Burgon's Confidence in KJB* by DAW ($3+$3)
[ ] Send *Readability of A.V. (KJB)* by D. A. Waite, Jr. ($6 +$3)
[ ] Send *NIV Inclusive Language Exposed* by DAW ($5+$3)
[ ] Send *26 Hours of KJB Seminar* (4 videos) by DAW ($50.00)

Send or Call Orders to:
THE BIBLE FOR TODAY
900 Park Ave., Collingswood, NJ 08108
Phone: 856-854-4452; FAX:--2464; Orders: 1-800 JOHN 10:9
E-Mail Orders: BFT@BibleForToday.org; Credit Cards OK

Order Blank (p. 3)

Name:_____

Address:_____

City & State:_____Zip:_____

Credit Card#:_____Expires:_____

More Materials on the KJB & T.R.

[ ] Send *Defined King James Bible* lg.prt. leather ($40+$6)
[ ] Send *Defined King James Bible* med.prt. leather ($35+$5)
[ ] Send *Heresies of Westcott & Hort* by Dr. Waite ($7+$3)
[ ] Send *Scrivener's Greek New Testament Underlying the King James Bible*, hardback, $14+$4 S&H
[ ] Send *Scrivener's Annotated Greek New Testament*, by Dr. Frederick Scrivener: Hardback--$35+$5 S&H; Genuine Leather--$45+$5 S&H
[ ] Send *Why Not the King James Bible?--An Answer to James White's KJVO Book* by Dr. K. D. DiVietro, $10+$4 S&H
[ ] Send *Forever Settled--Bible Documents & History Survey* by Dr. Jack Moorman, $20+$4 S&H. Hardback book.
[ ] Send *Early Church Fathers & the A.V.--A Demonstration* by Dr. Jack Moorman, $6 + $4 S&H.
[ ] Send *When the KJB Departs from the So-Called "Majority Text"* by Dr. Jack Moorman, $16 + $4 S&H
[ ] Send *Missing in Modern Bibles--Nestle-Aland & NIV Errors* by Dr. Jack Moorman, $8 + $4 S&H
[ ] Send *The Doctrinal Heart of the Bible--Removed from Modern Versions* by Dr. Jack Moorman, VCR, $15 +$4 S&H
[ ] Send *Modern Bibles--The Dark Secret* by Dr. Jack Moorman, $5 + $2 S&H
[ ] Send *Early Manuscripts and the A.V.--A Closer* Look, by Dr. Jack Moorman, $15 + $4 S&H
[ ] Send the "DBS Articles of Faith & Organization" (N.C.)
[ ] Send Brochure #1: "1000 Titles Defending KJB/TR"(N.C.)

Send or Call Orders to:
THE BIBLE FOR TODAY
900 Park Ave., Collingswood, NJ 08108
Phone: 856-854-4452; FAX:--2464; Orders: 1-800 JOHN 10:9

The Defined King James Bible

UNCOMMON WORDS DEFINED ACCURATELY

I. Deluxe Genuine Leather

✦Large Print--Black or Burgundy✦

1 for $40.00+$6 S&H

✦Case of 12 for✦

$30.00 each+$30 S&H

✦Medium Print--Black or Burgundy✦

1 for $35.00+$5 S&H

✦Case of 12 for✦

$25.00 each+$24 S&H

II. Deluxe Hardback Editions

1 for $20.00+$6 S&H (Large Print)

✦Case of 12 for✦

$15.00 each+$30 S&H (Large Print)

1 for $15.00+$5 S&H (Medium Print)

✦Case of 12 for✦

$10.00 each+$24 S&H (Medium Print)

Order Phone: 1-800-JOHN 10:9

CREDIT CARDS WELCOMED

Notes

Notes

Notes

Notes

Notes

www.ingramcontent.com/pod-product-compliance
Lightning Source LLC
Chambersburg PA
CBHW051045160426
43193CB00010B/1077